CUBA ON THE VERGE

CUBA

ON THE

VERGE

12 WRITERS ON CONTINUITY
AND CHANGE IN HAVANA
AND ACROSS THE COUNTRY

EDITED BY

LEILA GUERRIERO

ecco

AN IMPRINT OF HARPERCOLLINSPUBLISHERS

CUBA ON THE VERGE. Copyright © 2017 by Indent Literary Agency.
All rights reserved. Printed in the United States of America. No part
of this book may be used or reproduced in any manner whatsoever
without written permission except in the case of brief quotations
embodied in critical articles and reviews. For information address
HarperCollins Publishers, 195 Broadway, New York, NY 10007.

HarperCollins books may be purchased for educational, business,
or sales promotional use. For information please e-mail the Special
Markets Department at SPsales@harpercollins.com.

A hardcover edition of this book was published in 2017 by Ecco,
an imprint of HarperCollins Publishers.

FIRST ECCO PAPERBACK EDITION PUBLISHED 2018.

Designed by Suet Yee Chong

Library of Congress Cataloging-in-Publication Data has been
applied for.

ISBN 978-0-06-266107-4

18 19 20 21 22   LSC   10 9 8 7 6 5 4 3 2 1

CONTENTS

OUTSIDE

TWELVE ATTEMPTS

O f all the questions that journalism must ask (who, what, where, when, why, and how), there's only one that can be answered easily when we talk about Cuba: where. Everyone more or less knows where Cuba is. When it comes to the rest of the questions (What is Cuba? Who are the Cubans? What is Cuba like? When did Cuba start being what it is? Why is Cuba the way it is?) and the different variations and combinations of those questions, not only are there no easy answers, but everyone seems to have their own.

For some, Fidel Castro is a wise and admirable hero, but for others he is a tyrant who led a dictatorship for decades. For some, Cuba is a paradise made of palm trees, sun, and sea, with education and health care for all, while for others it's a country constantly suffering from shortages, filled with unbelievably smart biologists and architects working as taxi drivers. For some, Cuba is a model of equality and justice, but for others it is a place that sneakily replicates the blights of the West (corruption, the class system, social inequality). For some, it's a fantasy island. For others, it's a prison.

The twelve essays that make up this book try to distance themselves from these oversimplifications and, in telling us about this country, cover terrain that is much more dangerous, and also more interesting: that of doubt and contradiction. The journalists and writers who have participated in this volume— non-Cubans living in Cuba, Cubans who live in Cuba, Cubans who have left Cuba, non-Cubans who have visited Cuba—are writing about a country whose population has been educated in the most fervent atheism but also avidly drinks from the cup of African religions. A country for which the United States is an overbearing nemesis but which also carries baseball—the American sport par excellence—deep in its DNA. A country where women are queens and mistresses of their bodies ("Getting a curettage [abortion] done in Cuba is much more common than going to the dentist," writes Wendy Guerra), but where none hold a position of power, not even as the wives of its leaders. "An abyss lies between Fidel and a naked woman," Guerra writes. ". . . The current president of Cuba, Raúl Castro, is the widower of Vilma Espín, also a revolutionary fighter. He is said to be a family man, but no one knows anything about his life today. As for the female figure's relationship to Cuban heroes, leaders, and rulers, she isn't even in the background. She simply doesn't exist."

Leonardo Padura writes an ode to baseball, lamenting the advance of soccer over the sport that he once wanted to play professionally, and asks what will happen to the Cuban identity in the face of this and other changes.

The actor Vladimir Cruz remembers how, in 1993, in the most difficult moment of the Special Period, he arrived in Havana as a twenty-seven-year-old with two hundred Cuban pesos in his pocket:

> I had wanted to make it to the capital with my feet on the ground, and in effect there I was, but instead of my feet I had my back on the ground in the capital—on the floor of the capital's bus terminal, that is.
>
> I slept a bit and opened my eyes at daybreak, when the terminal opened. I got up, washed my face with a tiny trickle of water that dripped into the sink of the dilapidated and fetid bathroom.

That morning he won a breakout role in the movie *Strawberry and Chocolate,* and, though he was able to pursue his vocation in large part because of enormous support from the state, it was that same state that, with whimsical arbitrariness, prevented him from doing things such as attending the Oscar ceremony in 1994 when the movie was nominated for best foreign film.

Abraham Jiménez Enoa paints a vivid portrait of Ernesto, a *jinetero,* a man whose principal tool in his work is sex with foreign women.

Carlos Manuel Álvarez makes clear that emigrating, more than just leaving, means ripping a country from one's body, as he recounts his 2015 visit to his father who had recently emigrated to Miami, a man who in Cuba had been a doctor and now works knocking coconuts from trees in the gardens of luxurious homes belonging to others.

Iván de la Nuez wonders where Cuba is headed (after Obama and the pope and the Rolling Stones and the fashionable cafés and the Havana streets transformed for the set of *The Fate of the Furious)* and what road he traveled to arrive here.

An American, Francisco Goldman, returns to the stage he

visited decades earlier, the Tropicana, the capital's most iconic nightclub, and follows in the footsteps of a glorious past that no longer exists, or exists only in part, or exists in a different way.

The Spaniard Mauricio Vicent explores the history of the *bolita*, an illegal lottery brought to Cuba by the Chinese, in which numbers are associated with certain animals, people, or things, unveiling a sophisticated system of bets that brings together magic, poetry, the interpretation of dreams, and, of course, ambition.

On one of his first visits to Havana, the Mexican Rubén Gallo got to know Eliezer, the bookseller whose story he tells and in which converge different forms of sensuality, the tricks used to cheat the censors, and his expectations for the immediate future.

In *Mi Amigo Manuel*, Patricia Engel—a Colombian American living in the United States—tells us about the driver of an *almendrón*, the name for the classic American cars from the fifties that are sometimes turned into taxis. A man who seems to have crossed the threshold into all kinds of resignation, he works fifteen hours a day, he only rests on Sundays, and he says he would never leave Cuba, not for love of country but because he doesn't want to abandon his mother.

The American journalist Jon Lee Anderson recalls his experience living in Cuba with his family during the Special Period, as he conducted research for his biography of Che Guevara, and notes the contradiction between the hardships of the locals, forced to live with very little, and his privileged position as a foreigner.

The Chilean Patricio Fernández, using the background of a grim yet luminous cockfight, writes about the tensions that have rippled through the turbulent ocean of the Revolution:

The Revolution's great conquest was of time. Cubans are not in a hurry. The time agreed on for an appointment is only an approximate reference. Since public transportation is unpredictable, delay is easy to understand. What's more, little is lost by waiting. People who work assiduously are rare. Since the salary fixed by the state is around thirty dollars a month, chatting on the corner is almost as profitable as exerting yourself in a profession. More is obtained *por la iz-quierda,* or "to the left" (commissions, bribes, and all kinds of kickbacks that function at the edges of institutionality) than by obediently exercising a trade. When it came time to produce, the community's well-being turned out to be a much less convincing motivator than personal benefit. Efficiency disappeared the moment profit was forbidden. And with it, haste. If capitalism's success has led to a growing self-sufficiency, socialism's failure consolidated the need to rely on others in order to survive.

To retell the history of Cuba—like recounting the invasion of Normandy or the fall of the Berlin Wall—is to recount History with a capital *H*—an ambitious job. Here are twelve attempts.

—Leila Guerriero

INSIDE

MIAMI
THE COCONUT TRAIL

BY CARLOS MANUEL ÁLVAREZ
TRANSLATED BY ANNA KUSHNER

At the end of May 2015, I landed in Miami from Havana. I must have been one of the few Cubans who had ever set foot in that city not to migrate definitively, but only to visit. My plan was to spend two months with my father, Manolo, who had arrived a year and a half before to rebuild his life from nothing.

In the airport, I walked down cold hallways, crossed through glass waiting rooms and customs inspection stations. I was afraid. I realized later that it was a fear that didn't belong to me, because I didn't have any reason to be afraid, but there it was. It was the fear inside of all of us. They asked me questions, nothing out of the ordinary. They looked at my beard, I think: my funny year-old beard. When I got out, my father was waiting for me. He and I cried our respective melodramatic tears. Later, on an expressway headed toward the city, I asked myself if those tears hadn't been an exaggeration. At the end of the day, it had only been a little over a year since I had last seen him; other people never saw each other again or met again three decades later, when they were already something else, just shadows, broken without possible repair.

On the way, I saw so many signs that I didn't see any of them. I saw the face of Magic Johnson on the door of a bus. I saw the faces of lawyers on ads. I wondered what someone on an ad thinks when he sees his own ad. In a store, my father bought me some candy. He said he knew that I liked it. We weren't surprised, after the first few hours, by the ease with which we had linked that last day in Cuba to the first one here in Miami. We were surprised by the reunion: how smooth it was, how light, how little it weighed. Sometimes one doesn't leave to go outside, but to go inside.

"What do you do now?" I asked René Arocha.

"I'm a driver for a medical clinic for the elderly. I take them to appointments and then take them back to their houses."

"When did you separate yourself completely from baseball?"

"Five years ago. And since then, I've worked at this."

"Are you still passionate about baseball?"

"No."

"No?"

"No."

"Explain that to me."

"Everyone asks me if I saw the Marlins game, if I saw this, if I saw that. I don't watch ball. It's like when you stop liking a woman. I don't feel anything anymore. Before, I needed it. I dreamed of baseball. I lived baseball. Not anymore."

"Couldn't it be that you still like the woman and since she doesn't want to be with you anymore, you reject her out of spite?"

"No, no. Since I was little, ten or eleven years old, my grandfather would tell me to sit down and watch some game so I could learn. And I never did. Perhaps this is a regression. I stopped playing and now I'm not interested. Sometimes, I see a game, I don't know, the last one of the World Series, something like that, but nothing else."

"Do you watch other sports?"

"No. Nothing."

"What is baseball to you?"

"Being on the field. Especially in the mornings, when you go out to practice. Smelling the grass. You can really feel that fresh grass."

My father lived at 418 East Sixtieth Street in Hialeah, Miami's Cuban neighborhood, in a studio so small that, once inside, there was no spot from which I could not see him nor he me. Bed, closet, bathroom, and kitchen in a proximity that did not allow for distinctions. The spaces were less the fruit of architecture than of our imaginations. I slept on an air mattress at the foot of his bed, just below the grille that blew cold air from the ceiling. My former asthma came back. My coughing and expectorating kept us from sleeping. My father had to wake up at six every morning to distribute and fix air conditioners until well into the afternoon. He had a job at an old friend's refrigeration business that didn't pay much, about four hundred dollars a week, and then, at night, he went to school to learn English. Sometimes, back home, with his elbows propped on a small table, he would listen to several tracks to practice his pronunciation or fine-tune his ear, or he would look something up on Google, typing with just two fingers, as if he were a diligent typist transmitting life-

or-death messages from deepest Africa. Each time my father typed a letter, he looked at the screen to verify that the letter showed up. It took an insane amount of time for him to complete a word. He embodied these old ways of doing things that would have otherwise been lost. He was like a time capsule, preserving certain gestures—the medieval slowness of copiers—and keeping them uncorrupted by new habits. With his dusty soul, trying to learn a new language at the age of fifty, my father was all nostalgia. The wee hours of the morning were probably his finest, when he could dream in Spanish. But my asthma impeded his dreaming. So, although I had wanted to spend my visit with my father, I told him it would be better if I went to stay at a friend's house and he could pick me up on Sundays or in his free time. One week later—a week during which, for some reason, I didn't hear from him at all—he showed up at the friend's house where I slept and told me he had a new job: taking coconuts down from the backyards of houses and from the city's public spaces, then selling them wholesale in Hialeah. When he asked me to help him, I said yes.

He was a fighter and was happy with his new plans. I was a coward and felt sad for him. Although perhaps, after all, life was just being scrupulously fair. From a lost little rural village, with parents who went to school at the same time he did, Manolo had managed to study and become a doctor. The Revolution was the catapult that launched him. Later, that same Revolution, like Saturn devouring his young, made him decide to emigrate, after having managed the country's clinics and hospitals for almost thirty years. If the Revolution had not happened, two things would be different: Manolo would have many fewer contradictions than he does, and he would have always had to earn his daily bread the way he does now. Wearing overalls, knocking down coconuts around the city.

René Arocha stopped playing professional baseball in the year 1999, at the age of thirty-five. From then until 2010, he ran a children's baseball academy in Miami, where he discovered that he got just as much satisfaction from teaching as he had from being an athlete. He trained and groomed the kids until he had to close the academy due to financial problems. Perhaps the precociousness of Arocha's debut, rather than his early retirement, will help you to understand why he ended up indifferent and apathetic to the profession he had once practiced.

At thirteen, he played ball informally with the kids from his neighborhood in Regla, one of the fifteen municipalities that make up Havana, and he escaped to the Latin American Stadium, although he wasn't allowed to run around Havana on his own. At fourteen, as a member of the municipal team, he subbed in an insignificant game, and he did so well that he was soon promoted to Regla's first-division team. He pitched in the provincial finals, was responsible for ten consecutive strikeouts, and lost the game only in the eleventh inning. Later, he debuted in the Latin American Stadium, didn't allow any runs, and displayed the equanimity and skill of a much older player. When he was at the School for Beginning Sports Education (Escuela de Iniciación Deportiva Escolar—EIDE), he found out through the *Juventud Rebelde* newspaper that he was on the list for the Metropolitanos, which meant that he would be playing at a higher level and that he would participate in the National Series. And then, as you can imagine, his life changed. And his life changed very early: he was fifteen years old. At the beginning, he went to the stadium only on the days that he pitched, attending school the rest of the time.

"But halfway through the season, I understood that I wasn't meant for school, but for baseball," he says.

Thus, he began to travel to the provinces with the rest of the team. In his first season, he obtained 7 of his 104 victories in the National Series. He pitched tense, tight games, allowing the opposing teams few runs.

"If I had had luck, I think I would have won two hundred. There is no statistic saying so, but I lost, easy, thirty games by one run. Two to one. Three to one."

"What does a pitcher feel like when that happens?"

"I knew I was doing a good job even though I lost. And perhaps those tight games forced me to concentrate more, I don't know, to use my body more and not relax."

In 1982, several Metropolitanos players were involved in what continues to be the darkest chapter of the National Series. Metropolitanos was, until its disappearance about five years ago, the capital's second team, the underdog to the Industriales, perpetually condemned to a secondary role. In the same year, after having obtained a historic third place, a scandal was uncovered in which Metropolitanos had been paying bribes to win games, which ended with a definitive dismissal of several players. Within revolutionary amateur baseball, the showcase of the socialist brotherhood's highest values, the games that were presumed to have been fixed caused a shake-up similar to the one produced in the Major Leagues in 1919 when the Chicago White Sox sold the World Series to gamblers. In both cases, the innocence of the game's fans was forever shattered.

"That conflict, what was your experience of it?"

"It almost cost me my career. Out of nowhere."

"How so?"

"Because I also went to the DTI [Technical Investigations Department], and I was also interviewed, and they also wanted to blame me. I remember that when everything happened, the president of the provincial government and the provincial baseball commissioner called to tell me that the Revolution was benevolent, that they were going to let this one go. But they didn't have anything on me to let go. I was an eighteen-year-old kid. I didn't know what was happening around me, if it was happening—because at this point, I don't know if it happened or didn't happen."

"Did the Metros sell games or not?"

"Nobody knows, nobody says. I've talked to ballplayers who were in it and no one has said, 'Yes, I was sold.' So for me, it's nebulous. Because I don't believe that a team that was sold would get to the last day of a championship in the first place. Because no team has to be paid to win, you always want to win."

My first outing with my father was to Kendall. I remember the narrow, pretty streets, the low houses, all the same, the pruned little gardens, the garages. It was a little after nine in the morning and we were going at a slow crawl in a Ford pickup, spying those façades of a nearly unhealthy perfection, the roundabouts with their twisted corners, and the bunches of coconuts sticking out above the rooftops.

Kendall, like all of Miami, was infested with coconut trees, but no one opened the door to us at the first three houses. Manolo would park, go up to the house, ring the doorbell, and wait for one or two minutes, with his hands on his waist or walking around in small circles. Then he would return to the pickup, confused. It seemed like we were on a fool's errand. At the fourth house, someone opened a window and said no. We took it as progress that someone answered. We hadn't been at it an hour and everything seemed to be going too slowly for me. We were two Latino emigrants plunging ourselves entirely into the unchlorinated pool of survival. I knew that perhaps it wasn't that bad, but I also knew that being from Cuba meant being late to the world. Hoping that, with some luck, we could be useful for something. In the first house that gave us permission, there weren't more than a dozen coconuts, but Manolo reacted with a liquid happiness that nearly dripped.

"Up!" he said.

We took out our tools: a wheelbarrow, a cushion, a metal extension rod, and a sharp, curved, serrated knife. We had to be careful not to cut too close to the coconut, because if we took off the top, which was rather fragile, water would come spilling out, and broken coconuts, bled dry, couldn't be sold. There were many other requirements, but we were desperate neophytes willing to knock down any coconuts we were authorized to knock down. Manolo attached the knife to the end of the rod, extended it, and tried to place the knife in a strategic position amid the cluster of branches, dry leaves, and ripe or about-to-fall-off fruits that make up the always-tangled locks of coconut trees in the trop- ics. If the knife got stuck, there was no forcing it, just patiently freeing it. It was the only problem that required a certain amount of reflection in a job that was primarily physical. When I placed the first ten coconuts I'd ever collected in my life in the back of the pickup and, leaning over the side of the bed, I compared the space they took up with the space that was left—the work we had done with what remained to be done, my optimism with my laziness—the same feeling ran through me that I imagine runs through novelists after writing the first line of a novel.

The strategy consisted of knocking down coconuts one by one so as not to ruin them: decapitating them with a neat blow, quick and direct. Then I, the center field apprentice, would play ball with a small cushion in hand. It ended up being pretty amusing thanks to the mental tricks we invented to overcome the roughness of physical work. I was literally fielding, and the easiest thing to do was to invent an imaginary audience. Although for each fielding error, we lost almost a dollar: too much imagination would have been sacrilege.

Sometimes the coconuts fell in pairs. Or in threes. Or along with an entire branch. I bent over backward—without any luck—in order not to lose a single one. We also had a construction worker's helmet, but I thought myself agile enough to go without it.

Once the coconuts were knocked off, I gathered the spoils of our labor in the wheelbarrow and later unloaded them in the pickup truck. In theory, I played more than one role, but my contribution couldn't be compared—I know from the few times that we switched roles—to the main work, exhausting and rather melancholy if your father is the one doing it, of knocking down coconuts like one possessed. Sometimes seventy in a row, for seven or eight hours, never less. The pain in your shoulders, the cramped neck, the stiffness in your hands, the feeling of being a lamplighter, the creaking that comes from your body as it becomes tense.

That morning, we were lucky at a couple more houses. A fine and polite woman—we couldn't tell if she was Cuban or not—allowed us to deal with her three coconut trees, replete with yellow specimens, as we saw fit. Afterward, she offered us water and asked what many others might have asked: how was it that Manolo, a doctor, was knocking down coconuts? That made me feel somewhat ashamed. An unjustified shame, because in Miami, the immigrant lab, everyone viewed it as desirable that people should get ahead however they could. The woman asked if we could also knock down the dry coconuts for her, almost a hundred. Although they weren't worth anything to us, Manolo agreed. I whispered to him that we should go. He told me we had to do it because later that woman would allow only us access to the coconuts, and although that seemed like a reasonable motive—making a long-term investment—the truth was that it was all about his inability to say no. We had two ham and cheese sandwiches for lunch, drank Gatorade, and continued all afternoon, rather contentedly, until, after having gone unauthorized after a coconut tree located on that piece of grass between the street and the sidewalk that you never know whether it belongs to the city or is private, a neighbor threatened to call the police. As Manolo motioned to me to put the wheelbarrow, the rod, and the harvested coconuts in the pickup truck, he was telling the neighbor that the owner of the house had given us permission. The neighbor accused him of being a liar, because the owner of the house used coconut water for her kidney illness. Then she dialed a number on her cell and we didn't see anything else because we got in the Ford and screeched around the corner, like in a police chase in the movies.

In 1986, Arocha felt such pain in his arm that he seriously considered retiring from active sports. Beset by discomfort that had begun in the 1982 Youth World Series—where he pitched five of seven games—he couldn't hold his own even in provincial championships. He had lost the entire '83 season, the '84 and '85 Selectivas (all-star games), and the speed of his pitches had considerably lessened. "For those trifles, it's better to retire," his close friends told him. But later in 1986, after very rigorous training, Arocha made a comeback, recovering the speed in his throws and guaranteeing his entry to the national team.

"What does it mean to have made it onto the Cuban team?"

"Especially how I made it, after the injury I had . . . I tried to keep it up and I did, with ups and downs like any athlete, until '91, when, well . . ."

"Were you proud?"

"Of course, how could I not be? To have those four letters on my chest and go out and win, like, for example, in the Baseball World Cup in Italy, '88."

"Is that your best memory?"

"And one of my greatest disappointments."

"Why?"

"Because I was the one who started in both games against the Americans. And in the final, they pulled me from the pitcher's mound very quickly."

"Did that really affect you?"

"Of course, because I was all in, I was fighting my game, and it was early. I never understood why they took me out. There's no explanation. They never explain anything."

"I think it went very well for us."

"It's better than nothing."

"But is it good or not?"

"As a start, yes, but we have to do more. We have to try to do more than four hundred per day."

"Four hundred?"

"The old coconut gatherers do five hundred and six hundred, although they also have their advantages. People already know them, and at some houses, they save the coconuts for them."

"You're not satisfied."

"No, I'm fine. Don't worry."

"Is everything okay?"

"Yes, everything is okay."

"We'll get better."

"We don't have experience. And we have to switch out that rod, it's too heavy. Details."

"We can't get tangled up with the tall trees."

"I think they're too exhausting."

"And we fall behind. For five coconuts from a tall tree, we lose I don't know how many from somewhere else."

"True."

"But are you happy?"

"Yes, I'm happy."

We had those conversations. Manolo at the wheel. Me, barefoot, with my feet over the glove box. Sometimes Manolo would look at me: sometimes he slid his hand over my head. Sometimes he didn't look at me at all and kept his gaze facing forward, focused on the traffic or the airplanes crossing the city or the light change at traffic signals. The highway, gliding beneath us, was like a long dagger, as if instead of moving us forward, it was plunging into us. Just before four in the afternoon, we got to Ovidio's warehouse, on Thirty-Second Avenue NW and Seventy-Ninth Street in North Miami: a large building with hundreds of boxes stacked up, supermarket carts, a forklift, waste tanks, port-a-potties, and three or four workers who were smoking or hanging around or talking. They also looked like objects: spoiled things that the warehouse never threw out.

Ovidio had a good business: exhausting, but stable. He was about fifty. Tall, with a receding hairline, a Chaplin-like mustache and a lightning-fast way of speaking, as if his words were a waste of his time and he had to get them out quickly, squeeze them together. Ovidio was always walking away from you. He talked to you while going somewhere else, to show you that you weren't the most important thing. He immigrated in the nineties, and, since then, he had been buying coconuts from the city's coconut gatherers and packaging them to sell to a company in New York. I imagined some beach like Coney Island or Rockaway Beach, full of moneyed gringos wanting to sunbathe, slathered in expensive creams, lying on beach chairs at the edge of the sea and drinking, through straws, fresh coconut water from the coconuts we knocked down in a repeating series of scenes, monotonous, all the same, day after day. Manolo going over to my friend's house to pick me up around eight in the morning; me praying for a flat tire on the Ford, or for a windstorm, anything that would free me from that obligation. Later, me getting dressed, with my haggard face, asking myself why I should help Manolo, why he couldn't do it by himself. Us getting back on I-95 or on the Palmetto, sometimes for more than an hour, whether we were going north or south—Kendall, Naples, Broward, West Palm Beach—or staying in Hialeah itself. Us, morning fauna, the close cousins of tree surgeons and trash collectors and mailmen. Us stopping in any gas station along the way or beneath the shade of some corner tree to gulp down our snack. Manolo knocking on doors: yes, or no, or later, or I'm not the owner, or take them, or we know what it's like to make a living, or knock them down but don't ruin my garden, or leave me a few. Me sullen, or shy, or fed up, or jovial. Manolo defiant, taking shelter behind his glasses, a hat with earflaps to protect him from the sun, a hat like that of a Soviet in enemy territory. Me on the verge of passing out, my lips white, my throat like sandpaper, my hands trembling slightly and those mirages of heat—melted June—reverberating on the sidewalk. Manolo shaking down the trees of closed-up houses; me, helping him, afraid. Manolo expressing regret after a poor day: days without any coconuts, days with four hundred coconuts, mediocre days and bountiful days. Days on which we ran into other coconut gatherers and we sized them up suspiciously or greeted them affectionately. Me slowly exerting myself so that Manolo would work less, rushing to carry something before Manolo could carry it, trying to make my hand or my shoulder arrive before his hand or his shoulder. Me knocking down the coconuts with the rod and Manolo catching them with the cushion. Manolo with his tired muscles and me dreaming of coconuts, coconuts that spoke to me, coconuts that suffered if I let them fall, coconuts that asked us not to take them, mother coconuts crying for their baby coconuts, coconuts that sacrificed themselves, kamikaze coconuts, and broken coconuts that looked at me with languid faces and, shrouded in dignity, asked for a respectful burial.

At Ovidio's warehouse, there was enough time for the day's accounting. The delivery never took less than an hour. The first time, a nineteen-year-old kid who came from Las Tunas, in eastern Cuba, dealt with us. He had left behind his wife and daughter and told us that after a month, he still didn't know why he had come, that in Cuba he didn't work, he made a living from selling jewelry, and here, well, he was counting coconuts and boxing them up. The kid, depressed and pensive in the middle of a business led by a practical guy, with evidently little thought for matters of nostalgia, didn't last too long, so most of the time we dealt with Vladimir, the second in command and the only person whom Ovidio trusted.

Vladimir was fat and used a wide brace to ease his back pain. We liked him and he liked us. He called Manolo "doctor" and sometimes asked him about pills or some treatment. In reality, Ovidio and Vladimir were very generous. They paid us seventy cents per coconut, ten more than anyone else paid. And Vladimir would suggest which areas to go to, which coconuts we should knock down and which ones we shouldn't. But even if we knocked down suboptimal coconuts, he would pay half price for them.

Dry coconuts weren't any good. Coconuts in which you could hear the water weren't any good. Big coconuts, the male ones, weren't any good (and—as we learned later—there is a male coconut in every bunch, one that sacrifices itself for the others to prosper). Coconuts that were too odd, too scaly, were no good. Small coconuts were no good. Coconuts without any top were no good, and beat-up coconuts were worth less than others. Yellow coconuts were technically good, but the business in New York didn't appreciate them. The best coconuts were medium sized, consistent, and tough, between brown and green in color. Each box held ten coconuts, and broken coconuts were thrown in big plastic bins. The warehouse itself was a giant plastic bin where the city had deposited some of its defective coconuts.

Everything smelled like Cuba in that place. Memories, people, slang, the spiritual exhaustion dotted with ingenious jokes, and the solidarity of contraband. Sometimes, we stayed longer than necessary. Manolo liked to talk.

That was why René Arocha decided to emigrate: to not have to explain too many things to himself, especially anything outside of sports. Such as, for example, the two years an uncle of his spent in prison for carrying five dollars at time when it was illegal to have foreign currency.

"Five hard-won dollars so he could buy his wife some perfume."

Or the afternoons on which, exhausted after practice, with a game lined up for that night, he had to spend two hours sitting in the stadium listening to a meeting about some new Communist Youth directive.

"I was an athlete and that was my free time. I didn't understand why I had to go to meetings when what I needed was to rest."

On July 4, 1991, when the Cuban team had a layover in Miami, Arocha called his father and his aunt, who had been living in that city since his teenage years. He told them that he had time to see them and asked them to come get him at the airport. His father and aunt asked him if he had permission and Arocha told them yes, which was true. They went to get him and, once he was at the house of his relatives, with whom he hadn't had any contact since 1980, Arocha spoke, for the first time, of the thought he'd been holding on to for years: of going into exile, fleeing. His family ended up taking him in.

This made him the first Cuban ballplayer to abandon an official team. If there's a pioneer in the sports exodus from Cuba today, it's Arocha.

"What made you emigrate at a time when it still wasn't common at all?"

"It wasn't supposed to be in '91. It was going to be in '86. And it should have been in '79, when I went to Mexico. But it didn't happen in '86, for certain reasons."

"And why the delay until '91?"

"Because I had to find the perfect time and place, but I knew it would happen. Although, when I stayed, I didn't stay because anyone told me to stay, or because I was going to get millions. I stayed and thought my career would end there. I came to be just another citizen."

"Why were you so unsatisfied in Cuba?"

"Because I knew that they were telling me lies. Because everything was one obstacle after another. We couldn't even spend in Cuba the money that was given to us abroad. We had to spend it wherever we were. And on and on. Everything was a problem, even though we were worth millions of dollars."

"When the time came for you to stay in Miami, there was no fear?"

"No, no fear. Before leaving, I looked at the itinerary, and I knew Miami was the place."

"Is it true that you didn't tell anyone?"

"No one. Imagine! My ex-wife went to wait for me at the airport in Havana, when everyone else went back."

"And what were you thinking then?"

"When I woke up the next day, the only thing I was thinking was that the bomb had gone off, that was that."

"*Granma* immediately published a hostile piece."

"I have it saved. 'Baseball Player René Arocha Betrayed His Homeland, Seduced by the Miami Mafia,' et cetera, et cetera."

"How does one feel when one reads something like that?"

"The thing is, I didn't betray my homeland. I am Cuban, I continue being Cuban. My homeland betrayed me."

———

One day, the power steering belt came loose and we were left stranded in the middle of the highway: the steering wheel was stuck and we had no money for a tow truck, so we had to wait for a friend of Manolo's to come and pick us up. Another day, the air-conditioning broke. Another day, we forgot to tie down the wheelbarrow and it went flying off right in the middle of the interstate. Another day, we got a flat tire around West Palm Beach and we didn't have any tools to replace it. Two fat teen-agers were playing basketball with one of those portable hoops they have in every house in South Florida. I stood there, watching them; they didn't invite me to play. We were there for half an hour, until a near-albino from Camagüey, who hadn't been back to Cuba in over forty years and who had left behind all pigment of life on the island, lent us his tools. At times, the fatigue; the eighty-some-degree heat; my own nature, which shuns sacrifice; and matters of a metaphysical kind—like my tendency to perceive the world as an absolute dump—made me see Manolo as an enemy. But more often than not, even when exhausted, when drenched in sweat, when confused, we could turn on the radio and listen to songs that awoke a certain coded impulse, a messy candor. In other words: gratitude for being alive, a desire to not die.

I tuned in to 95.1 FM, a rock station that played "Layla," and "Sweet Home Alabama," and "House of the Rising Sun" by the Animals, and lots of Dylan. Manolo tuned in to 87.9, a classical music station that played Albinoni's Adagio, and the Lacrimosa movement of Mozart's *Requiem*, and the Poco allegretto movement of Brahms's Third Symphony. And all of that volcanic lava mixed with the coconut work, and the coconut work mixed with our anonymous B movie, wearing out the benefit of such a soundtrack.

Once in Miami, willing to leave baseball, Arocha only became convinced that he was good enough to make it to Major League Baseball when one of its representatives invited him as a spectator to a game between the Oakland Athletics and the Yankees. Like all Cuban ballplayers of his time, he thought that the Major League players were extraterrestrials. That if they, as Cubans, had a hard time beating college kids, what would happen when they were faced with the highest-level athletes? But that day, after seeing a couple of innings proving that the Major Leaguers were not Martians, Arocha commented to a friend that he thought he could make it. And he did. Manuel Hurtado, a former Cuban pitching star, began to train him. They contacted an agent and in 1992, after a thousand obstacles (they even had to wait for an okay from the State Department), René Arocha signed with the St. Louis Cardinals for $109,000.

After a very successful first year on the Cardinals' AAA farm team, on April 9, 1993, he debuted in the Major Leagues against the Cincinnati Reds. He pitched two sweeps in eight innings, struck out three batters, and achieved the first of his eleven wins that season. The Cardinals' fans began to love him. Joe Torre managed him. Ozzie Smith was his teammate. Arocha felt, at that time, something akin to happiness.

"It was what I wanted to experience in Cuba. And I wasn't earning millions, let's make that clear."

He stayed in St. Louis until 1996, the year he transferred to San Francisco, where he played for only one season. In 1999, he went to Mexico. In 2000, he came back to the United States and entered discussions with the Mets, but the Mets didn't offer too many guarantees and Arocha, who has never beat around the bush, decided to retire.

"What are the differences between Cuban ball and the Major Leagues?"

"Many. Abysmal ones. I thought I knew, but I learned how to pitch here. To pitch close, to throw a sinker. It's not pitching close and hitting them with the ball, it's knowing how to throw the ball less than an inch from your elbow and then getting it out, a strike."

"Your repertoire was famous in Cuba."

"In Cuba, I learned how to throw many things, but in reality, it was the same thing, different ways. A slider like this [he opens his arms], a slider like this [he closes them a bit], or a very short slider or against the floor. But a slider. And my curveball was good, especially my big curveball at the beginning, before my injury."

"So what did you learn here?"

"The slider itself, for example. I ran my fingers over the side of the ball and here, I learned to run them over the top, what Americans call 'staying on top of the ball.'"

"Is it more effective like that?"

"Of course. That way, the slider goes down, it doesn't float. Before, my slider floated. When the slider floats, the batter sees the ball here, he sees it there, and he sees it there. When it's not floating, he sees just one point. When it goes out and later when it falls, it's over."

There were hundreds of houses and, except for two incidents, I only remember pleasant moments. The teenage gringo whose paternal grandfather was Cuban and who helped us, in the middle of a rainstorm, to carry the almost one hundred coconuts he had gifted us. The decrepit woman who lived with another elderly woman, frugal retirees, who wouldn't allow us to leave before we tasted the dessert she had made. The forty-something homosexuals who saw my way of fielding as an example of extreme skill. And Mañi Gorizelaya, a haughty eighty-year-old who ended up being from my hometown and, to boot, had flirted with my maternal grandmother. My grandmother, although she liked Mañi, could not accept him because he was mixed race.

Nonetheless, the morning of June 25, 2015, was particularly intense and contradictory. We were traveling through the south and were still floundering in that indecisive zone in which a stroke of luck could determine our day. We knew from previous experience that if we took too long in getting it right, the bad signs would become irreversible: if, by a certain hour, you haven't been able to engineer your fate, providence tends to abandon you. Manolo had found a coconut tree in an area outside a house and, once again, we were unsure whether it belonged to the city or a private owner. We decided to take the risk, but a hysterical scream immediately stopped us.

On the other side of the street, behind the fence of the house, an Indian man was yelling and raising his arms. He wasn't speaking English. He was threatening us with a closed fist. We couldn't stand up to him because, although no one bothered us, knocking down coconuts from public trees was an illegal activity, and if someone made a complaint, the police could arrest or fine us. Manolo called the Indian man a faggot and we went back to the Ford and drove away. The man, we assumed, wanted the coconuts for himself, but didn't have any way to get them down. After a while, we went back and he was still keeping watch. Despite the fact that that coconut tree could have changed our day, I thought we shouldn't persist, but Manolo went back a third time. The place was clear. We took out the tools, knocked down a couple of coconuts, trying to make the least amount of noise possible, and suddenly, that beast's shriek sent chills down my spine. The man crossed the street and began to smack us. He knew we couldn't do anything to him. Manolo tried to talk to him, but the man just kept yelling. He took out a cell phone and took a picture of the Ford's license plate. Manolo was saying, why, listen, why are you doing that, son of a bitch. My muscles turned into knots. I could have cut that man's throat with the knife from the rod, as if his head were a coconut.

"Why does this bother you?" Manolo was saying to him. Who was he talking to? Was he talking to the man or was he talking to himself? What didn't my father understand? Gratuitous wickedness, perversion, treachery just because?

A man has a quota of justified blows to distribute throughout his life, and he shouldn't waste them, but he shouldn't hold back either, because that can backfire. We left and the man stayed beneath the coconut tree ready to chase away any trespassers. I can still hear him screeching.

Fifteen minutes later, still shaken up, as we got out at the corner of 119th Avenue SW and 188th Street, a small medic's van parked just behind the Ford and the driver came over to us. We looked at him skeptically. He greeted us, we returned the greeting, and then he told us he lived two blocks away, right on the corner, that he had coconuts outside and that we could take as many as we wanted. Manolo looked at me, surprised, but I vaguely began to recognize the driver. And, when I at last thought I understood who he was, I felt the open blow of an epiphany in my chest.

"What is your name?"

"Me? René," he said.

"René?"

"Yes, René."

I thought, frankly delirious, that that man was humoring me by saying what I wanted to hear.

"You know," I then said to Manolo, "this man is Arocha, René Arocha."

Manolo, surprised, said, "How is this Arocha? I didn't recognize him."

"And how did you recognize me, when you're so young?" he asked.

"I like ball," I said. "I've seen videos of you."

Manolo, who had seen him pitch, took over the conversation. I started to organize the mess of coconuts around us; I didn't listen to anything else, and then I heard this:

"I'm a doctor and here I am, knocking down coconuts."

"And I'm a pitcher. And here you see me, as a driver."

"That's how it is."

Then they hugged and said good-bye. The following week, on the evening of Thursday, July 2, I arrived at Arocha's house. He met me at the door and pointed out his coconut tree.

"You didn't end up taking any after all."

"They're no good. They're yellow and already dried up. They won't buy them like that."

"What are all of you looking for in the coconuts? Water?"

"Yes, water."

"Then you two don't know anything about coconuts. I knocked down two the other day and they had water, I could hear it."

"No. When you can hear it, they have little water, and that's why the water moves. When you can't hear the water and the coconut is heavy, it's so full of water that the water has no room to move."

"Ah, so you do know about coconuts."

"Yes. You're the one who doesn't know about coconuts."

Arocha smiled. Then he invited me to choose between the living room and the yard. He was wearing plastic sandals, a dark pair of shorts, and a light-blue tank top. His broad shoulders both had tribal tattoos, like vines. His hair, thinning, had not completely fallen out. His voice was powerful and his opinions were convincing. His ideas were deeply rooted. His gestures were pleasant.

At a West Palm Beach hotel, we asked the gardener for permission to scale two trees. He said no. No one had ever said no to us at a hotel. The gardener was Latino, Central American. Small and evasive, with dark spots on his arms and a round face. We asked him if we could knock down the coconuts from the trees across the street, and he told us that they also belonged to the hotel. He was grooming the lawn with a weed whacker and watching us out of the corner of his eye, as if we were his enemies or as if there was only room for one poor person here. I wanted to tell him that misery is poisonous and those who have been mistreated are the meanest, but I understood that I was only poisoning myself, and that, besides, Manolo would have replied with some superhistorical theory, exonerating our Central American brother of responsibility and blaming usurious capitalism.

We moved on about a quarter of a mile and, amid the mangroves on a very small and almost virgin beach, we found another coconut tree. When we finished working, a character from the hotel came in a golf cart, said a few things we didn't understand, put the coconuts in his cart, and threw the ones that didn't fit in the water. Manolo didn't say anything. Neither did I. We stayed, watching the coconuts, how the tide dragged them, the way the sea devoured them. We left in silence. Behind the hotel wall, spying on us, we made out the tattletale gardener. I still had a month left in Miami, but that was the last day I accompanied Manolo on his job.

———

"You keep a very singular distance from baseball."

"Because I have other hobbies now: cooking, spending time with my family, taking care of animals."

"Almost twenty-five years without going back to Cuba. What's left of your country when you spend so much time away from it?"

"I cut the cord from day one. I began to miss it, of course. My grandfather, my mother, my daughter, and my only sister were in Cuba, but I had many friends here and the rhythm of my life seemed to have stayed the same."

"That's a start. But today, what's left today?"

"If I get to Cuba, I won't get lost, but I will no longer be able to place certain streets. That has happened without my willing it. I have been living here for almost the same number of years that I lived there."

"You're not nostalgic for certain things?"

"Of course. Friends, my town, the house where I was born and grew up."

"Have you dreamt of Cuba?"

"I've had dreams, yes, but it has been a while. I dreamt that I got to Cuba and couldn't leave and I was telling myself, So now how do I leave, when I live in Miami? René, are you crazy, how are you going to go back now?"

"Was it a dream or a nightmare?"

"A tragedy, yes, a tragedy. I had that dream a couple of times."

"You're not thinking of going back at any point?"

"I can't say yes or no. Until now, I haven't taken the first step."

"But in the documentary *Out of Their League,* you're eloquent. You say, and emphasize, that you are Cuban, and that you're dying to sit down with a bunch of your guys to shoot the breeze in Havana's Central Park."

"Because those are the things that I miss. Because behind everything there is a political situation that perhaps no longer exists or that I've invented, inside myself, and because of which I have not wanted to return. Perhaps it is fear, I don't know. Everyone is telling me to go, that things have changed there, that nothing is going to happen, but I'm afraid."

"In the case of ballplayers, some have already gone."

"Ballplayers who have never made any statement against the government. I always said from day one that I came to this country in search of freedom. I've also talked about everything we athletes went through, the lodging where they put us, the mosquitoes that ate us up in the stands—because in Guantánamo, we had to sleep in the stands—and many other things. I hope that when I decide to go, it will be like they say and nothing happens. But, for example, one of the ballplayers who went told me that two minutes in, someone was pointing out the places he couldn't visit. If I go to Havana, how am I going to not be able to go to the Latin American Stadium? Why not? It's not like I am going with any political placards. If I go, I'm going to enjoy my game of baseball, period."

"There is, I fear, a distance in you that doesn't only apply to baseball."

"Yes, there is. René has this problem—he's removed, he's stuck in his house. Some people see me on the street and say I look like Arocha and I say, yes, I've been told that many times. You can't imagine the number of interviews I've turned down in recent years."

"Why?"

"I got tired of being used."

"Do they do that?"

"Of course. I got tired. At the beginning, they used me so much, because I was young and had the desire to let out everything I had brought from Cuba. All the TV shows called me. Every time something happened in Cuba, it was 'René, come here' and 'René, go there.' René the only Cuban ballplayer in the Major Leagues at that point, René the symbol."

"And when did you realize they were using you?"

"When I stopped playing, when I picked up and went home, and there wasn't a call or anything. That's when I realized it."

"So you don't go on TV anymore?"

"I've gone, but, you know, the last time I went, I got to thinking. To come home from work, shower, head out to Hialeah, to talk for two minutes there, because it's two minutes—no way, that's not my carnival anymore."

"Right."

"In other words, I value my time today much more. Come to me with a song, but leave with your song, because I won't do this anymore."

"So I was lucky. In the way we met, I mean."

"Yes, the way we met. I've been talking to you now because I saw you knocking down coconuts. Fighting for your life, just like I am fighting now."

Later, a millionaire cousin from my mother's side showed up and invited me to spend a weekend in Fort Myers, two hours from Miami. He showed me his three-story mansion, the movie theater in his house, his Maserati, his Mercedes-Benz, his wife's Audi 5. We went out fishing on his yacht. We had dinner at a Texas Roadhouse.

He lived inside an exclusive gated community, on an islet surrounded by a saltwater canal lined by coconut trees. I estimated that, if Manolo and I knocked down all of the coconuts around that complex, we could easily make more than six hundred dollars in one go.

My cousin was very generous. He made up a room for me that had a fridge and its own bathroom. He bought me clothing, shoes. He told me about my grandparents and great-grandparents.

On the last day, a few hours before he took me back to Miami, I placed the MacBook Pro he had lent me on the bathroom shelf and played "Forever Young" on YouTube, sung by Joan Baez. I turned on the hot shower and got under it. I felt stiff, orphaned. And at some point, without knowing how, I began to cry. I cried for three or four minutes, without stopping, without feeling ashamed. I wasn't crying for anyone. I wasn't going to tell anyone. The hot water dissolved my tears and burned a little. Was I thinking about my father? I don't know. I felt saved, as if that millionaire's house was an armored capsule to protect defenseless flesh. Later, I wasn't sad or hanging my head. Nor was I euphoric. It had been like a graduation-day cry.

CUBAN CAPITAL
TRANSITION (TO WHAT?) IN SEVEN PARTS

BY IVÁN DE LA NUEZ
TRANSLATED BY LISA CARTER

1.

In Cuba, everything that moves can be a taxi and everything that doesn't can be a rental property (either a restaurant, bar, hair salon, gym, or clandestine store). This is the new face of a private economy that is growing in real time, and through online ads, in plain sight. Welcome to the "primitive" accumulation of Cuban capital—with its own laws, its own tricks, and its own emerging classes, though not yet any sort of standardized capitalism (if there even is such a thing).

This new Cuban capital has both a symbology around money and a combination of agitprop and advertising that now goes beyond the old iconographic pact between Che Guevara and American Cadillacs; between the indestructible icon that sustains mythological life and the indestructible automobiles that sustain day-to-day life. Along this continuum, there is also a place to bring revolutionary tourists together with the last of the old combatants who now rent them rooms in their homes, with epic stories included.

I consider all of this one evening in March 2016. I'm in a building where almost every one of the owners rents to tourists. I'm on the balcony of an apartment belonging to a veteran diplomat who has mentored several generations of Cubans working in the foreign service. It's his birthday.

The conversation of the old guard turns to politics. Children. Businesses. One side is rhetorical, the other pragmatic. One is history, the other geography: all a matter of position.

The soiree is being held just a few days before U.S. president Barack Obama's visit to the island. At one point, someone checks their cell phone only to find a memo from the government sent to everyone who rents out their home.

It's . . . an antiterrorist measure! A warning about potential tenants from Middle Eastern countries—Israel, too, has been included—and an instruction for people to remain alert. The message suggests a tropical version of the Axis of Evil in which, sooner or later, the usual local suspects will play a role.

"They're preventing Havana from becoming another Dallas," a teenage girl says, alluding to the assassination of JFK.

"Don't worry, baby. Dallas didn't have State Security," her boyfriend replies.

It seems like Obama's visit is prompting a Cuban version of the Patriot Act. And preventive detention will no longer be a Soviet legacy, but a very contemporary American practice.

The Cuban capital's new private sector will either be antiterrorist, or it simply won't be.

2.

A few weeks later, my mother stands at her window, looking out at the teeming street. She doesn't dare go outside and doesn't understand the neighbors' explanation for the mounting chaos outside their homes: "They're filming *The Fast and the Furious* in Havana." (It is actually the eighth installment in this film franchise, to be called *The Fate of the Furious*.)

Today, in Cuba, everything is considered a turning point, an event we imbue with transcendent power to denote a before and an after in the life of this country. It might be geopolitical in scope, cultural, or purely frivolous; so it doesn't matter whether it's Obama's visit or a Rolling Stones concert, the opening of Galleria Continua or a runway show by Chanel.

The Fate of the Furious is no exception. In this neighborhood there's almost never anyone outside this early, but now inhabitants have to negotiate dozens of motorcycles, race cars, vans, "luxury" vintage convertibles, flashy dudes reeking of Prada, models, paparazzi, private security guards, extras . . . and the countless curious onlookers for whom all of this is "an unnamable fiesta," as the poet José Lezama Lima would say.

Not quite sure what to make of the full-fledged occupation of the neighborhood, my mother comes to the conclusion that we are witnessing the "American invasion" live.

She's not wrong.

For over half a century, and apart from exceptions like the docu-series *Cuban Chrome* (about the vintage cars found everywhere in Havana), we have never had American productions of this scale in Cuba. But now, one of the many business opportunities this country hopes to exploit is that of becoming an enormous Hollywood set, a virgin stage through which its unlikely superheroes can race—fast and furious.

This isn't to say that Cuba has been absent from the plotlines of American cinema, from Hitchcock to Coppola. But most often, as decreed by the embargo or the bureaucracy, it was re-created in the Dominican Republic or Puerto Rico. Nor was Cuba absent from television series like *The Agency, Law & Order, CSI, The Simpsons, House,* and *Castle.* In fact, those stories provide a clue as to what lies ahead for Cubans, as far as stereotypes go. It's all the same: an assassination attempt on Fidel Castro at the United Nations or a trillion-dollar bill the FBI sends Homer Simpson to obtain in Havana. It might even go so far as the case of a baseball player killed in Manhattan, solved by the writer-detective Castle, in which the Cuban suspects speak Taíno, an extinct language!

In any event . . .

For a long time now—on the left and the right, among tourists and the politically committed—Cuba has been a place people come not to discover reality, but to confirm a script. As such, its paradoxes are pushed into the background, its people condemned to be mere symbols squashed by the weight of prior judgment, of prejudice.

It's paradoxical that, while Cuban filmmakers have been fighting for a new film law for years, everything should run so smoothly when it comes to an American megaproduction like *The Fate of the Furious.* Caught between national lethargy and transnational speed, local filmmakers continue to demand independence. And, of course, they both fear and want to take advantage of the deluge unleashed by the thawing of diplomatic relations with the United States, precisely when the production of television series is at its peak and financial need forces them to participate yet carefully navigate the subordinate role they have been given.

Their challenge cannot be boiled down to a simple matter of independent filmmaking, but involves having a different discourse that would allow them to address this mash-up of tourism and the thaw of relations that is already feeding a new-old folktale in which even ideology is set to become just another chapter in the history of tropicalism. Such tension also reflects just how complex the opening up of relations with the United States is, and the delicate balance required.

From a practical point of view, this industry, which allows for the possibility of profit, technological updates, and work opportunities, is tempting and even necessary. From a cultural point of view, here at the outset of this new era, we are already heading back to the picturesque scenes of *Our Man in Havana*, where Cubans—maracas in hand—set the rhythm for the imperturbable avalanche of neocolonialism.

3.

The Seventh Cuban Communist Party Congress ended at almost the same time as the filming of *The Fate of the Furious*. And it did so arm in arm with another vintage fetish: that of unanimity. Pondering the topics discussed at the congress—and, more important, the topics that were not discussed—a group of old revolutionaries carries on its favorite pastime: fixing the country from a bar in Havana.

This is an ever-shrinking group, shaken by the permanent age-related departures it is experiencing. ("I'm next in line," my father used to say, until his turn came and he departed from both life and the group.)

All of these men rose up against Batista. Many of them carry the weight of more than one war on their shoulders. Almost all of them have children or grandchildren in Miami. Those whose homes are still respectable supplement their meager pensions by renting rooms to tourists. They are trying to retrain for these new times, never quite adapting, never quite surrendering, criticizing everything all the while. (Or everything that's "not the same but equal," as singer-songwriter Silvio Rodríguez would say.) Along with their discussions of *la cosa*—things, the situation—there is always rum. And an ambulance whenever one of them goes too far.

In Cuba, there is rum that marks the border between acceptable and dangerous. It is called Ron Planchao and a 250 cc Tetra Brik carton costs one Cuban convertible peso, or about a dollar. Connoisseurs of the spirit say these little Tetra Briks conceal a decent (though not always respectable) rum. The problem is that some of the veterans in this bar have, financially speaking, fallen beneath the waterline of Ron Planchao. And the combination of age and the harshest of spirits—that cocktail of hard liquor and soft currency—often put them in a difficult situation. Their distress also has as much to do with the passion of their arguments regarding economic reform, Obama's cleverness, the lack of a tangible plan for the future, and the fact that the new inequalities have placed them—"us, those of us who risked our lives for *this*"—in a precarious state.

From their twilight years, these old men ponder a revolution that, to their grandchildren, is nothing but an echo of the past. They keep waiting for a sign from their brethren in power about which political model will be followed, but all that comes out of the government are signs of economic reform. They hold tight to the days when Cuba proclaimed itself the first free territory in the Americas, yet the television at the bar portrays it only as the number-one attraction for foreign investment in the Caribbean.

Outside the bar where the old veterans are steeped in their alcoholic battles, you see the typical row of taxis waiting for tourists. It is a varied lineup, always a vintage American car, or a Chinese Geely, even a massive Soviet Chaika. In Cuba, outlandish cars are nothing new. But this Russian limousine goes beyond mere extravagance.

In actual fact, there are now ten Chaikas available for hire in Havana. The fleet was a gift from the top Soviet brass to allow Fidel to travel in safety. (No other taxi could presume to have such an illustrious pedigree.) Should you hire it, the driver will explain how this Communist limousine works, pointing out spaces for radio receivers and the escort detail, compartments for the auxiliary weapons. In terms of business, under the new Cuban economic system, this taxi is no different. "I have to pay thirty Cuban convertible pesos [about thirty dollars] to the company every day," the driver says. "Twenty-seven, to be exact."

Could there be a better example of how the scraps of socialism are being recycled in this new era? Could there be a clearer representation of the state of communism, where in order to become viable under the constraints of economic reform, it must draw upon El Comandante's fleet of vehicles?

If there were any doubts as to this symbiosis, they vanish once we reach our destination. The sperm whale of Cuban taxis drops us at the door to TaBARish: a "Soviet" bar filled with Communist memorabilia, where one can order caviar, vodka, soup, or pickles, surrounded by walls plastered in copies of the newspaper *Pravda*. Yuri Gagarin smiles out from them, and the red flag—complete with hammer and sickle—adds the finishing touch to the combined aesthetic of Soviet nostalgia and the new Cuban reality.

TaBARish turns, or attempts to turn, old communism into business. Here, and at the restaurant Nazdarovie (because TaBARish is not the only Soviet-themed business that has opened since private enterprise was allowed), you will find Russians and Cubans who once studied in the Soviet Union (tens of thousands of them did). Decorations include those famous matryoshka dolls, these ones dressed up for the occasion with the painted faces of Lenin, Stalin, Khrushchev, and Gorbachev. There is even one of Putin, a disturbing reminder to me that the Cold War ended when an agreement was reached between old Communists and new oligarchs.

As soon as the Revolution began, Cuban socialism began to conquer the old emblems of capitalism along its forced march. It began with the Hilton Hotel, rebaptized the Hotel Habana Libre, where Fidel Castro set up camp. This then cascaded all the way down to the old American cars, which continued to do battle with Soviet engines installed. Along the way, garrisons became schools, private clubs became workers' clubs, and so on with cabarets, fine restaurants, hotels . . .

Now, you can sense the exact opposite: within the heart of the flagships of socialism, you can increasingly hear the beat of commercial deals. Look no further than the Committees for the Defense of the Revolution, or CDRs, which now also guard private rentals. Or stop to hear how the language of police work has become part of the chorus of everyday life. *Come in, the captain will see you now. Run him through the system. Take it easy and cooperate.* To say nothing of the widespread use of a cell phone app that can provide the name, address, and date of birth of the caller. (Yet no one is shocked by the use and abuse of Cuban big data, maintaining that private enterprise and an end to privacy are perfectly compatible.)

4.

Sooner or later, everyone sits down to a banquet of consequences. So wrote Robert Louis Stevenson, a fan of islands. And that's what we are experiencing, right now, on the island of Cuba: a banquet of consequences. It comes in the form of a never-ending pageant of international visitors, which can range in a single week from a well-known artist (Frank Stella), to a president (Barack Obama), to a professional baseball team (Tampa Bay), to a famous rock band (Rolling Stones), to a designer fashion show (Karl Lagerfeld and Chanel).

Welcome to the long march, in the form of entertainment, that is leaving a trail of change in a country where it is more acceptable to consume the transformation than to discuss it. It's as if the cause had to be sacrificed in order to enjoy the consequences.

Let us think back to the time when the Revolution was in vogue. It was the 1960s, and intellectuals from all over the world were in Cuba, ever ready to offer theoretical support for the so-called Cuban way, a socialism that was green ("as green as the palms," according to Fidel), not red; that was Latin American, not Soviet; and that fed the fantasies of the West.

Today, however, in this Cuba of consequences, it is entertainment that makes the difference. Reggaeton, with its glamorous frivolity, marks the rhythm of this new life. Where once there was Sartre, now there is Beyoncé; where once we had Max Aub, now we have Paris Hilton. Graham Greene has given way to the Rolling Stones, and what was record turnout for the Maximum Leader's speeches now occurs for the electronic sounds of Major Lazer.

In the midst of this catharsis of controlled hedonism, even a trip as politically significant as Obama's was filtered through Cuba's most famous comedian, who performed a skit with the American president that was filled with double entendres, absurd jokes, and unofficial truths.

Even the historic table tennis exchange that took place during the time of Nixon and Mao was more solemn than this encounter between Obama and Pánfilo—an encounter, by the way, that forsook government protocol and left the opposition and exiles feeling out of place.

The United States invested millions of dollars in supporting the democratic cause in Cuba, and here all it took was a simple video of the president playing dominos with a comic figure who understands nothing for viewers to understand it all.

In this Cuba of consequences, no one can imagine Paris Hilton or Mick Jagger debating which is the best political model to follow. And that's because Cuban authorities themselves seem entirely uninterested in any form of ideological discussion, in a country that swings between illuminating the Bolivarian model and disappearing into the shadow of the Chinese model.

What comes next, after Obama? That's the question many asked themselves, on the left and the right, on the island and off it. It appears the government may carry on—as much as a government riddled with octogenarians can carry on—and yet there is also a sense of certainty that things need to change. And not just because of measures to open up the service industry— family-run restaurants, gyms, bars, and art galleries—but because the new economy has had an impact on areas traditionally considered sacred in Cuban socialism—education, health, and culture—that are beginning to brace for private initiatives that would have been unthinkable in the past.

A generation is now stepping into public life in the midst

of these reforms, at a time when the media is one step removed from its former political servitude, during a time of diplomacy and rampant hedonism.

The problem, though, is not change itself, but where change is leading. That is the tightrope on which this country, in which most people are unprepared for shock therapy, walks.

And while it's true that Cubans today are eager for money, they are also eager for time. They are eager for new business while still being eager to maintain the support networks that continue to pulse behind the everyday uncertainty.

5.

In January 2016, the government publisher Editorial Arte y Literatura released the novel *1984*. In a country that has been described as a utopia—geographically and ideologically—this dystopian novel by George Orwell contained all of the ingredients to make its publication a momentous occasion.

There were those who noted how long it took to publish this masterpiece. And there were those who, as Orwellians, demanded that *Animal Farm* (the blatant dissection of Stalinism barely concealed behind a universal diatribe against an abstract power) be published next.

Such grievances around the delayed encounter between Cuba and Orwell, the awkward author who was against Stalin yet fought on the Republican side in the Spanish Civil War, who opposed British colonialism and was a lifelong supporter of the "dark side" (as Spanish poet Jesús López Pacheco used to call the left), are not surprising.

But *1984* came to the island at the right time.

Because the Cuba that received this novel is increasingly like a dystopian country, ready to join the Orwellian revival that has taken hold since 2012, with new editions, comics, and announcements of film adaptations. (Hollywood has decided on a new telling of the story, following those already directed in Britain by Rudolph Cartier, Michael Anderson, and Michael Radford.)

In one way or another, we are all Orwellian. But Cubans are subject to "the damned circumstance of absurdity everywhere" in *1984* and *Animal Farm*.

From this point of view, *1984* is a survival guide, with GPS included, that can help us find our way along a path marked by socialist icons and the culture of entertainment, single-party states and tourism, science and remittances from abroad, anti-imperialism and the American deluge, the Chinese model and Cuban flavor—all bathed in the sweet-and-sour sauce poured over a world in which the free market and democracy filed divorce proceedings years ago. It's not that, in this Orwellian Cuba, we have bidden farewell to all Marxist discourse (or abandoned the Leninist concept of history, in which socialism is the ultimate end). But these ideas must wrestle with the fall of the Soviet empire that sustained Cuba geopolitically, and the collapse that has been described—how else!—as the death of utopia.

Against this background, Marx and Lenin must live alongside Huxley and Orwell in every nook and cranny of Cuba.

Within the utopian framework, the meaning of life was obscured by a future we were relentlessly heading toward. In the dystopian framework, we find that that future is already here, that it happened "the other day," while we were still planning for it.

And so tomorrow is just another day, a future that is neither perfect nor immutable. It is only *this*, what is happening right now, and it caught us by surprise on this Caribbean island, a place that is also—we must not forget—a model for the world.

In the midst of such change—which unleashes opinions as acrimonious as those around the delayed publication of Orwell's novel—we see a new generation that had its awakening in the twenty-first century, for whom the Revolution and the Berlin Wall are ancient history, a graduating class that grew up in the midst of the erosion of state monopoly over their lives, that has struggled from birth with a burgeoning economy as varied as their ideological references, topics, and life stories.

These Latin American millennials are developing in a world of social media and the international expansion of terrorism, in a precarious, do-it-yourself world in which they unabashedly examine national circumstances and are fully willing to participate in a globalized culture.

Rather than a spontaneous generation, this is a *simultaneous* generation, one that has known how to take advantage of the recent opportunity to become "self-employed" in Cuba, and taken it further, to *self-determination*.

This is not to say that they do not suffer from the usual Cuban complaints and conflicts, but something about their pragmatism reveals their insolence—they know they hold the keys to the future.

They are beyond utopia but before apocalypse. Perhaps this is because they live in the apotheosis, at the banquet of consequences in which every single dish of Cuban history is passing before their eyes.

6.

"We are not making a revolution for future generations. . . . We are working and creating for our contemporaries."

So said Fidel Castro at the National Library, during the monologue presented in two sessions that has come to be known as his "Speech to Intellectuals." It was April 1961, and both the speaker and the Revolution—the same revolution that was made *with* his generation and *for* his generation—were still young. This statement reveals a clear conviction regarding the generational nature of revolutions, and an overwhelming pragmatism: if a revolution is not generational, if it only plans for some yet-to-be-shaped person in the future, who then can sustain it while it is happening?

Attendees—the intellectuals who were listening to *the words*—were hit with this statement 105 minutes into his speech. (Today, we can hear the entire speech on YouTube, and who knows, maybe one day we will be able to watch it, too.) Just a short while earlier, Fidel Castro had offered his illustrious audience another phrase that would remain the guiding principle behind Cuban cultural policy: "With the Revolution, everything. Against the Revolution, nothing."

Given that history is also written in slogans, Fidel's statement regarding the generational nature of revolution—with and for that generation—was eclipsed by this other one, which established the boundaries of what was allowable, as if the limits of political contemporaneity were subject to the limits of artistic freedom: up to this point, you're *with*, and after this point, you're *against*.

Fifty-five years after his "Speech to Intellectuals," having turned ninety and fulfilled the destiny he created for himself, Fidel Castro ceased to exist. His death, and the subsequent mourning, plunged the country into a profound silence. The ubiquitous reggaeton that pours from taxi windows disappeared. The funeral procession bearing his ashes on their way back to the source—the guerrilla invasion in reverse—silenced even the hymns. A certainty opened up that an entire era was traveling along with Fidel in his funeral procession.

Because his death did not just pause the soundtrack of recent times—it revealed that the generation responsible for the Revolution was coming to an end. If there was any doubt in this regard, Fidel's successor soon cleared it up, stating he would step down as president in 2018 (though all indications are that he will continue to lead the Party until 2021).

Thus, Raúl Castro's last year as Cuban head of state, 2017, coincides with Donald Trump's first year as American head of state. And so the children and grandchildren of the generation that carried out the Revolution—for whom it was carried it out—will have to take the reins in Cuba.

The time has come for the "New Man" that Che Guevara envisioned—that collective Frankenstein shaped by those who never experienced the Batista regime—to get with the times, accept responsibility for his own political contemporaneity, and find, for the first time, a balance between the era he lives in and the power he holds.

With the death of Fidel Castro, various analysts predicted a U.S. naval blockade to prevent a mass exodus to Miami. They prophesied that the repressive political apparatus of the state would be dismantled. They foresaw the ultimate collapse of the system ("No Castro, No Problem").

But none of this happened. This may be because, having seen our future so manipulated, we Cubans have lost all respect for futurology. And yet this essay, written in February 2017, will also attempt to divine what is to come, so it, too, is no stranger to daring and indifference.

Now, in an era of post-Revolution meets post-democracy, someone born during the Revolution will most likely ascend to the presidency. This individual will undoubtedly come from the state and Party apparatus. It is unthinkable, however, that such an individual could ever possess the absolute power held by Fidel or Raúl. (They might even be a front man for the real power held by the army.) And the changes that began with Raúl will inevitably continue, as the options to go back become increasingly disastrous.

Handicapped by what it means to have potential in Cuba—essentially an invitation to beheading—Vice President Miguel Díaz-Canel (born in 1960 in Placetas, Villa Clara province) has a good chance to become this post-Castro Castroist.

But whoever becomes the next leader, he will not be commended to history and will have no mythical aura about him, but a life story very much like any one of his compatriots. He will have gone from school to work in the countryside, idolized the same sports heroes of Cuban socialism, and watched the same television series glorifying State Security agents. His family will be split between the diaspora and the island. He will have fought in Nicaragua, Angola, or another of the Cold War's hot zones. He will have listened to Nueva Trova ballads and answered the call to volunteer. He will have sworn allegiance to socialism and joined in the chorus of "We will be like Che!" He will be familiar with latrines, promiscuity, solidarity, and the cruelty of massification. He will know collectivization and impudence as ways of life under Cuban socialism, and the freedom of the flesh, or sexual freedom—where the spirit of the law is out of reach and of no effect. And he will come from a position of Absolute Truth to lead a country in an era now known as "post-truth."

The next government will be a direct descendant of reforms not Revolution, Raúl not Fidel, globalization not Cold War, at a time when the advantages of the Cuban Adjustment Act will end sooner than the disadvantages of the embargo. And so it will have to channel the discontent through fewer available escape valves. (Cuban immigrants in the United States will see their privileges disappear, and the normalization of Cuba means it will experience not only the justice that is found in other countries, but the injustices as well.) On the domestic front, Communist militants—an ever-shrinking group—will no longer be sufficient to make the government legitimate, and though the government's plans may not include opening up a multiparty system, it will have to allow more political diversity.

This New Man in power will have to exchange the future perfect for the future possible. And he will have to accept that socialism and capitalism are not, by any means, what the Revolution and the opposition promised they would be in their moments of glory.

Marx warned that people are more attached to the times they live in than to their parents. And the era that will embrace generational change in Cuba will face it in the midst of an extreme crisis not only in terms of Cuban socialism, but in terms of all political models. We have seen firsthand how the fall of communism led to calamity in the liberal world order and democracy itself, now in open conflict with the free market.

What, then, will Cuba become? A liberal republic, when liberalism is taking its dying breath? A post-Communist country open to shock therapy? An Antillean emirate with different laws for locals and foreigners, workers and investors, the powerful and the people? A dynasty? An exemplar of the Chinese model? Will it discover the formula that will allow it to, finally, combine socialism and democracy as it follows a new Cuban way?

For now, a combination of a one-party system and private enterprise is what's on the table, an emulation of the Vietnamese model. For a generation of millennials, messianism is not a viable political style and sacrifice is not the way to future redemption.

In 1960, a year before Fidel's "Speech to Intellectuals," Sartre spoke to almost the same audience, in the same place, the National Library. He, too, offered a few thoughts for posterity, which he later compiled in his book *Hurricane over Sugar*, in which he carefully examines the generational nature of the Revolution: "Given that revolution was necessary, circumstance appointed the young to carry it out. Only the youth felt enough outrage and anguish to undertake it, and only they were pure enough to see it through."

Presumably, Cuba after Fidel Castro will not be forced into another revolution. But this new generation will, at the very least, need to design its own political approach to its own times.

Whether he is absolved or condemned by history, Fidel Castro will surely never be forgotten by it.

7.

When society begins to collapse, hysteria tends to appear. But the opposite reaction can also occur: people go through a calamity behind a veneer of absolute calm. This is exactly what happened in the last years of communism in the Soviet Union, in a society built on the conviction that communism was eternal.

In the book *Everything Was Forever, Until It Was No More: The Last Soviet Generation*—a title that says it all—Alexei Yurchak called this state of shock "hypernormalization." Published in 2005, the book was used eleven years later as the basis for British filmmaker Adam Curtis's documentary *HyperNormalisation*. In his film, Curtis goes beyond the fall of communism to include the fake world that financial institutions and large corporations have designed for us.

When we speak of Cuban capital, it is important to point to the sense of eternity that has always accompanied political and economic life in Cuba, and the connection between the immortal socialism of the future and the remnants from a time in capitalism when things were built to last (from vintage cars to fridges, from houses to tunnels).

What is at risk now is not only a form of government or an economic system, but this sense of eternity. Cubans have a growing awareness of mortality—made more noticeable by the death of Fidel himself—which hints at the finite nature of everything that has been built.

At this juncture, our socialist side (wanting to maintain that socialism is eternal) insists that the transition *has already happened*. Meanwhile, our capitalist side (wanting to make liberalism eternal) insists that the transition *is yet to come*. For the former, Cuba improves, changes, evolves, but will never reject communism the way the Eastern bloc countries did. For the latter, the transition is not even here yet, for the simple reason that until there are multiparty elections, until the market economy has been implemented across the board, and until there is plurality of media, it simply cannot happen here.

What neither side seems to see is something potentially much simpler. It's not that the transition is unnecessary, as some would state. And it's not that the transition has not yet begun, as others would conclude. It's that, for a long time now, the only political reality in Cuba has been a state of transition. This transitional situation has become enormously comfortable, as it manages an endless limbo without a future.

Brilliant or cruel, the product of logic or superstition, longed for by the masses or fabricated by tyrants, for centuries the future defined history and relationships between people. It sowed power and inspired resistance. The pyramids and the Great Wall of China were the future. The catapult and the locomotive were the future. Da Vinci and Verne were the future . . . as were a dog in space and a man on the moon. The future was the French Revolution and democracy, the Bolsheviks and Mao's Long

March. The future belonged to the printing press and free trade, to the steam engine and communism.

Our parents worked, went to war, and participated in the Revolution precisely so their children could have a better future than they did. And thus the future is also everything that, one fine day, never came to pass.

The future's decline is not only connected to the end of communism, but has as much to do with the growing awareness of the finite nature of capitalism. The Spanish archaeologist Eudald Carbonell is convinced that capitalism will disappear in the twenty-first century not through revolution but through a process of "thermal death." He states as much in a book with the suggestive title of *El arqueólogo y el futuro* (The archaeologist and the future).

For an archaeologist to offer these clues about tomorrow could, at first blush, seem ironic. This is especially true because he does not speak metaphorically but from the perspective of someone who has spent a life digging in the ground, convinced that the mystery of our future cannot be found in foresight but through excavation. And that is because the future has not been postponed; it has been concealed. Thus we need to bring it into the light, not sit and wait for it.

If the future is already here, if it is *this*, what we are living through now, we had better dig through the surface layers that obscure it, not continue to ponder the layers of patina that cover it.

This is no easy task, of course. It is hard to speak of the future when we are surrounded by the refrain that our youth have no future. It is hard to clamor for the future in the midst of those who have been denied it.

A half century ago, in *The Book to Come*, Maurice Blanchot tackled something similar when he questioned the future of literature. One section, entitled "On an Art Without Future," could not be more explicit. The paradox, the novelty, is that it is precisely in this lack of a future that Blanchot found the code by which to map out a tomorrow. And because there is at least one advantage to the future of someone without a future: "the power and the glory" can no longer be a corollary to the process of the Revolution but is instead the exceptionally precarious condition on which to start all over again. "All great art originates in an exceptional fault."

That future Blanchot envisions brings Moby Dick to mind, the unattainable whale that stirs up dreams of greatness on the horizon. For us Cubans, it's not a whale, but a marlin. It is that beast besieged by sharks that the fisherman in *The Old Man and the Sea* knows he needs to haul back to the coast as proof of his truth and his greatness.

It is the beast we need to plant on the shore, to bear witness to the fact that we have battled it, that it is here, and that we can—at last—call it our contemporary.

THE PERSONAL MOVIE

TRIBULATIONS OF "THE GOOD DEMONS"

BY VLADIMIR CRUZ
TRANSLATED BY CECILIA MOLINARI

The *guajiros* of the Escambray Mountains, in Cuba's geographical center yet on the absolute periphery of the country's cultural activity, became acquainted with the movies before the theater.

Shortly after the revolutionary triumph of 1959, the mobile movie trucks arrived, sent by the recently founded Instituto Cubano del Arte e Industria Cinematográficos (ICAIC), and after the peasants' initial fright and fascination, the movies turned into something normal for them.

The theater arrived almost a decade later. It reminded the *guajiros* of the movies somewhat, although this time the truck didn't carry a projector and film canisters, but rather the actual artists, whom the *guajiros* observed as they prepared the stage, set up the lights, ate, and, at nightfall, gave the performance. In other words, unlike the ethereal figures projected by a beam of light onto a screen, they saw people in all their humanity, and perhaps that is why they began to call the theater "the personal movie."

It must be said that back then the adaptive capacity of the Escambray peasants, a traditional sector of society not at all inclined to sudden changes, was blossoming more profusely than the romerillo plant. In a short amount of time, those mountains had seen Che's column of rebels; the people who rose up against the triumphant Revolution, called *bandidos;* and the militia who battled those *bandidos.* And the peasants themselves actively took part in each one of those stages. In that same period, they went from agrarian reform, which gave them the land, to the cooperatives, which asked them to return it so it could be integrated into a collective structure. The process was not easy and caused an upheaval throughout the entire area, especially in the Lucha Contra Bandidos, the War Against the Bandits, of great importance to the consolidation and establishment of the revolutionary government, which forced each family to take sides, sometimes causing huge rifts, with one son on each team—there were even a few who, puzzled, tried to join a troop of insurgents who were characters in a play.

Those were revolutionary times, and perhaps fiction came to help the peasants understand the limits of reality, always so imprecise in Cuba, and to ease them into a new era.

However, I don't think any of them imagined, or had the time to stop and contemplate, that behind the well-lit and made-up characters on the screen, backed by the magical machinery of films, there were human beings as real as the ones getting out of the trucks to perform the plays, who also worked and ate, and sometimes got drunk, just like them, and even less that the distant lives of those people, their despair and misery, not just of the actors, but of all the people working in a movie team, are part of the film, influencing and sometimes determining its result.

Each one has his or her own real life behind those imaginary lives, and his or her own movie behind the one that reached the peasants.

My movie began one dawn in February 1993.

I reached Havana's bus terminal, which was closed in the small hours before daybreak. For some time, the terminals would close after midnight; no more buses would leave until the following day due to the fuel shortage. I headed toward the back of the building, where unlucky travelers huddled together with all the wildlife that, previously, when the terminal remained open, used to spend the night unnoticed in the waiting rooms. There were quite a few panhandlers, who had begun to appear in Havana more frequently. The area was packed, or at least the best corners to spend the night were, so, thanking my lucky stars for finding a piece of cardboard, I occupied the only available spot, under an incandescent lamp. I tried to sleep, but it was nearly impossible, not just because of how uncomfortable it was, but also due to my excitement about the unfolding events of the last few days.

I had reached Havana a couple of hours earlier, in a bus coming from Cienfuegos, a south central city, where I worked in a small experimental theater group. As soon as I arrived, I headed straight to my friend Susy Monet's house—she was an actress and former colleague from Grupo Teatro Escambray. This was the group that brought the theater to the mountains in 1968, hence the name, and where I began my professional life twenty years later.

Although I no longer worked with Susy, and we didn't see each other often, we were still close friends. I'd sent her a telegram announcing my arrival: *I'm going to make a movie and need to stay at your place because the production team can't get me a hotel room until a few days from now.*

She didn't have a phone, and back then we didn't even dream

of e-mail, so I resorted to the traditional telegram method, which worked quite well despite the challenge of never knowing if the recipient had received your message. Susy hadn't received it, and her house was closed when I arrived. I had no one else to turn to in those small hours, so I returned to the terminal to spend the night.

Since I couldn't sleep, I grabbed the script from my backpack and began to read: "Sequence 1: Havana. Exterior. Day. Free Cinema: Havana streets, a city where the macho is king . . ." The kick of a drunkard lying next to me, and his aggressive growl as a response to my complaint, convinced me that the script's first line hit the mark, and I realized how useless focusing on reading would be. Meanwhile, the bulb's light, like that of a torture chamber, was excellent at not letting me sleep but awful at allowing me to read . . . and I already knew most of the script by heart. So I decided to use it for a more practical purpose and covered my face with it. I remembered the meeting I had had a few days earlier with my theater group colleagues. The director had announced it as a simple fifteen-minute gathering to be held after our workday. It would be one of the most important meetings of my life, although I didn't know it at the time.

My group was one of those small "projects" that propelled Cuba's theatrical practice in the late eighties and early nineties, which up until then had been supported by stable companies. The projects were based on training, improvisation, and a series of ideas mainly taken from Eugenio Barba's books. We had enthusiastically welcomed the theories of the great Italian director and researcher, creator of the theater anthropology concept and considered by some to be the last great revolutionary of Western theater. We lived and breathed the theater. At the time, we had spent almost a year preparing for a performance following a process in which the actor's work became so personal that he or she couldn't be replaced by anyone else. If someone left the project, the entire group would be forced to start practically from scratch. The day of the meeting, we all sat on the floor and the director told my colleagues that I was going to share a circumstance about which they would have to make an immediate decision. I told them that the situation was very simple: the best film director in Cuba had called to offer me a feature role in his next movie, which had an extraordinary script, and I thought I had to go, even though this would affect our work as a group, because it signified my chance to enter our film history. I also said that, in any case, I was ready to abide by the collective decision. And I meant it. The director simply added: "Everyone knows what this means. I just want each of you to say what you would do if you were me and what you would do if you were him." They all said that if they were me, they'd go make the movie, and if they were him, they'd allow me to go.

I still think that if my colleagues had said no, I would've turned down the project and possibly given up my movie career. It wouldn't have been strange because, according to some of my friends, I've done everything to impede my career, starting with my decision to be the only one of my graduating class to go work for a theater group in the mountains, while the rest remained in Havana trying to make their way in the movie and television business. Even years later, when I felt the need to diversify my film work, I had no better idea than to write scripts, possibly the most arduous and unrewarding job in the industry. I think I have a fatal propensity to always choose the longest road. It must be a trauma acquired during my years of study—my acting professor, who'd studied in Moscow, placed so much emphasis on the process being more important than the result that I think we graduated without knowing how to accomplish anything.

When I finished the academy, overwhelmed by such an accumulation of theory, I felt I couldn't sit and wait for the movies or television to give me a shot: I wanted to immediately put into practice everything I had learned, to apprehend and comprehend it. And I thought theater was the right place to get my feet on the ground. That's why I left for the mountains.

And so I had wanted to make it to the capital with my feet on the ground, and in effect there I was, but instead of my feet I had my back on the ground in the capital—on the floor of the capital's bus terminal, that is.

I slept a bit and opened my eyes at daybreak, when the terminal opened. I got up, washed my face with a tiny trickle of water that dripped into the sink of the dilapidated and fetid bathroom, and, skipping breakfast, I headed straight to ICAIC.

When I reached the production office door, on the corner of Nineteenth and Sixth Streets, in Vedado, I was greeted by the movie's casting director. She looked me up and down with an expression that went from disbelief to astonishment. My appearance was pitiful: a pair of threadbare red pants, a striped shirt in the same state, and curly, sun-damaged, practically shoulder-length hair. I was so thin that my eyes and mouth took up my entire face.

The casting director couldn't believe that the person in front of her was the same one she'd spoken to several times over the phone during the week, and the one who would play a character that everyone had imagined would look quite different. She made sure I was me by asking for my ID card, then indicated I should wait by the door. I later found out that she'd gone to see the director and had said he was completely crazy. The director, without batting an eyelash, told her to let me in. I entered and was face-to-face with Tomás Gutiérrez Alea, who gave me an affable welcome. And that was the start of my first day at work on *Strawberry and Chocolate* as well as the beginning of my movie career.

I was twenty-seven years old, with five years of professional theater experience and around two hundred Cuban pesos in my pocket, which, at the real exchange rate, meaning in the black market, amounted to around two dollars. I had pesos rather than dollars because back then, prior to the legalization of the dollar in Cuba, I could've gone to jail for having that sum of money in dollars.

Let me note that, although in a practical sense I may have looked it, I was not someone who was impoverished, marginal, or unlawful, but rather a university graduate who worked every day in the career of his choice, with the maximum available salary for that position. I was as well or even better paid than many professionals. But, as I said, it was 1993, the darkest time of the Special Period.

The casting director didn't know me because the extremely extensive and complex main actor selection process had been personally led by Tomás Gutiérrez Alea, aka Titón. He was an exceptionally sensitive man and, rather than testing his actors, he tested his own ability to communicate with them. That's why he ended up choosing protagonists with completely different traits from those originally intended. Every actor in Cuba knew that the movie's leading characters were a university student and a homosexual a few generations his senior, therefore Titón was searching for a twenty-year-old actor and another one over forty. I had gone to the audition two months earlier, aspiring to play David, the young student, and there Titón said that I fit the role well, but I was too old at twenty-seven.

Each character presented great challenges when it came to choosing the actor, and David's challenge was his youth. They needed a very young performer, but with the experience and sufficient training to endure the pressure of carrying the movie on his shoulders. However, despite those difficulties, the first actor chosen by Titón was for David's role: a twenty-year-old guy, still a student, good looking and "well-fed," like Michelangelo's David. The team breathed a sigh of relief and easily got used to his image for the David in the movie. However, when rehearsals started, things didn't go so well, and Titón cried out for them to call me. I was saved by that rehearsal process, which allowed for the young actor's weaknesses to be revealed in time. If they'd gone straight to shooting, it would've been much harder to stop the film to replace him.

This rehearsal process, in some cases very intense, is one of the peculiarities of the way we work in Cuba. In other places, at least according to my experience, it isn't given the same importance, or barely even exists. I remember once, when we were filming *Che, el argentino,* I heard Steven Soderbergh, the director, mention that once, during filming, Al Pacino had asked him a question. He said it as if it were exceptional, because in Hollywood it *is* exceptional, but to us having questions is essential. We've always had to shoot with very few takes given the lack of money, especially when we filmed on celluloid. The raw material was extremely expensive; therefore, the intense communication and preparation between director and actors was indispensable so that they could arrive on set having done everything possible ahead of time. It may be a homespun way of working, stemming from need, but it's given us good results, especially in terms of the actors' work.

I remember reading back then in some magazine that Robert De Niro "warmed up" after take twenty-three. Big American productions don't have our issues—we've always had to film, even the Oscar-nominated *Strawberry and Chocolate,* in two or three takes per shot. Cuban actors always have to be "warmed up" by the time they arrive on set.

Twenty-something years and twenty-something movies later, in late June 2016, I arrived in Havana from Madrid to begin shooting *Los buenos demonios* (The good demons), a movie to be directed by Gerardo Chijona, my friend and the only Cuban director with whom I've filmed of late. Although I would've loved to continue working in my country, in order to talk about the issues that really matter to me and to address my native audience, during the last fifteen years I've worked mainly abroad. Projects with other Cuban directors, whom I also admire and respect, haven't materialized. The reasons remain unclear. Sometimes I feel that there's a subtle disconnect, because I work abroad, and in the worse cases some score-settling—although this is more subjective—with and on behalf of those who always work in Cuba.

Yet perhaps one of the keys can be found in the way Chijona himself approached me to see if I'd participate in his previous film, *La cosa humana,* shot in 2014, our second film together after *Un paraíso bajo las estrellas,* made fifteen years earlier.

Although we had become friends after that first experience, when he thought of me for a character in *La cosa humana,* he sent me messages to confirm a meeting with the casting director, the same one from *Strawberry and Chocolate,* with whom I have also been friends for years. I called him to ask why the two of us didn't just talk about it, since we knew each other well enough to do so, and he replied that he first needed to know how much I wanted to get paid, because he had a small budget and couldn't afford a high fee.

That may be the reason why I haven't been able to work with other Cuban directors: people think that you won't accept the

tacit agreement on minimum payment that is standard for act-
ing in Cuban movies and even for directing and producing them.
Very cheap movies, with such a low budget that it often influ-
ences the artistic quality—that's the only way Cuban films have
managed to survive the last few years.

I told Chijona that I wanted to shoot in Cuba again, to tell
me how much he could offer and that I would adapt to whatever
he said. And that's how we did it. At the time I couldn't help but
think about the first time we'd worked together, in 1998. I recall
it as if it were an old western flick: I'm sitting in my car parked
at the end of an empty block. Chijona's Lada drives down from
the other end and parks around three hundred feet from where
I'm waiting. We both get out and stare at each other (*the wind
howls and kicks up dust devils; we both squint and the neighbors shut
their windows*). He raises his hand first and tells me not to move.
We sit in my car. He tells me that the conversation we're about
to have is not happening. And if I ever repeat it, he will deny it.
(Therefore, I will not reproduce it here.) Minutes earlier, I had
quit his movie due to a salary-related argument. Chijona came,
spoke, gave me his word, and I returned to the set. I think it was
the first time I had an up-close look at the superhuman effort a
director has to make in Cuba in order to shoot his movie under
local conditions.

The salary issue always comes up, an unresolved problem in
Cuban films. First off, hierarchical movie salaries don't fit well
with the socialist philosophy where everyone is a simple worker.
Second, our precarious industry doesn't give actors much to
choose from, so they normally accept whatever they're offered.
Everyone knows a movie actor receives the best pay for the movie
he or she doesn't want to make. They'd pay to make the one that
they are interested in. For the one that they aren't, they ask for
double the salary, and that's what they get paid.

In 1998, after the worst of the Special Period, Cuban films had started to get back on their feet thanks to coproductions. That's when Cuban actors discovered that foreign producers were being asked to pay them a sum of money that never actually reached them. And the situation blew up just when we were working on *Un paraíso bajo las estrellas*.

To make matters worse, there was the two-currency issue: Cuban institutions pay in the "weak currency" and have very reluctantly been forced to add some of the "hard currency" in some industries with foreign investments and potential markets abroad, such as films. Begrudgingly accepting some market laws is the only way these institutions have managed to survive with minimal credibility. Additionally, during those years the difference between the official exchange rate and the one on the street was overwhelming, and that was the reason I left Chijona's movie (before the car scene), when the production company's director told me that they were paying us a lot because in fact the official exchange rate was one Cuban peso to one dollar. Taking into account that the exchange rate on the street was one hundred pesos to one dollar, I took this as an insult and said I was leaving, until Chijona came to my rescue.

Those differences in the exchange rate, five years earlier, in 1993, meant that for filming *Strawberry and Chocolate*, as lead actors, we earned the maximum allowed by the current rates, around four thousand Cuban pesos—with that money, shortly before, I could've bought a Soviet car—which at the street exchange rate amounted to less than forty dollars for three months of intense work. It may seem like a ridiculous figure, and it is, although to me, having started the film with only two dollars in my pocket, ending it with forty was not bad at all. In three months I had multiplied my capital by twenty!

Even those minuscule rates had been a victory because it's

said that they were even smaller before, and that they went up thanks to the day the great actor Reynaldo Miravalles was shooting a movie and discovered that the horse he was riding was making more than him. The owner had provided the horse on the condition that what they paid him be equivalent to what he could get from the horse's doing any other type of work, and it's likely that if the owner of the horse had found out that the owner of a cat, whose only role was to sleep on an armchair, made more than him, he also would've gotten upset. However, both owners, likely simple townsfolk, would've perfectly understood that the viewers wouldn't be going to the movies to see the cat or horse, but rather Miravalles.

It is said all this went down in 1978 during the shooting of *Los sobrevivientes,* by Tomás Gutiérrez Alea—although I wasn't there, there's almost no one left to ask, and I honestly don't remember Miravalles on a horse—and, to add to the animal tales, participating in that film were some Russian borzoi dogs belonging to Ramón Mercader, Trotsky's assassin, whom Alea had met by chance, obviously not knowing who he was, while Mercader was walking his dogs down Fifth Avenue in Havana. Alea had asked to use them in his movie (*Los sobrevivientes* involves an aristocratic family that owns exotic animals), and Mercader himself accompanied them on set.

I arrived in Cuba in June 2016 to shoot *Los buenos demonios.* After six months of working in Spain, my main professional base outside of Cuba, I carried a suitcase filled with costumes for the movie and the sense of optimism that we had breathed since December 2015, after the normalization of relations with the United States, which culminated in the reopening of the embassies. The first half of 2016 had been amazing in Havana, which had turned into history and entertainment's main stage. Parading through here were everyone and everything from Barack Obama to Chanel's latest collection to the Rolling Stones, and it all seemed to signal extraordinary things to come. Movie professionals were already cautiously optimistic because Americans were beginning to shoot on the island, with a Fast and the Furious and a Transformers film as their first productions.

However, in early July, the landscape changed radically, both in the economy in general and the film world in particular. The situation became much worse than I would've expected.

The fear was that Venezuela's crisis was finally affecting Cuba: that we'd once again be hit by the *fatum* of Cuba's economy, which always ends up depending on a sole benefactor, and that the Venezuelan oil tankers would stop coming, as had happened before with Soviet ships. People spoke of the start of another Special Period, although the government denied it and, meanwhile, announced oil rationing measures and financial difficulties due to the country's lack of liquidity.

I was rocked by the moment's similarities to those far-off 1993 days. As we say in Cuba, *El cuartico está igualito*—the room is exactly the same—and suddenly there we were, a group of people trying to tell a fictional story when reality is rattling and teetering everywhere, with the returning suspicion that we are once again dedicating our lives to conquering futility.

Filming on *Los buenos demonios* was stopped—twenty-four hours after it began—due to lack of fuel. Despair and uncertainty overpowered the entire team, which had been working for months. We all expected a difficult filming process, with the same limitations as usual, and moreover, it was the hottest time of the year, with children on vacation in an already-noisy city. But no one expected that kind of blow. We wondered, and asked the director, if we'd be able to continue. The director wondered, and asked the ICAIC administration why, if we'd been able to shoot during the most critical time of the Special Period, we couldn't do so now.

Finally, we found a way to continue filming, but with the sword of Damocles hanging over our heads, because the ICAIC wasn't what it used to be and was in no condition to defend its productions with the same strength as before.

That institution, which had proved to be so efficient in the sixties at distributing movies to the most remote corners of our country, among other things, is now an obsolete dinosaur, a hypertrophied and dysfunctional bureaucratic structure that everyone, even in the government itself, knows must be modified and radically updated.

The issue is the method to be used for those modifications. The first step came from the upper echelons, with a very conservative Transformer style far removed from the approach of the filmmakers, who advocated for one that was more *fast* and *furious*. After feeling they were being pushed into the background, they've now been meeting for three years, in open and spontaneous assemblies in a process that has been more *furious* than *fast* and has made evident the need for a film law that would regulate audiovisual productions in Cuba within the context of these new realities.

At this political-economic and institutional crossroads is where we began filming *Los buenos demonios,* sensing that the "exorcism" would be no easy feat. The project had faced, from its inception, inordinate obstacles. The first was the death, in September 2013, of its creator and the person who was supposed to be its director, Daniel Díaz Torres, which took everyone by surprise and left his collaborators incredibly frustrated. His lifelong friend Gerardo Chijona grabbed the baton and decided to finish the movie in his name.

No one found it strange that a project undertaken by Daniel had such disproportionate issues, because disproportion had plagued him during many moments of his life. Daniel was a good man, but he'd been turned into a demon. In 1991, his controversial movie *Alicia en el pueblo de Maravillas* catapulted him to the center of the country's political and cultural scene. The film is a satirical metaphor that gathers and exaggerates the worse defects of the socialist society that Cuba had been attempting to build; it was made "to disturb and provoke active reflection" (in the words of the director), but it was very badly received by the "guards" of the revolutionary ideology, hardly inclined to an exchange of ideas and lacking a sense of humor. The historic moment was conducive to ideological radicalism: the fall of the Berlin Wall and the Eastern European socialist bloc had left Cuba in a desperate situation. At screenings of the film, Communist militants took over movie theaters to repudiate it, sometimes violently, and it placed Daniel on the scandal's marquee, facing censorship like never before.

It also led to the first big crisis for the ICAIC, when the government considered merging it with the television office and abolishing it as an independent entity. Filmmakers resisted, and the always-latent tension between them and the country's political leadership was exposed. Daniel's moral integrity was of enormous help in resolving the conflict, and it allowed him to continue living and working in Cuba. His honesty was so evident that even those who had demonized him had to accept it.

Somehow the process was reversed and Daniel went from being a demon to being good. That's why, now, twenty-five years later, those of us who knew and loved Daniel believed that finishing *Los buenos demonios* in his memory was an act of poetic justice.

It is said that during those difficult times in 1991, when poor Daniel was being shaken by all types of forces that wanted the film to be censored, one day he and Manolo Pérez, the head of a creative group inside the ICAIC, went to see Alfredo Guevara, the fabulous president of the institution, newly arrived from Paris. Guevara was also a good and bad demon. Good for everything he did in favor of Cuban and Latin American films in general (the so-called New Latin American Cinema, which he defended to his death), and bad for many other reasons. He was always a powerful man, and he'd been called upon to appease his people and put out the fire. After founding the ICAIC and doing many important things as president, he'd been away for a while in Paris and was now returning to save us all, like a musketeer, with his cape on his shoulders.

Among the president's strange characteristics was that he always traveled with his small, hairy dog, so soft it seemed like it was made of cotton, in his arms, and it had likely also come from Paris. The president's image became so associated with the little dog, named Bacus, that it's said that when the elevator doors slid open on the ICAIC's seventh-floor office and Bacus walked out, people straightened up as if it were the president himself, although these may be water-cooler stories.

What isn't a water-cooler story is the meeting between Daniel and Manolo and the president (or at least it hasn't been denied by the only one of them who is still alive). The president received them standing behind his desk and didn't invite them to sit down. They explained the issue that had brought them there while the president listened, serious yet somewhat absent, although they were speaking of nothing less than the national cinema's survival. Suddenly, the president interrupted them with just one phrase in an imperative tone: "Get up here!" Daniel, overwhelmed as he was by the potential consequences of what was unfolding and in hopes of finding a confident and wise voice that would tell him what he had to do, looked at the table trying to find a free spot to climb up on, and he was about to do so when Bacus jumped onto the president's chair, clarifying the situation. Daniel breathed a deep sigh of relief when he realized he'd just avoided one of the most compromising moments of his career. The president is no longer with us, and neither is Daniel. I doubt Bacus is still here, because it's been twenty-five years, and Manolo admits he doesn't remember that day but says that the dog thing could've happened. The limits of reality are always vague in Cuba. In any case, I prefer to see it as a story that should have been true even if it wasn't, because it does a far better job at explaining the things from our past that have brought us to our current problems than many other analyses. The president had lights and shadows, and one of his demons, perhaps not one of the most aggressive ones, was his indifference, which hurt me personally: it kept me from attending the 1995 Oscar ceremony, the year *Strawberry and Chocolate* was in the running for Best Foreign Language Film, the only Cuban film that has ever been nominated.

The Academy invited the directors of the nominated foreign films, not the actors, to the ceremony, although the actors did everything they could to be there, paying their own way (which was impossible in our case) or being invited by producers or distributors. My costar Jorge "Pichi" Perugorría and his wife got in touch with Miramax, our movie's U.S. distributor, and the Americans said that they would be delighted to have the actors attend, but that they could only pay for our stay once we arrived on American soil, so we had to pay for our tickets.

It cost three hundred dollars to get to Miami. Pichi was able to round up the cash, but I didn't have enough and had no one to ask. The president had requested a visa to travel to the United States and attend the ceremony, but it had been denied, which seems to have greatly affected him. That's when Pichi came into the picture to intervene on my behalf, telling him I had a U.S. visa because they'd given it to me when I traveled to a festival in Puerto Rico, and all I needed to attend the movie's grand night, a movie I was a key part of, was the three hundred dollars for the ticket to Miami. The president said that he couldn't take care of this request at the moment because he had a migraine.

I didn't travel to Los Angeles and I was likely one of the few, perhaps the only, participating actors from the nominated movies who watched the ceremony on TV, in a remote satellite dish factory in Santa Clara to which I had to travel several miles by bicycle.

Attending the Oscars would have been a magnificent reward for the effort and all the difficulties we experienced while making this film, something I would have never even dreamed of that night in Havana's bus terminal; however, to be rabidly positive, after seeing all those uptight people in their tuxedos and ties, I think I was much more comfortable watching the ceremony in my shorts and T-shirt.

The film didn't win, and fifteen years later, in December 2010, Nikita Mikhalkov came to the Havana Film Festival—he was the director who had won the Oscar for Best Foreign Language Film that year, beating *Strawberry and Chocolate* with his movie *Burnt by the Sun*. He was honored at the festival's closing ceremony, and in his thank-you speech he spoke a little Spanish, explaining that his nanny had been a Spaniard.

Outside the Teatro Karl Marx, it was pouring rain when Pichi and I saw Nikita, who'd been surrounded by people all night long, completely alone and waiting for his car. He's an impressive, tall, and elegant guy, and even taking shelter from the rain under the theater's tiny eaves, he couldn't conceal the confidence and poise emanating from each of his gestures. We approached him and asked him very seriously if he knew who we were. A light cloud of worry crossed his face and we realized that he was discreetly looking for an exit to escape these two guys who, with a far from mollifying appearance, were harassing him against the theater's façade. That's when we said, "We're the actors from *Strawberry and Chocolate,* the movie you took the Oscar from in 1995." After a brief effort to recognize us, he burst out laughing, hugged us both at the same time with his Russian bear paws, and whispered, "Since I've come to Cuba, everyone is telling me the same thing." I think that the fact that everyone in Cuba thought that the Oscar should've been ours, and that they blatantly said it to the winner—well, that was our real award.

Nikita Mikhalkov is also a good demon. With a stunning body of cinematographic work, he's ended up flirting with politics, becoming the Russian film institute's president, and making very unfortunate comments about homosexual rights. (Perhaps he hesitated to hug us because of our movie's theme?) However, the scene of the three of us embracing under the Teatro Karl Marx eaves has undeniable cinematic value. And if I had to choose an ending for the film fragment that this *guajiro* (I'm also a *guajiro,* although I'm from Santa Clara) has been capable of making with his life up until now, I'd probably choose this one.

Yet it's a false ending; Mikhalkov got into his car and left, and we stayed back there a while longer watching the enormous downpour over Havana. We then also gave each other a hug, which to us (and possibly to the Cuban audience) was more significant than the one with Mikhalkov, and said good-bye.

I remained alone, watching the water fall, and thinking about how the only thing that keeps us alive and fighting is our next project and the need to tell stories that can help people live and experience their own "personal movie."

I glanced around in search of something to protect me from the rain and found a piece of cardboard. Picking it up, I recalled the bus terminal. In the end, that night had been a perfect way of ensuring I'd have an ascending career: everything that came after, necessarily, had to be better.

———

In September 2016, as I protect myself with a similar piece of cardboard, I exit the production car in front of the ICAIC studios in Cubanacán. It's been raining for four straight days, and water is filtering through the studio's roof in abundant leaks that continuously ruin the scenes' sound. It's rumored that the foreign company that repaired the roof and was supposed to maintain it had to leave Cuba after not being paid, and now it was a lost cause. It's also said that this happens frequently, yet once again, these could be water-cooler stories, although my first day of filming had to be canceled because the location where we were scheduled to shoot, the Sierra Maestra restaurant at the Habana Libre Hotel, had a piece of its roof fall off due to the rain.

I look up at the sky searching for an explanation, only to find an imperturbable gray. Seems like things will remain the same. I think of Daniel and in my mind I say to him, "See if you can do something up there, my friend. Try to at least find a vice president, and even if you have to climb on his table, give us a hand, we're almost done . . ."

I enter the studio. Chijona is waiting for me with the team, stoically weathering the storm with hurricane-proof determination. And so begins the last week of shooting *Los buenos demonios*.

GLAMOUR AND REVOLUTION

BY WENDY GUERRA
TRANSLATED BY ROBIN MYERS

1.

If we study images of Havana from the early 1960s, if we return to our parents' and grandparents' photos from the early decades of the Revolution, we can sense a certain air of effervescence, an elegance, much like the ambience treasured by the French in their own black-and-white albums from the sixties.

Slightly later, the cliché of the *barbudo*, the bearded revolutionary—along with the delirium that awoke guerrilla norms like a virus in those early years of new life and prêt-à-porter—made it impossible to find the time or space for contemplating or attending to the self. Starting in the 1960s and '70s, the body became an instrument of work, defense, and reconstruction.

Ideology mined aesthetic spaces: the image of an overly made-up woman clashed with the revolutionary thinking. An elegant *compañera* didn't suit the times. She needed a uniform and an olive-green face if she was to make her way through those hard years as part of the whole.

The economic circumstances following the missile crisis (namely shortages), as well as the sexist prejudices imposing ideo-aesthetic limits that were permitted in those years, worked against the preservation of revolutionary female beauty. The "New Man" couldn't possibly be beautiful.

Legend has it that the famous Cuban model Norka Korda—wife of the photographer Alberto Korda, who took Che Guevara's most emblematic portrait—paraded about the House of Dior in Paris before returning to Cuba, in the years of real political commotion, to don military trappings and face each dearth and drama that the crisis caused.

How have we succeeded in both resisting and safeguarding our beauty, coquetry, and tropical glamour amid genuine deprivation? How can we *convertir el revés en victoria,* as the revolutionary maxim goes—turn the setback into a victory? And how, beyond the slogan itself, can we continue to be beautiful, making use of natural, organic recipes in a country like Cuba: devastated, bereft of resources, where sun, salt, and diet conspire against our physical harmony?

RECIPES FOR RESISTANCE

Cucumber face mask
Avocado hair mask
Mascara made from shoe polish
Tanning lotion made from butter and iodine (assuming
    there's butter and iodine)
Grapefruit peel steak as a substitute for meat
Toasted peas to supplement scarce coffee beans
Dresses made from recycled suit linings, slips turned into
    miniskirts
(The list goes on forever.)

2.

LITERACUBA

I spent my teenage years at art school, boarding in a coed dormitory. Hurricanes or bad weather would often collapse the partition walls or compartments used to separate girls from boys, and it was then that the sexual restrictions melted away. The map of gender differences was gradually erased and our promiscuity became essential: a vital ingredient in our collective memory.

In Cuba we use the word *blúmers* for underwear, underpants, panties. I remember the clothesline hung across the dorm—a place where sleeping or showering was truly a group endeavor, with certain touches of drama, mischief, creative delirium, and absolute ignorance of the defenselessness we'd subjected ourselves to. This sense of resistance is what still unites its alumni, many of whom are now dancers in the Royal Ballet, visual artists with work in the permanent collections of MoMA or the Reina Sofía, or prominent actors and playwrights in Cuba: we all grew up together in a state of extreme overcrowding.

The *blúmers* exposed over the bunks. A public intervention into our few brief private affairs, betraying our biographies.

Do Cubans have private lives? No. The private is still seen as suspicious here. Each and every one of those *blúmers* tells a story, narrates a status. People say there have never been social classes in Cuba, but our underwear says something different.

We grew up in a country where you could buy one set of underwear a year. To do so, you used a ration book: coupons O-22 or E-13 or A-12. These coupons also enabled the purchase of cloth, needles, thread, and cotton sheets—which meant you had to choose between underwear and sheets to cover yourself with.

If you wanted anything else, you had to get married. The state provided a set of basic items, as well as drinks or sweets, to those who wanted to hold a wedding amid such financial strain. How many friends got married just so they could get hold of an iron, a box of beer, some of the famous Cuban sponge cake, blankets, bedspreads, some underwear? Only matrimony would grant you this special privilege. I received many marriage proposals just so the men in question could procure some of these essential items. I always refused.

Ripped, worn, mended, everyone-and-their-mother's *blúmers:* pieces of nylon with tattered, discolored, hot, shapeless elastic bands. This garment was unquestionably the property of a girl who had no relatives abroad. Her parents lived solely off their wages. They were workers, farmers, steadfast revolutionaries, austere souls who had little to give their children.

Socialist passion-killing *blúmers:* cotton underpants, always enormous, decidedly unsexy, covered with little Misha bears and blue or purple flowers against a white background, whimsical snowflakes, smiling matryoshka dolls. This girl's family certainly included a student in the old Soviet Union or a diplomat in the former socialist bloc, or maybe a sister married to a German, someone the state had classified as a "foreign technical expert."

New, brightly colored lace *blúmers,* or the famous *semanarios,* "weeklies," stamped with the day of the week you should wear them: it was wise to start bidding this co-student farewell; she was certain to desert the island soon. She'd have a grandmother, an aunt, or a sister in Miami or Madrid, someone who selected sexy garments at a distance in order to "save" the teenage girl from crude Soviet aesthetics. She always loaned us hers so that we could go out with our latest boyfriend. Where might she be living today? How many girls lost their virginity in those borrowed *blúmers*?

A philosophy of scarcity was written in our dorm bunks, a narrative that cast prudery aside and took up herd mentality as an instrument of resistance. Many of our novels are clearly rooted in this state of mind.

Daughter of a humble leftist intellectual, I went commando during my teenage years. Dorm culture, the upper bunk at boarding school, is a privileged place for a writer, and the post-battle landscape is a true subgenre of literaCuba: stark autofiction. The self stripped bare.

3.

WOMEN'S LIBERATION IN CUBA

My mother used to say that women's liberation wasn't a slogan; it meant having an electric washing machine and a can of food so she could conjure up a meal after her long workdays at the radio station. Women's liberation, in her case, involved finding practical ways to make her life easier so she could keep tending to social activities and to me. She'd spend twelve hours at a stretch in the broadcast car, waiting to transmit the arrival of various socialist-bloc presidents: Erich Honecker, Nicolae Ceaușescu, Leonid Ilyich Brezhnev. It all made her nervous—the ideological pressures, the security measures, the crowds. And when she returned home, what was awaiting her there? A small child, nothing or almost nothing to cook with, a pile of dirty laundry, dishes to wash, and no detergent.

While revolutionary heroines Haydée Santamaría and Celia Sánchez were indisputably popular among and beloved by the Cuban people, they always maintained a certain political discretion that allowed them to work on their own projects in the background, without affecting the male leaders at center stage.

Today, however, things have changed. Confrontations between women and the police are hardly uncommon. Women want to march; the police obstruct their demonstrations. The Ladies in White, for instance, demand the right to march peacefully for the release of brothers or husbands serving time as political prisoners, and they are frequently suppressed. There are female bloggers in Cuba, too, who write freely about their realities. Cuban women are gradually opening their own businesses, deserting the so-called state sector, seeking their autonomy, defending it from the obstacles of power.

My mother died young, but there are questions I wish I could have asked her: Could all of this be part of a new women's liberation movement? Will we have a female Cuban president someday? That said, and despite the "macho Leninism" of our leaders, women after 1959 started distancing themselves from the traditional domestic model—devotedly throwing themselves into revolutionary tasks as the family shifted into second or third place—and countless laws were passed to guarantee equality for women. For example, few countries have a longer mandatory maternity leave than Cuba: here it starts during pregnancy, at thirty-four weeks, with eighteen more weeks of paid leave after childbirth. Later, if they wish to, mothers can opt for an even longer leave period, up to a year, but receiving only 60 percent of their typical salary. In addition, divorce is a swift process in Cuba, allowing people an easy exit.

Not all such developments are the fruits of the revolutionary saga. An abortion law, for instance, has existed in Cuba since

1936. Back then, a woman could have an abortion if her pregnancy resulted from rape or endangered her health. Later, in the early revolutionary years, this right was gradually expanded. Indeed, my generation now views abortion as a means of contraception. Actual contraceptives grew scarcer and scarcer, while promiscuity, overcrowding, troop mobilizations, and economic deprivation meant that the rate of undesired pregnancy rose considerably on the island.

Monsignor Antonio Rodríguez, dean of the Seminario de San Carlos y San Ambrosio, a Jesuit school, explains that the tolerant attitude toward abortion shouldn't be seen as a phenomenon caused by the Communist Revolution of 1959: "Catholicism in Cuba was never deeply rooted; it has always been a minority religion. People before the Revolution believed that women should be able to abort."

Perhaps this is why the freedoms introduced by the revolutionary government were so swiftly adopted by most Cubans—and why social changes were assumed so naturally, without blame or resentment or surveillance, by a church that was increasingly fading into socialist society. Going to church was seen as a betrayal, but getting a curettage abortion was considered a routine medical procedure. A Cuban woman can have a curettage performed or undergo menstrual regulation and continue on to school or work without being instilled with the idea that she has committed a physically or emotionally traumatic act. Getting a curettage done in Cuba is much more common than going to the dentist. Every neighborhood outpatient clinic has a modern menstrual regulation facility. In this sense, I can say that Cuba is the country with the highest number of legal pregnancy interruptions in the world. When women go for a checkup and a pregnancy is detected, the doctor always asks the same question: "Are you going to leave it in or take it out?" It's usually the second option, and we don't always inform the men or let them participate in this process. We're the ones who decide.

However, beyond the law and whatever empowerment it might bring, the island is full of women who must face life alone. One in every five Cuban women is abandoned due to political or economic exile. One in three marriages or consensual unions ends within five years. And Cuban women, domestically speaking, are the ones who negotiate between reality and fantasy in order to survive: we all know that a child in Cuba can't live on just forty Cuban pesos (less than two American dollars) a month. But that's what divorced fathers legally contribute to mothers who hold custody of their children.

As for me, I've been censored in my country for describing women's realities. This means that I've published very little of my work in Cuba. Every time I finish a book, I think of the other female poets and novelists who are restricted by this dense editorial silence. And then I hope for the best and send my work to publishers or media sources in the rest of the world, thinking, every time, Will something happen to me in Cuba because I've written and published this text?

4.

BETWEEN FIDEL AND A NAKED WOMAN

Where did Fidel live? Who were his female companions, his partners, during the fifty-seven years of his rule? What are his children like?

Do heroes and martyrs have families, marry, divorce, behave like human beings?

The only physical observations I've read of two important figures in the Cuban Revolution, the only comments on the size, gestures, and clothing styles of Fidel himself and of Celia Sánchez, I found in an issue of the magazine *Bohemia*, while researching my novel *Nunca fui primera dama*. Ironically, the text was written by the American actor Errol Flynn after visiting Fidel's top-secret hideout in the Sierra Maestra, the nest Celia Sánchez equipped for the two of them.

The subject of Fidel's intimacy is entirely sealed off. The details of his personal life have been protected to the point of total mystery, his connection to Celia Sánchez even more so. Their habits and rituals, as well as her conduct in the Comandante's presence, are little known. Here is Flynn's description of his encounter:

ME AND CASTRO
by Errol Flynn

[Fidel] placed his ear against the tiny speaker of a radio receiver. Lying on a table, less than half a meter away from him, was a Belgian revolver: a dreadful-looking weapon. For a moment, he paid no attention to us, and then his eyes scanned the room. It was medium-sized, lightly furnished, with the appearance of something set up in haste, giving the impression of constant bustle, of people coming in and going out every minute. Celia Sánchez had a pink orchid pinned to her right shoulder. I held out my hand to her and lowered my eyes to the height of her waist. Hung there from her thin silhouette was a .32-caliber revolver.

My slight unease didn't prevent my clinical Hollywood eye from taking action. I instantly noticed that she wasn't built like most Cuban women; she was slender. I looked at her beautifully formed body. I'd calculate her measurements at 36-24-35—not those of the average Cuban woman. Very dark hair, brown skin, and luminous eyes that never missed a single detail, that missed nothing at all, constantly returning to the Comandante. Once the transmission was over, Castro lifted his head, saw us, and stood.

He is more or less my height; that is, six-foot and half an inch tall. There is a grace and simplicity in his movements and a humility in his manners that I confess I hadn't expected to find. In sum, he wasn't the imperious figure I had imagined meeting; these weren't the gestures and figure of a man with his authority.

My first impression was of his natural composure, one accentuated by reserves of strength and energy. He doesn't look like someone who has been browned by the sun. He gave no signs of having spent five and a half years in jungles, in the mountains, outdoors, which is what I thought I would encounter. His face is soft, as are his hands. Actually, his hands aren't soft, not at all, but they gave an impression almost of delicateness, without veins close to the skin. They looked much more like the hands of a man who has spent his time at a desk, not behind a machine gun. His handshake was firm but not especially vigorous. In a way, I expected to feel nerves of steel between my hands, but there was nothing supernatural about his physical appearance.

He was wearing glasses, and as he began to speak with me, I observed that his secretary, Celia, tended to him with utmost consideration. While he spoke, she removed his glasses, without him seeming to notice. She cleaned them and slid them back on, affably but subtly, as if to avoid bothering him. An interpreter helped us converse.

"I suggest," he told me, "that you go to the town of Palma Soriano. This place has just been freed by the liberation forces. The people there will be happy to see you, and you will see how Cubans feel about being released from Batista's grip."

That was when I asked what I should call him and when we settled on Fidel and Errol.

(From *Bohemia*, February 1959, p. 50.)

The Cuban secret services care a great deal about having uninterrupted access to our private lives. As a result, the Comités de Defensa de la Revolución (Committees for the Defense of the Revolution, or CDR) were born: entities responsible for the constant surveillance of every neighborhood. For those people who erect large barriers to prevent neighbors from seeing into their houses, a housing law exists to fine them and make them expose their inner world to public view. A Cuban with privacy is a suspicious element, a red flag.

Leaders, moreover, don't typically allow themselves to be glimpsed in a domestic, family-oriented environment. An abyss lies between Fidel and a naked woman; the vertigo of love unsettled him. Our leaders don't present themselves as mortals: they don't like to display this affinity with us *criollos*, passionate beings derailed by love. Apparently, Cuban heroes neither suffer nor divorce. They aren't susceptible to desire and they don't feel pleasure. Legend has it that Fidel Castro didn't know how to dance, had no interest in music or parties, and struggled to spend time with his family. People also say that Fidel had multiple romances, all short lived—the result of his obsession with staying active around the clock as he ran the country. And that he had a wife named Dalia Soto del Valle and several children from different marriages or relationships. For security reasons, very few know the precise location of "Punto Cero," where his true home was said to be.

Cubans' private lives, then, must be officially public, but the lives of the politicians who govern the country are mysteriously private.

The current president of Cuba, Raúl Castro, is the widower of Vilma Espín, also a revolutionary fighter. He is said to be a family man, but no one knows anything about his life today. As for the female figure's relationship to Cuban heroes, leaders, and rulers, she isn't even in the background. She simply doesn't exist.

5.

FASHION IN CUBA TODAY

Before the revolutionary triumph, we were a country of suits and ties, drill jackets, straw hats, and pearl necklaces. We were also a country of discreet elegance, poor but stylish. People went to work in their finest attire, starched, ironed, and mended. All of this appears in countless films or archival images.

Decades of sacrifice followed, forcing us to recycle our clothes: we made dresses from old suit linings, drew lines up and down our legs with eye pencils to simulate the effect of a fine stocking sheathing the stretch of flesh from calf to thigh. Then came the harsh years of khaki pants, uniforms, and work boots. Those who left or died handed down their belongings to us, and in 1980, with the so-called *viajes de la comunidad*—community trips, the first attempts at contact between exiles and islanders to be tolerated by the revolutionary government—we started receiving packages full of imported clothing. These garments replaced our basic items with designs that were rarely appropriate for our climate or lifestyle.

The secret service appropriated guayabera shirts; women started going out in curlers and household clothes. There were always people fighting for some sort of stylistic coherence, but an army of bad taste was enlisted against them, armed to the teeth with shields produced by the country's economic realities.

Dressing well, for the few who could, was an ideological problem, a petit bourgeois form of conduct. You would only see Cubans in uniform—or, at most, in khaki slacks, humdrum Yumurí-brand shirts, or crude, heavy Jiqui-brand pants.

In the late 1970s, from her post as the secretary of state councils and ministries, Celia Sánchez Manduley created the Taller Experimental de la Moda, the Experimental Fashion Workshop—a business devoted to producing Cuban styles based on fresh, modern, accessibly priced fabrics and designs. In the eighties, Caridad (Cachita) Abrahantes launched another fashion business, Contex. There, as the head of the men's design department, the Cuban designer Lorenzo Urbistondo astutely and creatively revived the sacred Cuban guayabera shirt, proved it was possible to devise new styles from our roots, made women's shirts lighter, and did away with the horrible safari suits that Cuban leaders were so fond of wearing when they weren't in uniform. In 1987, Cachita inaugurated the fashion house La Maison, headquartered in an exuberant mansion in the elegant

Miramar neighborhood. The goal was to offer tourists, as well as Cubans of a particular stratum or background, a catwalk with beautiful *criollo* models, displaying the finest fashion produced on the island—an island subsumed in the profound crisis and isolation precipitated both by the U.S.-imposed economic embargo and by the revolutionary leadership's self-blockade.

In this universe of the "square under siege," which lasted a little over three decades, we learned almost nothing about what the world identified as trends, fashion, or style. Only minimal exchanges with the so-called socialist bloc allowed us to clothe our bodies with items that, frankly, never seemed very tropical, and which certainly weren't designed to embrace the sizes and curves of Cuban men and women. Around this period, Catarritos appeared—a brand of horrible Russian shoes easily disintegrated by regular tropical downpours.

In those years, the loan and sales shop El Louvre opened its doors, presenting "elegant" coats and clothes for people traveling to countries in Eastern Europe or elsewhere in Latin America. But this store was only patronized by the privileged few, who could leave the country under exceptional circumstances. As of the mideighties, girls turning fifteen had a place to acquire a pair of shoes for their *quinceañera:* the store was called Primor and it offered heels that had been popular in 1950s Havana. Briefly, a crafts market was allowed to set up shop in the plaza in front of the Havana Cathedral. There, at least for a while, we bought sandals and shoes more suitable for our sultry climate—but the state's resentment of the profits of those who manufactured these wares put an end to their sale.

Telarte was among the best initiatives to appear in Cuba. Founded in 1974, it produced textile products from 1983 to 1991. This business, funded by the Ministry of Culture in conjunction with Contex and the Fondo de Bienes Culturales (Fund for Cultural Assets), was a marriage of visual artists and the textile industry. Luckily for us, this unprecedented experiment resulted in fabric designs by important local and international artists—figures like Mariano Rodríguez, Robert Rauschenberg, Raúl Martínez, Luis Camnitzer, and Manuel Mendive. For a few years, they dressed bodies that had long been eager to distinguish themselves from the uniformed masses.

But the Special Period began in the early nineties, after the fall of the Berlin Wall, and during this terrible phase—which no one here has ever declared to be officially over—we experienced a frightening precariousness. Everything was scarce: soap, oil, toothpaste. We stopped receiving underwear from Eastern Europe. Cuban industry didn't produce a single garment that could clothe us. Staying clean and shod became an odyssey. Some families decided to exchange their inherited jewelry at the so-called casas del oro y la plata, houses of gold and silver, which belonged to the CIMEX department at the Ministry of the Interior. Jewels were traded for food, household appliances, shoes, and casual clothing, generally of Panamanian origin. The Cuban state needed an injection of gold, silver, and precious stones, and in order to collect such assets it opened exchange bureaus and shops specialized in unequal trade. The fashion offered in exchange included "prewashed" jeans, blouses and shirts referred to as *bacterias* (describing their printed pattern), bathing suits, and cheap underwear. Swapping their family memories, the Cuban people began to dress differently. These designs weren't known for their tastefulness, but the broad color palette seeped into our surroundings.

How do Cubans dress today? With very little information on international styles, and without a clear sense of appropriate attire in places like hospitals, churches, or theaters, you'll often see Havana residents wearing shorts, flip-flops, and tank

tops in settings usually associated with sobriety and decorum.
The boundary between household clothes and going-out clothes
has been erased. The makeshift stores have gradually rubbed out
our identity altogether. Recycled clothing and cheap knockoffs
have invaded our bodies. From Miami and Panama, we receive
contraband of the shoddiest order. From Ecuador or Chinese
markets on the outskirts of Madrid, snuck in through Cuban
customs, we receive jeans studded with rhinestones, phospho-
rescent Lycra, odd neck scarves stamped with sundry patterns,
squeaky wooden shoes, garish handbags, and terrible imitations
of classic purses. In Havana, as in many other places, it isn't at all
expensive to sport a Vuitton bag.

I watch people walking around my beloved city, but I don't
recognize them, nor do I recognize this confusion of bodies and
colors. We were different: we once had a way of expressing our
life stories through our wardrobes. What has become of them—
our years of instruction, our aesthetic education, our museums,
still open today, that boast the finest Cuban art, work that lifts
us up and makes us proud? I wonder, too, what has become of
our bodies, flaunting our (deluded?) insignia.

6.

PHYSICAL EDUCATION

We were born in a secular, nonconfessional state; the church
has had no role in education for the past four generations. We
grew up in a nation where scholarships (boarding schools for
needy students, or for those from other parts of the country who
receive study grants from the government), rural schools (com-

bining agricultural work with standard academic subjects), and overcrowding are all part of life.

Starting in fifth grade and through secondary school, students are given short readings on sexual education. Natural science classes include a program that addresses types of intimate relationships, human reproductive organs, different sexual identities, and even the risks of promiscuity and its possible effects on our health. What's striking, though, is that we already know quite a bit about these subjects by the time we study them in school. I don't know any fifth-grade pioneer who can't recite many of the lessons from memory that the teacher dictates from the blackboard.

We Cuban kids usually find our first "boyfriend" or "girlfriend" in preschool. Our first kiss comes in elementary school, and in middle school and then high school and precollege programs—at which point we're nearly the same age as our teachers—we're likely to be exchanging theoretical and practical knowledge both in the classroom and beyond it. Here, in the words of poet Sigfredo Ariel, "You only lose your innocence once, and life is long." Sexual life in Cuba is an open book that everyone interprets in his or her own way.

Our parents assumed dense intimacies, formed brief connections, fleeting marriages that faltered as infatuation waned. They had no material things to protect. Previous social norms were thrown into the socialist bonfire; family ceased to be the altar of personal sacrifice. It was no longer necessary to stoically endure a tired marriage for the sake of children, parents, or external judgment.

And so we grew up with our house keys hung around our necks so we could let ourselves in—our parents would be back late. Adults didn't necessarily know everything about our parallel world, and adult life bore a strong resemblance to our own: brimming with adolescent emotion and peppered with sexual encounters similar to ours. A generational fusion softened hierarchical distinctions until it melted them together. Antonio José Ponte's essay "Tener veinte años toda la vida" (Being twenty forever) describes this system of eternal puberty and minimal commitment that afflicts us Cubans.

When people hit their forties, the divorces begin and young lovers join the fray, slipping in and out of former family homes in the wee hours. Those homes, meanwhile, have now become the nests of single women who still feel like teenagers. The beds of women born in the 1970s and '80s are visited by young men born during the Special Period, and—what a surprise—my generation has replaced our parents' noble "peace and love" with generally sexist behavior. This conduct is harsh, corrective, occasionally rude, and nearly orthopedic as far as casual sex is concerned; blows, as part of what could be playful erotic language, replace tenderness, and gestures shift from caresses to slaps in a single night.

1. Turn around, baby.
2. Get on top, girl, and move your body, come on.
3. Turn around or I'm leaving you right there.
4. Come on, girl, I want it right now.

Vulgarity, herd instinct, and reggaeton culture have infiltrated sexual encounters in Cuba, which seems to have become a completely different country within a single decade. These tendencies crop up equally among intellectuals, scientists, engineers, workers, musicians, or theorists finishing their Ph.D.s. Physical violence is overpowering tenderness; coarseness overcomes the simple act of gallantry, flirtation, or infatuation. All-out war erupts between bodies: erotic punishment with military trappings and physical pain as a vehicle of pleasure.

What could have been a marginal habit is now a peremptory norm that marks and muzzles the sexual spirit of a country where the body has always been and remains a white flag.

7.

SEXISM IN CUBA

Sexism isn't expressed the same way in Cuba as it is elsewhere in Latin America. First of all, Cuban men have had to take up child-rearing. Given the many roles the Revolution has assigned to women, men often find themselves alone and juggling domestic tasks. It's quite common to see a Cuban father braiding his young daughters' hair in the early morning, sewing on buttons, ironing, and taking his neatly dressed children to school. For many different social and political reasons, these families have been divided, and the father frequently performs both roles in what Latin Americans from outside Cuba would consider a highly unorthodox household.

Lifestyle models in Cuba, as well as domestic gender roles, are a far cry from what Western parameters define as normal.

We Cubans can't freely access statistics on death or separation due to domestic abuse. But what we can observe in daily life, closely scrutinized by the mass organizations that begin in every neighborhood's Comité de Defensa de la Revolución and continue in schools and workplaces, is a perpetual struggle for equality among all citizens. From adolescence onward, the Cuban men and women of my generation learned to shoot firearms, generally Russian, as part of our mandatory military training. It would be odd for a woman trained to "defend the homeland," instructed to "vanquish or die" in her formative years and ever since, to let a man hit her without some sort of emphatic response on her part. Our character is built through the slogan *Cada cubano debe saber tirar y tirar bien*—every Cuban must know how to shoot, and shoot well.

Infidelity in Cuba is rooted in the informality of human relationships in the resistance movement. Guerrilla groups, mobilizations, coexistence at boarding schools far from home, have made us fickle and fleeting in our emotional commitments. As a result, both women and men can decide to end marriages abruptly after finding love, desire, or admiration elsewhere. Women often maintain long-term parallel relationships that may continue indefinitely. Here, a woman can be as unfaithful as a man; she can abandon a household and then start over, just as a man might, whether she has children or not.

But once again, while female empowerment has taken root in many realms, it remains excluded from the political and ideological one. Today, female political leadership is still unthinkable. It would be impossible to have a female president; the "macho Leninism" of our historical leadership impedes it. That said, women now participate in many sectors where they had no role before the Revolution. There are women sappers, gunners, machinists, and parachutists. Of course, we Cubans would also like to have women government secretaries, news directors, and military leaders. But this kind of equality has remained elusive: such posts have always been held by men, trained in a gender-based tradition that goes farther back than the rules we learned in 1960.

If you try to envision the political leadership headquartered in the Plaza de la Revolución, you'll see mostly men in olive green, gathered behind the monument to José Martí as they assess a military parade (composed, in turn, of virile soldiers).

Why have there never been female presidents in the socialist world? Why isn't there a feminist movement in Cuba? Might feminism actually run contrary to the nation's revolutionary, Marxist, socialist precepts?

For a female Cuban writer, translating the codes of such an idiosyncratic society is no simple matter. The credibility of its actions and figures has no basis in the traditional codes that Western readers are used to. Our situation is not only rooted in magical realism; our very existence has been hounded by isolation and autophagy. To outside eyes, our actions seem absurd, disproportionate, indecipherable, or exotic. The body as the sole space of freedom, our sexuality, our complex relationship with our own customs, surveillance, witchcraft, scarcity, the informer culture, our detachment, our complicated relationship with power, the decisive control of politics over our entire lives, censorship, music, rum consumed as an everyday drug to help us bear the impossibility of taking our own existence by the reins, our ownership by the state, and the interpersonal relationships forged over years of resistance—these are challenging things to narrate. Keeping common sense alive in such an absurd and unusual context is our most difficult task, and we undertake it every day. From within this war, a Cuban woman, naked, wearing only a hat, sweating amid the *tropidrama* of her island, writes in the sand.

DREAMING IN CUBAN
A CHRONICLE
IN NINE INNINGS

BY LEONARDO PADURA
TRANSLATED BY ANNA KUSHNER

To my father, Nardo, an Almendares fan,
And to my uncle Min, an Equipo Habana fan.

FIRST INNING

My father's great dream was to be a baseball player. A *pelotero*, as
we say in Cuba. As far as dreams go, his wasn't very original: for
150 years, the desire to become a *pelotero*, renowned, lauded, and
beloved, has been one of the most common among men born on
this island as well as the one that has been most often thwarted.
Of the millions of Cubans who have grown up and lived with
that aspiration, only a few hundred have fully achieved it and
just a couple of dozen have made it into the pantheon of the im-
mortals.

As a child and for part of his adolescence, my father devoted
all the time he could to playing baseball. He did it on the bar-

ren terrain of Mantilla, the Havana neighborhood where he was born, with kids from the area, but never as frequently as he would have wanted, since, at the age of seven, he was forced to start helping my grandfather and my older uncle in the fruit-selling business that supported our family. Nonetheless, it was thanks to this work that, saving one penny at a time, he was able to afford the tremendous luxury of buying himself a left-handed glove in order to play more and better ball.

Years later, when my father already knew that he would never make his dream a reality—not for lack of effort in his attempts to see it through, but because his diminutive stature made things more difficult—he wished to pass down to his oldest son that cherished aspiration. Before undertaking this task, my father had commended himself to Our Lady of Charity, for whom he had a long-standing veneration although he was not particularly religious, and had asked her that his first child meet three re-quirements: that he be a boy, that he be left-handed, and that he have the distinction of being the famous *pelotero* he never man-aged to become himself. And he promised that if she granted at least the first of these petitions, that firstborn son would have Our Lady's name, in other words, Leonardo de la Caridad.

Leonardo de la Caridad was born on October 9, 1955, and two days later, when he was taken from the clinic to the family home his father had built a year earlier, in the crib purchased to receive him were the trinkets that usually surrounded newborns at the time: noisy rattles, a stuffed teddy bear, some rubber toy or other, and . . . a baseball.

Eleven months later, when there was no longer any doubt that Our Lady of Charity continued to indulge my father, since his firstborn lifted his spoon and shook his rattles with his left hand, he tried to accelerate the process. He went to a sporting goods store and bought a small baseball player's uniform with the blue color and the insignia of his dream team: the Almendares club. As a magnificent reminder of that effort, one photo remains, in which Leonardo de la Caridad, dressed in his *pelotero*'s uniform, takes his first steps in the backyard of the family home. The die was cast, and, going forward, they could always count on Our Lady's generous assistance.

One of Leonardo de la Caridad's unforgettable childhood memories was his first visit to an official baseball stadium. His father took him there on a Sunday afternoon, probably in 1962, when he was six or seven years old. By then, the boy Leonardo had proven through his family, social ties, cultural ties, and even genetic makeup that he was an absolute fan of the game of baseball. Of course, at that moment, Leonardo de la Caridad had no definitive notion of how the Revolution happening around him affected nearly everything, including the game of baseball. Nor did he know that the visit to the Grand Stadium of Havana (which would soon change its name to Latin American Stadium) would be the last his father would make to that great sanctuary of Cuban culture and life until the night on which Leonardo de la Caridad would again accompany him, twenty or twenty-five years after that magical and unforgettable afternoon.

When my father agreed to forget his bitterness and return to the stadium, too many things had occurred in his country, in his city, in his house, for him not to have begun a reconciliation with his past, or at least with his passion for baseball. The solicitous Our Lady of Charity had not been able to carry out the task he had commended to her. Although his firstborn was a boy and left-handed—a privileged condition for baseball players—and had become a fan of that sport, similarly infected with the dream of becoming a great player, Our Lady's powers were not enough to make him a good ballplayer. Despite Leonardo de la Caridad's spending hours, days, months, years in that effort, playing ball with his neighborhood friends in the same places where his father had thirty or forty years before, the all-too-common and terrible fate had repeated itself. My father's oldest son would know almost everything that can be known about baseball, he would love and suffer for baseball for the rest of his life, but he would have to park his great desire to be a famous player in the warm, dark spot where all thwarted dreams go. All because neither my father's efforts, nor the most propitious social and cultural environment, nor the miraculous Our Lady of Charity managed to make a good ballplayer out of me.

SECOND INNING

The Havana of the 1860s was a social, political, and economic hotbed. The capital of the prosperous island of Cuba had all the aspirations, possibilities, and dreams of the Cuban people concentrated in its territory and spirit. It was this Havana that the boy, adolescent, and then young poet José Martí walked through, in which he forged the indomitable desire for independence to which he would devote his entire life and even his death a few years later. It was a Havana in which whether you were a native-born Cuban (*criollo*) or a Spanish-born *peninsular* began to signify a pivotal conflict, two opposed expressions of belonging. Further, which side one fell on influenced one's opinions about politics, whether one saw the future as breaking with or continuing the colonial condition that regulated life in the country.

Havana of 1860 saw the return of a group of young people who had, after years of living as students in North America, in New York, Philadelphia, and Boston, become fans of playing a new sport called baseball that was already a hit among the Yankees of the great cities of the north. It was a sport with complicated rules, in which—as opposed to other ball games in vogue then and later—the competition was not a fight between two armies on a battlefield with the goal of taking the enemy's main square. Baseball had a different philosophy: the individual player attempted to return to the house from which he had left ("home"), and the winning team was the one that, with the collaboration of all of its members, managed that victorious return the most times. The rationalist and typically nineteenth-century philosophy of that concept, lacking the military structure of sports like soccer, made baseball a practice that was distinct, modern, intelligent—and chic.

But those first young men from Havana who were baseball fans had another important motivation: this sport, with its slow and deliberate pace and its outlandish uniforms (which were even considered lascivious), was the antithesis of the crude and backward *peninsular* pastimes, such as the violent bullfights of which Spaniards were such fans. Playing baseball, then, became a way of culturally distinguishing themselves as *criollos,* of relating to the world from another perspective, of being modern, and it soon became an expression of being Cuban.

It was precisely during the decade in which the Great War for Cuba's independence unfolded (beginning in 1868 and concluding in 1878 with an ominous pact that left the Spanish in charge) that baseball achieved its initial popularity in Havana; soon thereafter it spread to the rest of the country. To get to that point, some fundamental changes had to take place in the configuration of Cuban culture and identity. As the first baseball fields appeared around different parts of Havana and the first games and tournaments were organized, a deeply integrating and, to a degree, democratic current emerged. To stimulate its dizzying expansion, the sport that a few years earlier had been imported by some young aristocrats had to become a popular

activity that counted on the participation of Cubans of all so-
cial classes and colors, a process that was already quite visible
by 1880. In addition, that symbolic representation turned into a
feast of cultural confluence when baseball games became popu-
lar open-air parties where there was eating and drinking, flirting
and conspiring, and, above all, music and dancing to the rhythm
of the *danzón,* the music created by and performed by blacks and
mulatos that would become the Cuban national dance. Baseball,
music, society, culture, and politics coincided on the sports field
in a rich and dynamic configuration of Cubanness.

From then until today, we are Cuban because we play ball,
and we play ball because we are Cuban. Thus, my father's dream
and mine has been the same as that of so many millions of people
born on this island in the Caribbean throughout these 150 years.

THIRD INNING

Baseball, *la pelota,* is a sport, but it is also a way of understanding
life. And even of living it. And in my case, I can say that I am a
writer thanks to the fact that I couldn't become a baseball player.

The neighborhood on the outskirts of Havana where I was
born, and where I still live, did not have a field with the neces-
sary conditions for playing ball according to regulations. But,
as in dozens of other Havana neighborhoods, the kids of my
generation learned to play ball in alleys and more or less suit-
able barren fields, where we sweated out the need that, when it
became an extreme passion, we called "the vice of ball" in my
day. On the corner of my block, in a school yard, in a vacant lot
near a quarry, in a sandy plot on the outskirts, I played ball every
minute of my life that it was possible to do so. With or without
improvised uniforms, with or without gloves, with the bats and

balls that turned up in the years in which the greatest shortages prevented us from acquiring those implements, my friends and I devoted ourselves to playing and dreaming of baseball.

In my case, the "vice of ball" acquired the proportions of true addiction: besides playing the game, I lived it. In my school notebooks, I sketched baseball fields and imagined games. When I ran down the street, I imagined I was doing so in a stadium, and I ran through the square because I had hit a decisive home run. I clipped photos of Cuban ballplayers of the time and glued them in a notebook. I watched the games broadcast on television and became a fan of one club, some of whose players became the greatest and best idols I've ever had or ever will have. I lived surrounded by baseball, inside it, because my neighborhood, my city, my country were an enormous field on which an eternal game was unfolding. And life was a baseball.

If I owe my father for the injection of that overwhelming Cuban passion, then it is my uncle Min, as we all called him, to whom I am grateful for many of my best memories regarding the game. As opposed to my father, who was always a disciplined and compulsive worker, Uncle Min was a party animal who would drop everything to go to a game in any of the parks around the city. Almost every Sunday, for several years, I went with him and his drinking buddies to games at the Latin American Stadium. But many mornings and afternoons, I got into his pickup truck with other fans like him to go see lower-division games in neighborhood stadiums in different parts of Havana.

When I was ten or eleven years old, I began to practice the game in a more organized way and learned many of its many secrets and the greatest of its mysteries: baseball is a strategic sport in which, when it seems like nothing is happening, the most important thing could be happening. My father, who was friends with Fermín Guerra, a great Cuban star of the 1940s and

'50s, managed to persuade the maestro, who was already retired, to accept me at his small academy on the fields of the Ciro Frías sports area, a few kilometers from my house. Later, when I was about fifteen years old, I joined a team that played games on Saturday afternoons and Sunday mornings on the fields of Havana's Sports City and of La Estrella chocolate factory, and I continued learning, competing, and dreaming of glory.

Two or three years later, when I realized that I would never be a fast pitcher or a powerful hitter and had to recognize that the baseball elite was not a category I would be able to join, I very rationally decided that, if I wasn't going to be a player, then I would be a sports commentator. What counted was being close. But that dream was also cut short because, even though I had the required high grades, when I finished high school, I was told that that year there would be no spots available at the University of Havana's School of Journalism, since someone had decided that there were enough journalists in the country. With my dreams abandoned, I ended up at the School of Letters, where the fate I had not dreamed of awaited me, although I now believe it was written in my chromosomes. Because it was there, upon seeing that other classmates wrote stories and poems, that my latent competitive spirit as a ballplayer pushed me in that direction: if others wrote, why shouldn't I? Thus, out of that competitive spirit, I started to write and embarked on the definitive path of what has been my life: that of a frustrated-ballplayer-cum-writer.

FOURTH INNING

Out of necessity, a public spectacle with a mass following creates myths and legends, leaves its mark on spaces and times. The history of baseball and of Havana is plagued with them.

Beginning in the late nineteenth century, illustrious youth from Havana such as Julián del Casal, one of the great voices of poetic modernism, wrote chronicles and commentaries reflecting the presence of baseball and its stars in the sports, culture, and daily life of Havana. At one of the emblematic places for youth gatherings back then, the Louvre Sidewalk (so named because of the café in that spot), converged writers, dilettantes, independence activists, and young people who were practitioners or lovers of baseball, and consciously adopted it as an expression of belonging and a banner of nationalism. And so the first myths about Cuban baseball were founded.

Throughout the twentieth century, Cuban popular mythology continually added the names of white, black, and *mulato* players, such as Emilio Sabourín, the martyr baseball player of independence; Carlos Maciá, the first great star of this sport; Martín Dihigo, called "The Immortal"; Alejandro "The Knight" Oms; José de la Caridad Méndez, crowned "The Black Diamond"; Orestes Miñoso, nicknamed "The Cuban Comet"; Manuel Alarcón, alias "The Coppersmith"; Omar Linares, known as "The Boy"; Orlando Hernández, nicknamed "The Duke," like his father, Arnaldo, among many others. Although without a doubt, the most mythical of all the great players Cuba has produced was Adolfo Luque, for whom one nickname was not enough—he had to be given three, one in Cuba and two in the United States: "Papá Montero" in his country and "The Perfect Havana Cigar" and "The Pride of Havana" in the lands to the north.

Adolfo Luque's adventures and great feats fill half a century of Cuban baseball history and fulfill an important mission: that of a nationalist reaffirmation in a period of deep national frustration, following the long-awaited independence that was also mediated by a North American intervention, and an onerous amendment to the new constitution that gave us neocolonial status. This is why Luque generated many anecdotes on and off the playing fields, inside and outside of Cuba, and, in many ways, his personality and the impression he made as an athlete synthesized the character and quality of being Cuban, both on and off the island.

His career as a player, in the 1910s and '20s, unfolded in the Cuban Professional League and in the U.S. Major Leagues, where he was one of the first Latinos to join and to win, inspiring other Cubans to believe that they could also achieve something like that. In Havana, he mainly pitched for the storied Almendares club, although he also lent his services as pitcher to the Havana team, the former's archrival. In the U.S. Major Leagues, he mostly played for the Cincinnati Reds, with whom he had a season of twenty-seven wins and eight defeats—quite a feat. Later, as a coach, between the 1930s and '50s, he worked in the United States, Cuba, and Mexico. And wherever he went, he left his imprint as a born and bred man of Havana.

It seems that Luque's main characteristic as a person and as a baseball player is that he went from festive to irascible with little in-between. A drinker of rum and beer, a dancer, and cigar smoker (to which his northern nicknames alluded, inspired by two very well-known brands of cigars at the time), he embodied the essence of his time and place: being impulsive, aggressive, and unpredictable was part of his Cubanness. Despite being white, his nickname of "Papá Montero" was given to him because of how similar his personality was to that of a famous black *ñáñigo* (member of an Afro-Cuban religious sect), who was known for his skill at dancing the rumba ("a louse and a rumba dancer") and his penchant for cockfights, women, alcohol, and, by unavoidable logic, brawls.

The peak of Papá Montero or the Pride of Havana's baseball fame seems to have come in 1923, during the season in which

Luque won twenty-seven games; upon his return to the island, he was received with a massive parade running through the streets of the capital and to the most important field of the time, the Almendares Park, where he was met by a new car, purchased for him by the people of Havana. In the procession, according to what I've read, was a *danzón*-playing orchestra strumming "¡Arriba, Luque!," a song composed by Armando Valdés Torres in his honor.

FIFTH INNING

The myths of Cuban baseball by necessity had an influence on practical life. Without a doubt, baseball diamonds were the center of intense sporting and social activity and have been considered sanctuaries. Havana has had three great "cathedrals of baseball": Almendares Park, founded in the nineteenth century; La Tropical Stadium, famous in the 1930s and '40s; and the Grand Stadium of Havana, opened in 1948, later renamed the Latin American Stadium, still active in the working-class neighborhood of El Cerro. In them, several generations of Cubans have experienced initiations similar to mine.

But the rest of the city was also invaded by baseball for decades: photos of players and teams, banners, colors, and uniforms made the presence of baseball and its idols common in houses, streets, and the city's public places. Almanacs, cups, plates, fans—the most varied objects were emblazoned with the insignias of the best-known teams: the Almendares scorpion, the Havana lion, the Marianao tiger, and the Cienfuegos elephant. In every neighborhood, there was at least one field where you could play the game.

At the same time, the people's language became filled with

phrases and situations taken from baseball: being "caught between bases" was to be surprised while doing something wrong; "I'm three [balls] and two [strikes]" was an expression of enormous doubt; to be "wild" was to be mistaken. Meanwhile, baseball was the subject of many popular songs, tobacco brands were introduced with names referring to baseball, and people of all sorts took to wearing baseball T-shirts.

To my mind, no other social and popular activity—with perhaps the exception of music—has had a greater influence on Cuban cultural life, in the making of identity and in the sentimental education of so many people born on this island.

SIXTH INNING

For twenty years, my father, such a lover of baseball, turned his back on its development in Cuba. His reaction was visceral: with the Revolution's elimination of professional sports on the island, in 1960, the former Cuban winter league disappeared, along with its most representative teams, among them the Almendares club, of which my father was a devoted fan.

Even today it's difficult for me to process the depth of the frustration my father must have felt seeing the team he loved for his whole life vanish. But I can begin to understand it, starting with a proof I would call ontological: a man can change identities, citizenship, political parties, lovers . . . but it is very difficult to switch sports alliances. And my father, who had lost his team, could only make that transition over the course of twenty years, throughout which he lived without watching or wanting to know anything about baseball in Cuba.

A curious thing also happened after 1961, when the so-called National Series of Amateur Baseball was instituted in the country, and nine new teams were founded (although one of them was still called Havana, like the city and the province). With very little difficulty, people took to the new banners, to players who were almost unknown until then, and gave them their favor and fervor. The only explanation I find convincing is not political, social, or sports related in nature, but rather, has existential and identity-related origins: Cubans cannot—or couldn't—live without that sport that was theirs, through which they thought and expressed themselves, for which they existed.

The history of the baseball that was played in Cuba starting in 1961 is undoubtedly glorious. It was perfectly connected with a robust tradition despite its having been introduced, politically, as a break with and improvement over the past, since there was talk of the "victory of free baseball (amateur) over enslaved [baseball] (professional)." This new baseball grabbed the country's attention, created new fans, generated other idols, and filled the vital space that Cubans had always devoted to that sport.

Twenty years after that radical change, when the dream of becoming a baseball star had already ended for me and I was writing my first stories, I convinced my father to go with me one night to the Latin American Stadium to see a game with the team of which I had become a fan when I was a boy: Havana's Industriales. And my father fell into the trap that he had avoided for two decades because the prospect of entering a great baseball stadium, seeing the lights shining on the reddish soil and the green grass of the diamond, breathing in the smell of earth and glory, seeing the players' multicolored uniforms, and feeling the pulsing of a national passion were enough to vanquish even the most deeply rooted rancor. At some point before the beginning of the game, while the players were warming up and the air was charged with that sticky magic of baseball, my father asked me the name of the team dressed in blue, like Almendares, and I told him it was the Havana Industriales, then he asked me which one was my team, and I confided to him that it was the very same Industriales. Later, as the game went on, my father told me that he, too, was rooting for the Industriales. And he continued to do so, from that day until his death, with the same passion, with the same enjoyment and suffering and feeling of belonging that he had had as an Almendares fan for the first thirty-three years of his life.

SEVENTH INNING (THE LUCKY INNING)

Although I could not be a star on the ball field, and I couldn't even work as a sportswriter focusing on baseball, my passion for this tangled-up, cerebral sport never disappeared. I was never cured of the "vice of ball."

People like me, born and raised in a baseball culture, are attracted to any ball game. The attraction is stronger than your will. That is why, frequently, as I walk down some street in Havana and come upon a group of kids playing ball, I stop to at least watch the end of the play. As if it were important. And it is important.

I enjoyed my great moment as a doubly frustrated ballplayer and sports commentator in the 1980s, when I was kicked off of a cultural magazine and, as punishment, sent to work for the evening newspaper *Juventud Rebelde*. And there I had to become a journalist, practicing journalism. I was lucky that, precisely because I was not a press professional, my work stood out amid that of my colleagues because of its heterodox, literary style and I soon enjoyed a rare privilege: I could write about what I wanted, how I wanted, and as much as I wanted. So I proposed to my colleague Raúl Arce, the newspaper's official baseball chronicler, the project of interviewing a group of old ballplayers, the same ones who, twenty or thirty years prior, had been our idols.

It was thus that I was able to fulfill a delayed dream: for two years, on every propitious occasion, we would meet up with some of those veterans who had brought us so many joyous moments. To meet them, understand them, make people remember their greatness, their failures, their humanity, was a privilege I still feel today, because thanks to them, I came to understand many things about the dramatic and deep relationship between Cubans and the game of baseball. Their personal stories relating to baseball, with all the peculiarities belonging to their era and its social and family context, had been very similar to mine: that of a vice, that of a greater passion.

Those interviews published in the newspaper were later collected in a book called *Soul on the Playing Field,* which was published for the first time in 1989 and that today, in times that are less propitious for the publishing industry and for Cuban baseball, is still in print and being read.

EIGHTH INNING

After the Almendares team uniform that my father bought me before I was a year old, I didn't have another complete baseball outfit until 1968, when my uncle Min emigrated to the United States and gave me the one he used to wear. That revolutionary decade of the 1960s, in which even the nature of baseball on the island changed, was one of such shortages that it became nearly impossible to get a ballplayer's outfit.

I remember like it was yesterday the pride with which I left the house when I slipped on that uniform of Uncle Min's. Before that, my mother had had to subject it to general repairs so that it would fit my thirteen-year-old frame, and, in the process, I asked her to replace the number 22 it originally had on the back with a number 3, the one used by Pedro Chávez, the Industriales player who was my first great sports idol. Although the letters, the socks, and the cap were red and not blue, the kid who went out to play ball that day, dressed in his flaming uniform, had to be the happiest in all of Havana.

It has been almost fifty years and, as Martí would say, an eagle has flown over the sea since then. More than an eagle, actually. My memory remains intact, but I can't see myself in the city, can't find myself on the streets or on an improvised neighborhood field wearing that outfit: because no one, almost no one, goes around the streets of Havana in a baseball player's uniform. In contrast, I see dozens of young people walking around the city (and through all the cities and fields of Cuba) with Cristiano Ronaldo and Real Madrid shirts, Messi and Barcelona, Müller and Bayern Munich. What has happened? Have the city and the country been switched on me, and with them, the passions of their inhabitants? How is it possible that for decades, they played baseball, talked about baseball, lived for baseball, but they now play soccer and dream of the teams of the Spanish league, the English league, the German league? Is this only a generational change of paradigms, or is it something deeper?

Cuban baseball is living through its deepest crisis today, in all senses. The arrival of the hard years of the 1990s, when everything was lacking and the country was practically para-lyzed, deeply changed Cuban society, for good and for bad, or for neither: society simply changed, so one of its basic expres-sions also changed—baseball. In recent years, for economic reasons, there has been an unstoppable hemorrhage of Cuban players of all levels and ages who leave the country by the most diverse paths, in search of fate and a professional baseball contract, preferably in the United States. The mysticism capable of allowing three decades of Cuban players to opt for "free ball" over "enslaved ball," that preserved a high competitive level in the national championships and the fame of unbeaten records in international tournaments, no longer exists. Economic pragmatism has imposed itself over physical proximity and ideological propaganda, thus hundreds of Cuban ballplayers have left the island in search of fulfillment, in both sports and business.

Parallel to this, the official Cuban media, which did not broadcast a U.S. Major League game for fifty years, began to give greater space to professional soccer programming, especially European soccer, and thus soccer fans were created. Why favor professional soccer over professional baseball if they both have the same economic nature? Because if Cubans become passionate about soccer, nothing happens: it's a fever without any larger complications. In contrast, if they become familiar with another kind of baseball, in which some of their emigrated compatriots even shine, the political and social results are different.

But even when no possibility of watching much professional baseball exists (for the last two or three years, a few edited games are broadcast per week, better if there are no Cuban ballplayers involved), the result is the same: the players who can and want to will continue to emigrate. There is no reversing that process.

What is happening in Cuba, what I see and, above all, what I don't see in the streets of Havana, is not a simple phenomenon of fashion or sports preference: it is a cultural trauma of unpredictable consequences for the Cuban identity. In Havana's alleys and barren fields, children play soccer and not baseball, they dream of being like Cristiano Ronaldo and Lionel Messi, they suffer over Real Madrid or el Barça, implying a serious wound in the nation's spirituality. Could we reach the point at which we

Cubans cease to be baseball players and become soccer players? Anything can happen. But, if it happens, it would imply many losses, because without the passion, without the "vice of ball," Cuba would be renouncing one of its essential, defining brands.

NINTH INNING

The history of Havana and of its residents would not be the same without the sustained presence of baseball throughout a century and a half. Havana's pride is intrinsically linked to the practice of that sport. In the cathedrals of Cuban baseball echo the screams of fans who saw, among so many memorable things, Adolfo Luque's and Conrado Marrero's artful pitching, Orestes Miñoso's colossal hits, Agustín Marquetti's decisive home run in the 1986 series, and so many indelible feats that flood our shared memories.

The city's culture and history are also made with baseball games, with baseball players, with the national passion for ball. And now, has the game ended? I hope not. Because it hurts deeply to lose a source of pride, to no longer have a worthy dream.

—*Mantilla, Havana, July 2016*

THE HUNTER
ERNESTO THE *JINETERO*

BY ABRAHAM JIMÉNEZ ENOA
TRANSLATED BY ROBIN MYERS

I t was raining cats and dogs in Viñales, 183 kilometers from Havana, and Ernesto had the Italian girl naked on the kitchen table in a rented house when his phone started to vibrate. It was the French girl. After lunch, as the Italian girl was washing the dishes, Ernesto had come up behind her, pressed the length of his muscles against her, the breadth of his bare pectorals, his entire virile self, and had begun to kiss her softly along her neck, shoulders, and back, before turning her around and undressing her right there. He'd forgotten that the French girl had e-mailed him the day before to confirm her arrival that very morning, and she'd already spoken with her family—the French girl had Cuban relatives—about introducing him. So Ernesto devised a way to leave the Italian girl alone for a few minutes, shimmering with arousal, so he could go to the bathroom and answer the French girl's call.

ERNESTO: *Salut, mon amour, est-ce que tu es bien arrivée?*
FRENCH GIRL: Yes, *mon amour.* When do you get to
   Havana?
ERNESTO: *Aujourd'hui, ma chérie.*

The Italian girl was flying home the next day, in the evening,
which was a problem. Back from the bathroom and carrying on
as if nothing had happened, Ernesto knelt on the kitchen floor
and kissed his way up her legs, like someone scaling a scaffold,
until he returned to her face and made love to her for the fourth
time that day. Then he lied: "My sister says my mother's gotten
sick again—I'll have to leave for Baracoa right away."

It was two in the afternoon when they finished, exhausted,
slicked with a cream of sweat, and the Italian girl, quenched and
rapturous, stretched out across the cooking pans and cutlery as
if on a waterbed.

———

I met Ernesto in August 2015 on the sad, rough sands of Gua-
nabo, a beach east of Havana. It was the second time the French
girl, Fadih, was coming to Cuba. They'd met four months earlier,
when she visited the island for a Cuban cousin's wedding. We all
ended up at the same summerhouse with a pool, rented by the
mother-in-law of a friend of mine who comes once a year to see
his two daughters and his mother-in-law. The mother-in-law, in
turn, has been married for over twenty years to a Congolese man
of French origin and divides her time among Congo, France, and
Miami. One of the Congolese man's nieces is Fadih. Fadih was
born in Brazzaville, Republic of the Congo. She's enormously fat;
she must weigh about 250 pounds. Her skin is black as charcoal.

She is thirty-three and bespectacled. Her family had never seen her with a boyfriend until Ernesto appeared.

"I captured Fadih in the airport when I went to drop off a Spanish girl. It was her first visit to Cuba and she ran into me on her way out the door. A sign, right? It's all going great," Ernesto told me that day in the beach house. Then he plunged elegantly into the Guanabo water in his nylon briefs, neon yellow, fitted closely to his thighs.

Fadih's trip to attend her cousin's wedding was supposed to last five days, which evolved into two months. Her run-in with Ernesto at Exit #4 of Havana's José Martí International Airport would change her life.

"You have to be ruthless. She looked sort of lost and I pounced. I immediately pocketed the address of where she was staying and her phone number at the house. And, of course, I whipped out my most seductive face to see if I could hook her."

Every night that week, he called her or appeared outside the building where her relatives lived and invited her to go sit on the pier. Fadih would drink beer; Ernesto, fruit juice.

"It just so happened that she showed up when I didn't have any girls here, so I could spend a lot of time convincing her."

Fadih ultimately changed her return ticket and set off with Ernesto to explore Cuba. They went to Viñales, to Trinidad, to Pesquero in Holguín, and ended up in Baracoa, where she met Ernesto's mother.

"After all that me-time, no woman can resist. They lose it. Bringing her home was a point in my favor. I know how to work the foreign girls. I peddled her everything beautiful about Cuba, plus my own assets, you know what I mean? In the end she really believed that I didn't just want to go on vacation, that I wanted to get serious."

In the early 1990s, with the fall of the socialist bloc and the disintegration of the USSR, Cuba fell on its hardest times. The national economy abruptly stopped receiving the metric tons of commercial privileges that its sister nations had been sending to stock the country, and the island sank into a swamp—an outcome even the gloomiest forecasts hadn't predicted. Financial crisis gradually swallowed up the great social achievements made by Fidel Castro and the triumphant Revolution of 1959. Cuban society started to experience a metamorphosis.

The hunger, scarcity, and discontent sparked by the 36 percent contraction of the GDP—between 1990 and 1995, according to statistics from the Centro de Estudios Económicos de Cuba, every Cuban adult lost between 5 and 25 percent of his or her body weight—brought dormant perversions to a boil. Prostitution was an emergency exit out of the crisis. During this so-called Special Period, some decided to weather the storm by clinging to their convictions alone. Others threw themselves into the struggle for survival. And so, in this savage time, when everything was justified in the name of getting by and the government offered no response at all, *jineterismo* was born—the range of illegal or semilegal activities, including prostitution, undertaken to acquire money, comforts, or mobility from foreign tourists.

The Special Period ravaged Ernesto's household. His mother, who had a government job, was laid off in one of that era's massive budget cuts, and his father died suddenly of a heart attack when Ernesto was only eleven. He had no choice but to go out and earn a living as a child, which is how he ended up joining forces with the other boys in his neighborhood; together, they'd go to the most heavily touristed area of Baracoa and ask foreigners for money. He dropped out of school, but at first he didn't tell his mother. He let her wake him at six thirty every morning and dress him up as a little red-kerchiefed pioneer. He'd leave the house with a backpack full of books, but instead of continuing on to school, he'd hide the pack in a derelict two-story house, untie his neck scarf, pull off his white outer shirt, and run off to the old historic part of the city: the hotel zone.

"My mom found out, man, because I'd always come home chewing gum and bring her baskets of bread and jam and cheese and cans of soda and American coins. Where was I going to get all that? She couldn't say anything, because if I didn't bring stuff home, we'd starve."

A month after our first conversation in Guanabo, Ernesto and I met up in Havana to talk some more. We sat in Café Mamainés, in Vedado. Fadih was in Paris and Ernesto was coming from Varadero, where he'd sent off a German girl who called herself Judith and had just flown back home. The next day he had to go to the airport and pick up an English girl. That night he would sleep alone in a rented room in the Miramar neighborhood, and the next morning he'd set out for a hotel in Varadero with the English girl—the same place he'd checked out of with the German girl less than twenty-four hours before.

<hr />

Ernesto only officially finished the first part of middle school, but by age fourteen he could already communicate in English and Italian. He'd transitioned from stalking tourist buses, clamoring for gum and sandwiches, to prowling around the historic district, where he'd recommend restaurants and charge commission. He went from begging for quarters, fifty cents, a dollar, to selling Cuban bills stamped with the faces of José Martí and Che Guevara. Until he realized that he could obtain far superior dividends by making foreign women fall in love with him. "At the end of the day, they're here for us," he told me the day I met him on the Guanabo beach, turning his back to Fadih's Cuban family.

All his international shoulder rubbing made him a polyglot; he enriched his repertoire with German, Portuguese, and French. He started doing gymnastics and conjured a university air: he used to say he was pursuing a bachelor's degree in physical culture.

"Man, I know I'm hunky and sweet and my skin's the color those foreign chicks are looking for, but no one likes a moron. Sometimes I read the *Granma* paper, you know, and I watch news on TV so I can talk about the world, too."

One day he decided to start systematically eating breakfast at the expensive cafés in Havana, all the tourist spots, and in hotel lobbies and restaurants. But this tactic yielded no results other than financial losses.

"I realized that wasn't the way. If I was going to conquer the foreign chicks, I'd have to dazzle them Cuban style: rum in hand, salsa, catcalls. And you can only pull that off at a nightclub."

The reigning scarcity imposed during the Special Period meant that Cubans saw foreign tourists as veritable gold mines. The Cuban government tried everything to prevent the proliferation of this attitude. For years, the government legally forbade its citizens from visiting hotels and tourist centers. It was an authoritarian shield worthy of a preschool: Cubans didn't know how to behave around visitors, so they couldn't have anything to do with them. It wasn't until 2008 that a series of new legislations, promoted by Raúl Castro, allowed Cubans to enjoy many of the rights held by foreigners. Even so, this change couldn't altogether eliminate the tension surrounding the outsiders who come to relish things that insiders can't experience at all. The Revolution had unwittingly shot itself in the foot: in confining Cubans, it transformed foreigners into superior beings, aliens. Which is why, no matter where you are, you'll so often see Cuban/foreign couples, romantically imbalanced and united by money. You can tell with a single glance that one of their pockets, the woman's or the man's, is the sole attraction. Old ladies trying out stylish outfits and walking hand in hand with their latest catch, exhibiting him: a burly, brown-skinned, charismatic, Caribbean twenty-something, a good dancer, with dreadlocks or braids. Or a grizzled foreigner relentlessly smoking his Cuban cigar while talking to a slim, honey-skinned girl with curly hair and full lips.

The *jineteros* are everywhere, especially in tourist areas and ever-proliferating trendy bars. They're bona fide squadrons, armed with the gift of gab, soldiers who have transformed their Cuban identity into a pointed dagger they'll sink into the flesh of the foreigners who have long yearned for this particular pain.

———

It's been over a year since Ernesto last traveled home to Baracoa, Guantánamo. He says the next time will be to say good-bye to his friends and family, to leave the country and never come back, because he's sick of living in squalor.

He's a nomad who lives all over the island: from one end of the country to the other, from rented house to rented house, from hotel to hotel, or in the houses of his clients' friends. No fixed whereabouts: his clients always fund his stays, and they're the source of the money he sends his mother each month. Ernesto's mother is seventy-six years old, healthy as a horse, and she uses this money to fund her business selling grated-coconut candies in Baracoa.

———

"I'm a professional and this is my job," Ernesto told me, smiling, at Café Mamainés. In order to carve out a niche and ultimately triumph in such a vast market, he added, he had to focus and distinguish himself. "There's lots of competition, lots of people in the same business. I don't eat fatty foods, and if drinking can't be avoided I prefer rum and whiskey. I avoid beer at all costs—I drink it only if the client deserves it. I just kiss the edge of the glass without swallowing much yeast, wetting my lips with the foam, which helps me keep the ladies excited. I'm not a vegetarian, but I prioritize vegetables. I have to stay fit."

When he doesn't have clients to attend to, he concentrates on physical exercise. He doesn't lift weights. He prefers planks, pull-ups, and the parallel bars, combining everything with various types of sit-ups. He also goes running, though he doesn't overdo it; he doesn't want to get too thin. Ernesto's body looks handmade, a Roman statue from head to foot. His skin is light brown. His eyes are almond shaped and his hair is long, curly, just grazing his firm shoulders. At age thirty-four, he has a gymnast's build. No flab, all muscle, but not over the top, either. He knows he has to tempt all tastes: he lives to serve, a mannequin on permanent display. His goal is to attract the attention of absolutely any foreign woman: blond, black, Chinese, olive-skinned, fat, thin, tiny, tall. He waits for a woman to fix her eyes on him, and this will lead to a few days of leisure, eating in restaurants and private joints, going to the beach, sleeping in air-conditioned rooms, before he scrapes some money off his foreign companions in the form of the commissions he charges at the places he takes them or through various dirty tricks (he'll sell them tobacco, rum, or some other merchandise at a higher-than-normal price). When the dreamy days come to an end, anything—some sandals, an iPhone—serves as payment. There are no set rates. Just perks. A subtle agreement, barely tangible and never mentioned, that the foreign women know to heed.

"We don't talk about it, but most of them already know. No need to sign a contract. There are others who don't realize, poor things, and they figure the whole thing out when they're already over the moon."

If the client is satisfied with the performance and pleasure of the service offered, and if the fling continues to evolve over the Internet, it may well culminate in a wedding. And, more to the point, in Ernesto getting off the island. Moving to another country. Any country; it doesn't matter which.

Ernesto has a scar on his lower abdomen, a knife slash he received in a prison fight. There, in jail, over ten years ago, was the last time he tasted bread. Today he feels repulsed by the mere sight of it.

"Man, the last time I ate that stale garbage was in prison. I did three years in Santiago de Cuba for prostitution and tourist harassment."

Three years of his life in the Cárcel de Boniato. During the summer, sprawled out in his bunk, he felt like he was melting in the heat that seeped from the narrow walls. In the winter he suffered from the humidity and he missed bright light and the wind.

"In Baracoa the police had warned me about getting too close to the tourists, but I wasn't afraid of them. Until one day I got reckless, leaving the salsa club with a group of Brazilians. They stopped me and boom! Into the cop car without a word. Trial and three years in the can. I lost that sweet Brazilian girl—she was crazy for me, man, totally nuts. Imagine it: bad guys, really bad, fighting to survive. And I was just a kid; I was twenty-one years old when it happened. I had to get tough. Anyway, I'll have this mark on my body for the rest of my life. Two guys even wanted to rape me."

"And you didn't learn your lesson?"

"No way, man, the other way around! I left jail even more determined to win over all the foreign chicks around, so someone will get me out of this shitty country."

That day, in Viñales, Ernesto left the Italian girl and went out in search of his French girl.

"The Italian girl is leaving tomorrow and she's only here to party, anyway. No chance of marrying her and no way of her getting me out."

He went to the beach house in Guanabo. When he opened the door, he found Fadih's entire Cuban family gathered there. This was an audience he wasn't used to: Ernesto always performs his shows for foreigners. Before he went in, he worried that his charade might be exposed. And that's exactly what happened.

"Cubans know perfectly well how to identify a *jinetero*, but I'm not worried; there's no fear in this body of mine. They're the ones who made me put on the whole show."

Fadih's Cuban relatives couldn't understand how she hadn't noticed Ernesto's intentions. Behind his back, beside me, Fadih's aunt said, "Let her be—if she gets him out of Cuba just to have some fun, she'll lose him as soon as they arrive." Her cousin responded, "But Mom, where else would she ever find a hottie like that?" Fadih, meanwhile, looked radiant with pleasure, as if she were having a sublime experience. Ernesto approached and whispered something into her ear. She smiled and made a gesture that landed as a caress near his neck.

Incredulous stares followed Ernesto everywhere he went: when he got up to go to the bathroom, when he lifted a forkful of food to his mouth, when he pulled off his T-shirt and strode off to the pool, when he walked up to Fadih and murmured sweet nothings.

"Her family's judgment is normal because they're Cuban and they can smell it. But no fear. When you're good at your job, the rest doesn't matter. The girl's in love, and this didn't start just yesterday."

According to the Cuban Ministry of Tourism, about four million tourists visited the island in 2016, a record figure that Ernesto maximized for his own purposes. Throughout our conversations, he has never for a moment put away his cell phone. His list of contacts is immense. "I've been doing this for years now. I have to check my e-mail and Facebook every day to make plans and so all the ladies don't show up at the same time. I don't go out much to hunt anymore; I've got my own business taken care of and I don't have to compete with the others. My catch is guaranteed. It's taken me years to get to this point," he said once, his iPhone 4 in hand, scrolling through the female faces in his WhatsApp list.

"At first it was hard for me because I'm a shy kind of guy. But I got over that pretty fast, man," said Ernesto in Café Mamainés. He then launched into a detailed explanation of his modus operandi.

"First you attack with your eyes, pierce them with your gaze, so you've got a head start in the conversation, less ground to cover. If a foreign chick looks at you and maintains eye contact and then looks at you again in a matter of seconds, she's easy prey—she's yours. You have to be nice and start ahead in the tab. If she's willing to keep talking, you have to treat her first, start with an advantage, and then you start ordering more and more and learn to feel confident enough that you don't react at all when the check shows up; you don't pay a cent."

Once he's dazzled his prey, the true challenge begins.

"The real work happens in bed. The rest is just protocol, a duty you have to fulfill."

According to Ernesto, many women come in search of Caribbean heat, and heat means a high dose of sex. So you have to give it to them. Mercilessly, ruthlessly. At night, in the morning, before lunch, after lunch, in the bathroom, in the kitchen, in the bed, on the floor, behind a leafy tree, in a bush, on the stairs.

"You have to drive them wild, man: six, seven, eight times a day and they're hooked. No one in the world can do that except for Cubans. And how do I do it? With my mind, man. I focus, I concentrate, I'm having sex but I'm not looking at her tits or thinking about them—just about what that body's going to deliver when I'm not on top of it anymore. Professionalism, man, professionalism. What little I've got in this world, I owe it to my cock and nobody else, man, nobody else."

But none of the foreign women on Ernesto's long list could imagine exactly how this man has become an expert in the art of sex.

"After you fuck a chicken till it clucks really loud, after you drill a pig or a goat, then you're ready for combat, man. Only way to learn that is being a kid in the east, in the countryside. Animals are hornier than women and that's how you learn to control yourself and not come too fast."

"Do you keep count of how many foreign women you've slept with?"

"Nah, man, I wish. I always regret that. The other day an associate asked me the same thing and I didn't know what to say. But the number's got to be pretty high, because I'm not picky—whatever smells like a foreign girl, I'll smoke it. The fatter and uglier the better; those are the ones who could really use some love."

In July 2016, Ernesto traveled to Baracoa and spent a week at home. His mother says that he didn't go out at all, not a single night, and he only left the house to connect to the Wi-Fi in the park downtown. He spent seven days in an armchair in the living room, staring out the window, turning a gold band around and around on his right ring finger.

"He said he'd come to say good-bye, that he'd gotten married and was leaving the country with the French girl he'd introduced me to last year. I actually can't remember which French girl she was."

OUTSIDE

EVEN THOUGH
HE'S DEAD

BY PATRICIO FERNÁNDEZ
TRANSLATED BY MEGAN MCDOWELL

A man without some kind of dream of perfection is quite as
much of a monstrosity as a noseless man.
—G. K. Chesterton, *Heretics*

NOVEMBER 1, 2016, THE DAY OF THE DEAD

On December 17, 2014, Barack Obama and Raúl Castro stood before the cameras and declared that they had decided to reopen diplomatic relations between their two countries. Up until a few months before, when both heads of state were in South Africa for Nelson Mandela's funeral and made news by shaking hands, only one U.S. president had been face-to-face with a Castro. The first and last president who met with Fidel was Richard Nixon, who at the time was vice president, in 1959. After that came the Cold War. Che Guevara even said that if, in order to continue the socialist revolution, "it were necessary to embrace the atomic cloud, I would embrace it." Ronald Reagan baptized the Soviet bloc "the Evil Empire," and before a 1984

radio address in Washington, while he was testing the micro-
phones, he slipped in a joke that made the world tremble: "My
fellow Americans, I'm pleased to tell you today that I've signed
legislation that will outlaw Russia forever. We begin bombing in
five minutes." The truth is that the capitalists won and their faith
spread over the entire world; that of the leftists, meanwhile, went
to hide like dust within the folds of the triumphant ideology.

That December 17 was the feast day of San Lázaro, or Ba-
balú Ayé, the most miraculous of the orisha saints inhabiting
the island, where Santeria concealed itself within Catholicism
and never succumbed to Marxism. People in Havana could not
believe the news. Many people hugged before their TVs. Phone
lines were overloaded. More than a few people remembered the
saint, and in several of Havana's churches, as soon as the news
was public and without anyone giving the instruction, the bells
started ringing.

It was a war finishing, families reuniting, isolation ceding,
and an era reaching its end. The empire had given up on inflict-
ing political defeat on the Castros (in this, Cuba won). Instead, it
was leaving their subversion in the hands of the market, which, as
experience showed, corrodes convictions with an efficiency very
difficult to resist. "There's no going back" was what many con-
cluded. I was among them, and in the following days I decided I
wanted to witness the end of the story.

I reached Havana in early February 2015. It was cooler than
usual, and the subject on everyone's lips was the cold wave that,
according to the newscasters, should be arriving at any mo-
ment. On TV they were warning of temperatures dropping to
forty-eight degrees Fahrenheit, which had many people going

out wearing unusual and unjustified coats. The air didn't have that sticky heat that keeps bodies damp and prohibits any kind of formality in the Cubans' dress—they are used to shorts, unbuttoned shirts, and plastic sandals—but it was a far cry from shivering cold.

"Here, what you expect to happen never happens," Gerardo told me the day I met him. I was looking for a car so, when I needed to, I could move beyond the circuit of the *almendrones*—which is what Cubans call the American vehicles from the fifties that pick up passengers along the large avenues—and Regla, the black woman who cleaned Señora Ruth's house, where I rented a room, had assured me that the best thing would be to come to an agreement with this friend of hers, who very soon became a friend of mine. "Anything you need, Gerardo can make it happen," Regla told me.

At eight in the morning the next day, Gerardo was waiting for me steps from Señora Ruth's house, at the corner of Eleventh and G, talking on the phone and sitting on the hood of his car. The gadget pressed to his ear wasn't really a mobile phone, but a tablet the size of a notebook, and when I got close to him and he guessed I was the person he was waiting for, he began to say good-bye, first with tender words—"yeah, sweetie, I'll call you, I swear"—but once I was close enough for a handshake, he started to show signs of annoyance—"I gotta hang up, girl, my passenger's here . . . Yeah, yeah, I told you I'll call you for sure. Yes, for sure! . . . I mean, how do you want me to say it?! I'll call you! I've told you a thousand times, by God, I'll call you!" When I was beside him he started to hit the tablet: "Piece of shit contraption!" he shouted while he brought it close to his eyes to be sure it had turned off correctly. "You're Patricio, right?"

I still hadn't explained what I wanted from him, and it didn't seem to matter much to him; when a *mulata* girl walked past, thick thighs and red Lycra pants that showed her underwear in front and back, he didn't take his eyes from her ass when he asked me if I preferred them like that, or if I liked them "skinny." "I like them just like that!" he said, raising his voice so "the female," as he called her, would hear. She smiled, but didn't look at him. "Have you tried a *mulata* yet?" he asked me. I replied that I hadn't on this trip, and he concluded: "You got time."

He had a white, rusted-out Lada, on which only the driver's-side door closed normally. He used it as an informal taxi, and also to move merchandise of any sort, although most of the time he used it to contact his buyers and sellers of dollars. He worked, as I found out later, in the currency black market. His main clients were Venezuelans who came, as he told me, to *raspar cupos* (roughly, "scrape quotas"), a financial exercise that ended up making their trips profitable through a mechanism that, in spite of his efforts to explain it to me, I never managed to understand. "Forget it: just some capitalist funny business to get some benefit from socialist rules."

Gerardo and Regla became my friends from everyday Cuba. I wandered the streets with him, and with her I'd talk over breakfast or while she did the cleaning for Señora Ruth, her boss, a Communist who was nearing eighty and who considered Fidel to be "the most beautiful man in the world." The day I arrived, Ruth told me not to believe anything I was told, because there were people who took advantage of foreigners to "blow nonexistent problems all out of proportion." She was a history professor and spoke like a teacher. As soon as she left me alone, Regla, who never took the kerchief from her head, came over to me to ask if I wanted some *fruta bomba* juice (what Cubans call papaya juice), and when she saw that Señora Ruth had disappeared into her room, she clarified that "Ruth doesn't know anything because she never leaves the house; at most, she makes it to the park on the corner." Regla was not an enemy of the regime. In fact, during those days she was very grateful because the office of City Historian Eusebio Leal was repairing her apartment in Habana Vieja, near the courthouse. But she stressed: "The things we lack, we really lack. Things are tight." Regla brought me to a house where they sold fish. She showed me the pig they were raising in the laundry room of the apartment. And she told me that the Revolution wasn't evil, but it was blind.

The other Cubans I saw, the ones whose houses I visited or who I went out to eat with in one of the new private restaurants that began to proliferate with the promise of the country's opening up, belonged to the elite. This is not an elite that lives in luxury, although neither does it feel the scarcity that the rest of the population does. It's very small, as in all the continent's countries, and within it coexist the heirs with eminent last names, new entrepreneurs, visual artists, musicians, and writers. There are almost no black people among them. It's not that these people explicitly reject blacks or have racist attitudes, it's just that black people don't make it in. It's very unusual to see an interracial marriage in those circles.

The artist Felipe Dulzaides told me, "Cuba must be the only country in the world where ours is the best-paid profession." Since Cuba has come into fashion, people in the rest of the world want to find out what's happening in this country of resistance. It's no longer seen as a danger, but as a curiosity. The gringos are no longer the enemies (they never were, for the general population); the gallerists of Miami and New York—and Canada and Europe—regularly come through the workshops looking for homegrown talents to export to their countries. The paradoxical thing is that only in the touristy street circuit, which is more artisan that artistic, does "revolutionary folk" painting abound, while in these new, expanding markets, highly sophisticated, conceptual, postmodern, and antiestablishment art predominates. Even Kcho, the darling of the regime, makes installations with rafts and sharks, where it's impossible not to see references to a dangerous and desperate escape.

What's happening today to visual artists has long been occurring with musicians, either because they exalt the longed-for Caribbean happiness or because they glorify the revolutionary era—that is, the archeology of a dream. The tourists seek out the music, and the Cubans who emigrate find each other through it, so that if having a guitarist in the family used to be cause for shame, once the Revolution was under way, it became a life raft. Lawyers, engineers, doctors, architects, or economists—people of liberal professions—receive a salary fixed by the state, which today is no more than thirty dollars a month. And since neither prostitutes nor waitresses (the other profitable professions) have the prestige required by any elite, it's the musicians and producers, the writers and painters who are the true protagonists of that elite. The artists are not only the life of the party, they're also its owners.

At this point everyone criticizes the government, some more than others, but in a way that denotes closeness, almost like complaints about a family member. There is no one on the right in that world. Those people left long ago. (According to the writer Wendy Guerra: "Everyone leaves.") None of the participants in this cultural elite would want Cuba to become a business haven, because there's a rhythm, a coexistence, in this country's daily life that they don't find other places when they travel, and lately they travel often. Pichi Perugorría, who has played some of the most uncomfortable characters in Cuban cinema—the most emblematic of all being Diego, the homosexual in *Fresa y chocolate*—said one afternoon, between Cuba libres: "Don't ask me to understand it, but Cuba is where I feel free."

Every one of the members of this elite has a chosen moment to explain when the story went sour: either it's with the sovietization, or the Five Gray Years, or General Ochoa's execution, or the Special Period, or the raft exodus, or Raúl. But there are no "dissidents" among them, just people who are critical and people who are very critical. "Dissidence," to tell the truth, has few advocates—Guillermo Fariñas, Antonio Rodiles, Laritza Diversent, and not many others—and finds no sympathizers among the citizens. They talk to foreign media, but they have no way to talk to media in Cuba, and even if they did, the truth is that their complaints don't seem urgent for the average Cuban, who is more worried about the price of tomatoes than freedom of the press or abuses of authority. Nor are there any strong organizations outside the government through which any opposing discourse could take root. Maybe the church, but it is very cautious with Cuba. Since John Paul II visited the island in 1998, the church is no longer a direct enemy. That was the year Christmas was declared a holiday again, after it was suspended in 1969 and officially abolished one year later. As Pope Francis himself let people know when he visited in 2015, there are many values that Christianity and the Revolution share.

In the year and a half that I've been visiting the island, I have not met anyone who talks to me about democracy. And except for the Ladies in White, who demand the freedom of their relatives arrested for political reasons and who number no more than fifty-something, no one talks about human rights, either. It's true that if you dig deeper you uncover pain, the frustration of what could have been and was not, or, in the younger people, the boredom with what they never wanted anyway, a feeling of premature failure that relaxes and distresses at the same time. But it's domestic problems—electricity, water, the infrequency of *almendrones,* the price of onions, the disappearance of beer—

that dominate conversations. The press, the radio, and television never give bad local news. Terrible things only happen outside Cuba.

━━

I covered almost the entire island following Pope Francis in September 2015. We saw him in Havana, in Holguín, and in Santiago. As we drove, we listened to the pontiff's speeches on Radio Rebelde. My secret hope was that, as a lot of people gathered to hear him, spontaneous protests would break out, cries of unrest. That's what had happened in Chile when John Paul II visited during Pinochet's regime. Every one of his appearances became an excuse to make all kinds of denunciations so the whole world would hear. Popes bring in a lot of international press. But nothing like that happened here, where people aren't living with an unsustainable tension and there are no cauldrons about to boil over. His visit didn't even awaken the slightest religious fervor. A large portion of the crowd attended because they were brought by their respective Committees for the Defense of the Revolution (CDRs). Gerardo himself preferred to wait for me in the car drinking a beer while I attended the homilies. He didn't feel any curiosity.

During that trip, we crossed thousands of hectares given over to that robust weed called the sickle bush, plus old sugar factories that had engendered some of the largest fortunes in the west (estates that have become infinite plains, interrupted only by shrubs and white-bellied royal palms) and ex-plantations of citrus (Oriente had been an important orange producer), now barely cultivated in small plots plowed with oxen that pass alongside the ruins of old Soviet machinery. If Havana was paused at the height of fifties modernity, the life of the peasants—*guajiros*—

has returned, technologically speaking, to the abandoned poverty that existed during those same years. They aren't lacking in medical attention or in schools (the Revolution's two great achievements in the countryside), but they have made no material progress. According to them, people in Havana are materialists corrupted by money. And it's in the rural towns that fidelity to the regime remains most fervent.

Over the course of the trip I saw Gerardo enter into action several times. The same night we arrived in Santiago de Cuba, he asked a waitress to close her eyes and think of a number. The waitress, who was not exactly young, did it. Then Gerardo asked her to tell him what it was. And she obeyed: "Three." He raised his arms and shouted: "Girl, I swear I can't believe this! I was thinking of the same number! This must mean something. Let's get together when you get off work?" That night, however, he went to bed with another woman. While I'd been chasing the pope, he'd worked out the details of the date. The next day, while he was saying good-bye to the girl, I saw him pass her some bills. He explained that it wasn't because she charged him, but she did expect something. "I give her ten CUC [Cuban convertible pesos] and we all leave happy," he said. "The truth, Pato"—he rarely called me that, because in Cuba they call homosexuals "pato"—"is that around here, all the women are whores. I don't even trust my wife, or my sister, or my mother, or my daughter. There isn't a woman in the world who gets undressed faster than a Cuban one. And there's no woman in the world I like better."

Perhaps fifty or a hundred years from now they'll be able to write objectively about the way of life we called socialism. Without all the tears and obscenities. They'll unearth it like ancient Troy. Until recently, you weren't allowed to say anything good about socialism. In the West, after the fall of the Soviet Union, they realized that Marxism wasn't really over, it still needed to be developed. Without being worshipped. Over there, he wasn't an idol like he'd been for us. A saint! First we worshipped him, then we anathematized him. Crossed it all out. But science has also caused immeasurable suffering—should we eliminate scientists? Curse the fathers of the atom bomb, or better yet, start with the ones who invented gunpowder? Yes, start with them . . .

—Svetlana Alexievich, *Secondhand Time:*
The Last of the Soviets

"I was never a Communist. My father was, but I just wasn't made for it. I like to have a good time, brother. Have myself a rum, grease a girl, and I don't ask that I always eat well, because as we say here, 'He who eats well and eats badly ends up eating twice.' The ladies have been my vice since I was little, ever since a neighbor lady brought me to her room for the first time. As you know, man cannot live on bread alone.

"I get by with what I earn. My family doesn't lack for anything and they don't have anything extra. My wife sometimes complains there's no meat or potatoes, but since the Special Period, you can always get rice and beans. Now that was a hard time. We ate whatever turned up. In the food basket they'd give you six pounds of rice per person per month. That's not enough for anything. Three pounds of sugar. A packet of coffee per person. Oil only showed up every once in a while. All fowl and meat disappeared from our diets. The minced meat they gave you at the butcher's was supplemented with soy, and you hardly ever even got that. Everything else you had to order on the black market. There was no fuel, no transportation. You could lie down to sleep in the street with no problem. There was almost never any electricity, and that's why we didn't talk about *apagones,* or blackouts, anymore, but of *alumbrones,* or "light-ons." There were plenty of family men who worked for a normal salary that wasn't enough to buy anything. Hunger, hunger, hunger, no, but with six pounds of rice per month along with the little piece of bread you got once a day, well, if you had a teenager in the house and you saw how things were, you had to give your rice to him, my friend, and then you'd eat a little less. Then that family man with no way to find a little extra, he'd take his bicycle to work, and there were a lot of people who fainted in the street from the physical exertion, since sometimes they hadn't had breakfast. That was when this country started to go down the tubes. We've always had prostitutes, but they used to be more reserved. Now you got these hookers, and along with them come the police. Since they were supposed to combat prostitution, they jumped all over the girls, and then the corruption started. Since there was no superior to mediate, everything got fixed with a few CUC. Instead of chasing down crime, they went around fucking with the girls.

"During that time my older brother left, not long after the tugboat *13 de Marzo* tragedy. He didn't tell anyone he was going, especially not our father, who got furious if he even saw someone chewing gum, because according to him that was a *yuma* habit, only for Americans. Imagine that! He hated gum for being capitalist! He never forgave my brother, and only after Obama's visit did he let my mother tell him how my brother had gone to sea in a raft made of eight truck tires, with fifteen other people on it, one canvas sail and another one of plastic. It took them four days, and by some miracle they all made it alive.

"A month ago, my brother came to visit. He brought his two

sons—George, fifteen, and John, twelve—and he told us that he's been separated from his wife for two years. He's a pretty calm guy, not like me; I've been married three times. He came loaded down with presents: he brought my mom a suitcase full of clothes, perfumes, soaps, things like that, and he gave my dad some Puma soccer shoes like the ones Fidel's started wearing. That's what he told him when he gave them to him: 'They're the same brand Fidel uses, Dad.' And the old man laughed. Then he started to cry."

"One night we stayed up drinking rum, me, my brother, and my dad, and the old man, once he'd had a few, started complaining that the Revolution has stolen his life. He repeated several times that he'd given everything, he'd even sacrificed the love of a son, and then he did something I never thought I'd see in my life: he asked my brother to forgive him. He said, 'I should never have judged you, I'm sorry,' and while my brother hugged him the old man cried like a baby, and I had never seen him cry like that, I swear. He said life had passed him by, that this fucking revolution had rotted his soul; he felt poisoned, because he saw how the people who left were now coming back as conquerors, and the same guys who'd called them shit-eating worms and antisocial scum were now offering them businesses and possibilities that they, the ones who stayed, would never get. 'What are they going to offer us,' he said, 'when we've already learned to be happy with nothing!' He said, 'They cut off our balls!'

"I like Cuba, Patico. I swear it on a virgin's pussy. I like the people, I have what I need—although I have to save up CUC so I can send the Lada to the body shop and freshen her up—I have fun with my friends, my kids have education and health care, and if things change, I just hope it's for the better. Because it's true that we lack some things, but there are also a lot of things we could lose if the *yumas* show up with their suitcases full of dollars. I'll give you just one example: You think anyone would get into this heap if one of those companies can offer a new car? And the females—what do you think?"

Gerardo told me these things and more the morning of August 13, 2016, before he brought me to Karl Marx Theater, where an event was to be held in celebration of Fidel Castro's ninetieth birthday.

The four days that Barack Obama was in Cuba at the end of March 2016 led to unthinkable consequences: with his ease and warmth, he captivated a population used to aged, hierarchical leaders, and he contradicted the imperialist discourse that would have been predictable in a U.S. president. He declared the failure of his country's historical policies toward Cuba and said he wanted the two nations to understand each other through their differences: "You have a socialist economy, we have an open market; you have a single party, we have a multiparty democracy. . . . The important thing is that it's the Cuban people who decide their future." He said the Cold War was over, and he went with his family and Raúl Castro's to see a baseball game during which, with a packed stadium watching, they laughed together. He won over the Habaneros by telling them that they had unusual talents, a genius that can achieve complicated solutions with precarious tools—they make replacement parts for their cars using tin cans—and he told them that with the education they possess, they can go far. He had a meeting with small-business owners, attended by hairdressers; designers of books, pamphlets, and refrigerator magnets; and another twenty-odd *cuentapropistas* (freelancers), which is what everyone who doesn't work for the state is called. Afterward, people were left with the feeling that it was Obama who was coming to offer unattainable utopias, except that, to show that these utopias were possible, he had a successful U.S. small-business owner speak and asked him to tell about how he started out and how far he had come. Obama's words and his figure were the subject of conversation on every corner. His visit to the island came to revolutionize the Revolution.

The great absence during those days was Fidel Castro. Not only did he not show himself, but his name was not mentioned in any of the speeches during the visit of *el negro,* which was how some people referred then to the U.S. president in this country where most people are black or mestizo. He only appeared a week later, to remind people who was in charge: "My modest suggestion is that he reflect, and not try to elaborate theories about Cuban politics for now," Castro wrote in *Granma.* In the same text, he said that Obama had used "convoluted" words, and he rejected the proposal to leave the past behind: "What about those who died in mercenary attacks on Cuban ships and ports, an airplane full of passengers blown up midflight, mercenary invasions, multiple acts of violence and force?" he reminded people.

After that, official TV and newspapers, and the Web site Cubadebate.cu, threw themselves into redirecting the feeling after the *yuma*'s visit. Fidel had drawn a line. There were multiple analysts who, falling in line behind his orders, wrote columns pointing to Obama's disgraceful willingness to erase history and the importance of upholding the nation's values. Obama's trip to the island had resonated more widely than expected. In Cuba's current process of opening up, one of the greatest concerns of the upper echelons is keeping control and regulating the speed at which things happen, and after the president's visit they felt the reins were slipping from their fingers.

Many people expected that the Communist Party's Seventh Congress, which was held in April, a month after Barack Obama's departure, would indicate the next steps on the path to liberalization, from which, regardless of obstacles, it now seemed there was no turning back. But that's not what happened: the "Obama effect" had the opposite result. Instead of designing the new map of power in the post-Castro era, power was reconcentrated in the old guard, and especially in Raúl's family. State Security was put into his son Alejandro's hands, and the economy into those of his ex-brother-in-law, Luis Alberto Rodríguez López-Callejas. The congress's final call was "for the achievement of a sovereign, independent, socialist, prosperous, and sustainable nation." For those who follow the island's politics closely, this showed that the brakes had been put on all the exuberance.

Fidel is seen or heard from only on the rarest of occasions. After that editorial in *Granma* in which he talked about the U.S. president's visit, he has appeared only twice: during the Seventh Congress, when he gave a speech that sounded more like a grandpa saying good-bye than an all-powerful statesman, and on August 13, for his ninetieth birthday, when he published one of his reflections. In it, he remembered his father and his childhood in Birán, writing that "the human species today faces the greatest risk in its history," and he took the opportunity to chastise the head honcho of the American empire (his eternal interlocutor) for his speech on May 27 in Japan, when "words failed him in excusing himself for the massacre of hundreds of thousands of people in Hiroshima, though he was aware of the bomb's effects."

That Saturday, August 13, 2016, the day he turned ninety years old, Fidel attended an event organized in his honor at the

Karl Marx Theater. The area was full and the stage overflowed with military men. He could barely stand up. He was wearing a white Puma sweat suit. He was accompanied by his brother Raúl and the president of Venezuela, Nicolás Maduro, but the tribute's central figures were the children who sang and recited odes in his honor. All the children in all the island's orphanages did the same, and in all the schools and many CDRs of the capital. To those children, Castro is that little old man who looks like Santa Claus, not the illustrious warrior or the authoritarian father of contemporary Cuba. I was in a bar when a scene came on TV of Fidel in the Sierra Maestra, and I heard a little girl ask her father, "Who is that?" The man, surprised, laughed uncomfortably and replied, "It's Fidel Castro."

August was entirely dedicated to Fidel. Looking in the windows of stores where they sold crispy fried chicken, or in the markets that are less well stocked than usual because of the new crisis in Cuba after Venezuela cut its contribution of oil (in Havana's outer districts there have even been blackouts, bringing back nightmare memories of the Special Period: "The people here can't take another special period" is a frequent refrain), you can read the same slogan painted with the same handwriting and the same colors: "Long live July 26. Fidel, 90 and many more." The carnivals that had to be held in commemoration of the Moncada Barracks siege were moved to the weekend of his name day. Documentaries about his life, and interviews and round tables about the significance of his work, played nonstop on TV. *Granma* published a special issue dedicated to glorifying him: "Every age has its man who marks it in history; the 20th century belongs to Fidel" (Juan Almeida); "Fidel, in a few words, is the truth of our epoch. Without prejudice, he is the greatest world statesman of the past century and of this one; he is the most extraordinary and universal Cuban patriot of all time" (Ramiro Valdés); "Let us go / fervent prophet of dawn / down hidden, wireless paths / to free the green alligator that you love so . . ." (Ernesto "Che" Guevara).

There are two ways to read this Fidelist upsurge on the occasion of his birthday: one would point to the effort to retake the historical reins of the Revolution after Obama's visit brought on such a hunger for reform, and many Cubans came to feel that the cultural and economic opening-up was just around the corner. Only three days after Fidel's birthday, Madonna rented the entire terrace of the restaurant La Guarida—where they filmed the interiors of *Fresa y chocolate*—to celebrate hers. Ever since the Rolling Stones came at the end of last May, it's not unusual to see rock and pop stars on the city's streets.

But there is another way to read this grand finale of Fidelism. It's clear that the Comandante has little time left, and love him or hate him, he's not just any man. The Cuban Revolution is not the work of a people, but rather of an individual, and the Cubans know that well. Even his worst enemy recognizes in Fidel the greatest of his kind. Fidel is also a bad aftertaste left over from the nineteenth century, an anachronism from a more nationalistic era. The only Cuban who doesn't dance. A guy who the present left behind to become a personage of History with a capital *H*, which he was always addressing, and which he himself, before he turned thirty years old, claimed "will absolve me." His true enemy was never capitalism. Fidel will die fighting the United States.*

---

* Editor's note: This essay was written on November 1, 2016, the Day of the Dead. Fidel Castro died on November 25, 2016.

The day after Fidel's birthday, Gerardo had planned to bring Giro, his fighting cock, to the Wajay cockpit. He had owned this rooster for five months and had raised him with good food in the yard of his house, in Marianao. Though at first, knowing nothing about cocks, he'd laughed when some cousins gave him to him for his forty-third birthday, one week later he was imagining the animal's great exploits that would bring him glory. One day as we were entering the Old Square—which, with its recent sprucing up, is regaining its sophisticated Italian feeling despite the poor neighborhood surrounding it—he told me that his cock crowed "real loud" and that it had "the dick of a pig." He got himself a chicken foot, tied it to a stick, and used that instrument to goad the cock, to train his anger. When he wasn't doing that, he had Giro in his arms. As he told me, he'd started to care about the animal from so much dreaming about his warrior exploits, admiring his curved beak and his intelligence when he attacked the foot tied to the stick. After they'd spent five months together, one of the cousins assured him the animal was ready for any showdown and put him in touch with a certain Amadeo, owner of the Wajay ring, where that very Sunday they were holding cockfights.

Gerardo arrived at Señora Ruth's house in Vedado before noon to pick me up. He had Giro in a cage in the Lada's backseat: white feathers around his neck and like straw over his chest, black beak stained with lime, his crest blood colored and wrinkled like a burned little finger, and a shining gray body. He looks more like an ambassador, I thought when I saw him, than a murderer. Gerardo's cousin had given him fifty CUC to bet, and Gerardo was betting two hundred, almost all he had saved up to send his car to the body shop.

Wajay is some twenty kilometers from downtown Havana in the direction of the airport, very close to Fontanar, in the area of Chico. The earth is red and pasty there, and serves as a quarry for potters. You had to ask around to get directions to the place, starting from the exit off the highway. A man who was going to the cockfight on a bicycle guided us. When we reached a house at the side of the road he recommended we park the car there, where he was going to leave his bike, and continue on foot. If the police came and found the vehicle at the cockpit, they could seize it. Cockfights were supposedly illegal, though everyone knows that the upper ranks of the hierarchy include several fans. It was at a cockfight, on February 24, 1895, in the city of Bayamo, when a group of patriots gave the cry of *"Libertad!"* (Freedom)—the cry known as the *Grito de Oriente* because the War of Independence started in Oriente, the western part of Cuba—that began the Second War of Independence in Cuba. "In any case," explained the man who suggested leaving the car, "ever since some guards went into the cockpit at Río Cristal and four people were stabbed to death—two guards and two cockfighters—now they may call the owner, but they never come in."

We walked along a path to a ravine you descend into through sickle bush; there, beside the "well of death," as one guy with a mermaid tattoo on his back called it, two women were selling beer, soft drinks, fried plantains, and mortadella sandwiches. Otherwise there were around fifty men, almost all of them gathered around the *espueladores*, who attach the spurs to the cocks' feet. One man held the animal while the other filed the natural spur that grows from its feet, after cutting off the excess with a saw. When he drew the first drop of blood, just a red dot at the center of the filed protuberance, the *espuelador* cleaned it with disinfectant that also served to seal the wound. Then he spread silicone paste over the scab with a little spatula, evenly over the flat surface of the claw. There he mounted the spur, a long, sharp piece of metal with the slightly curved shape of an elk's horn, and with the silicone that overflowed, he fused the edges of the join between cartilage and weapon. This was what Manuel and Hortensio, the guys in charge of the maneuver, did with both of Giro's feet.

Then they handed the cock to Gerardo, and, surrounded by a crowd of bettors who sized him up to decide if they would take a chance on him or not, Gerardo carried him to the scale that hung from a tree like a cloth cradle, where the judges checked his weight. One of them was wearing Bermudas and a straw hat; the other had a mustache and an unbuttoned shirt. Giro weighed 2.4 kilograms, half a kilo more than recommended, according to Hortensio. Gerardo regretted having coddled him so much. Giro had feathers on his legs, unlike his opponent, Indio, an upright and nervous rooster ready for the cooking pot or for war. Most of the bettors went with him, and when his owner and Gerardo entered the cockpit with their respective animals in their arms, the shouts that arose left no doubt: "Sixteen bucks on Indio!" "Twenty on Indio!" Only one shouted, "I'll take Giro!" Once on the battlefield, with people crowded around the railing, their owners brought the animals face-to-face in the air until they nearly collided, and then they were set loose in the ring. Gerardo moved to one side without leaving the fight, and both animals opened their collars of feathers like umbrellas or shields and started pecking at each other in flight, trying to land blows with their weaponized feet.

Indio's fury quickly prevailed over Giro's elegance. Our rooster hadn't even finished intoning his gentlemanly call to battle when Indio, like a bruiser from any tough neighborhood, stuck him in the side with both spurs and started pecking at his skull. "There!" "There!" "There!" the spectators shouted until their throats were raw. Giro reacted and tried to get his own blows in, but after a few minutes it was clear that it would be a massacre. More than once the two roosters got stuck, and their owners went in to separate them. While Gerardo merely blew on Giro's face and lowered his wings to encourage him, Indio's custodian stuck the rooster's whole head in his mouth to clean and freshen it. Then he spit.

After fifteen minutes both roosters were bleeding, and the long attacks gave way to tired flapping and sporadic stabs, mostly suffered by Giro. When he tried to escape, limping and with one of his wings raised, I asked why they didn't just call the fight, since it was obvious he could no longer defend himself. But the teenager next to me was clear and concise: "It's to the death." The shouts from the public grew louder as our rooster's agony intensified: "Finish him!" "Get him!" "There!" "There!" There!"

At a certain point, Giro stopped fighting. "He's blind," said Hortensio. It was true, you couldn't see his eyes in his face anymore, it was one big stain of mud and blood; he stopped walking and lay down. Indio turned his back scornfully, while Giro rested his beak on his chest.

Gerardo told me that when he went to get Giro the cock was still trembling. Gerardo himself was covered in sweat, as if he had shared the effort and the agony. He left the dead rooster hanging head down from a branch so he could tie his shoes, then he picked him up by both ankles, between the spurs (which now seemed inoffensive) and the still-warm claws, and we left without saying good-bye to anyone. I had also given Gerardo a hundred U.S. dollars to bet, but what I'd lost was nothing compared to the fortune Gerardo had forfeited. Even so, he cared as little about the money as I did. The next day, he had Giro stuffed by a taxidermist.

Back when the Cuban Revolution seemed infinite, I was among those who saw it as a prison sentence. I came of age when it had already lost its enchanting air, and at least from afar, it was more like one man's obsession than the will of the people. When I sensed its end was approaching, as happens with parents who lie dying, I decided to stand by its deathbed and hear its last words. For Latin Americans in the past half century, the Revolution was either a dream or a nightmare, and for some it was both.

During the time I've spent here, there have been fewer changes than expected. Most people's lives are largely the same as before. The cities have the same worn-out look, and money is far from being central the way it is almost everywhere else on the planet. There is still little to buy, although you have only to lift up a rock to find the shadows of foreign speculators waiting for the proper moment to swoop in. More than a few are acquiring property through Cubans. McDonald's already has a map of Havana with dozens of corners marked, where they'll open franchises as soon as it's possible. These changes, however, are not yet visible. For the moment, change is an underground force that manifests in an increased willingness to criticize and in the almost complete disappearance of the word *socialism* in the official discourse and conversations in the street. As I write this, there is, however, a spreading sense of immobility. As my friend Grillo says: "We are still 'blocked,' from outside and from inside, and right now nothing moves in Havana, not even the flies." Few work, and many wait. For what? The next minute, their turn in civil offices, potatoes, a chick to walk past, a guy to approach her.

The Revolution's great conquest was of time. Cubans are not in a hurry. The time agreed on for an appointment is only an approximate reference. Since public transportation is unpredictable, delay is easy to understand. What's more, little is lost by waiting. People who work assiduously are rare. Since the salary fixed by the state is around thirty dollars a month, chatting on the corner is almost as profitable as exerting yourself in a profession. More is obtained *por la izquierda,* or "to the left" (commissions, bribes, and all kinds of kickbacks that function at the edges of institutionality) than by obediently exercising a trade. When it came time to produce, the community's well-being turned out to be a much less convincing motivator than personal benefit. Efficiency disappeared the moment profit was forbidden. And with it, haste. If capitalism's success has led to a growing self-sufficiency, socialism's failure consolidated the need to rely on others in order to survive. It's true that there are corners where capitalist energy is starting to rise up again from the ashes. In Calzada de Monte, for example, once the commercial territory of the Polish before the Revolution, people who live on the lower floors have opened their doors to the street and turned their living rooms into hair or nail salons, their kitchens into cafés or shops selling prepared dishes, their storage rooms into spare-parts shops, scrapyards, or workshops doing all kinds of repairs. Clandestine businesses exist all over the capital, and the truth is that with a little effort you can find anything, even jewelry from the world's most prestigious brands. The general tendency, however, is to manage with what's there rather than obsess over what you lack. It's something that no politician could ever propose to a people, but for those of us who live in abundance and competition, this tendency constitutes a rest.

That's how the journalist Abraham Jiménez, twenty-seven years old, explained it when I asked him why he didn't leave Cuba if things were as hard as he said: "Because I like the people's self-confidence, I like that they don't beat around the bush, I like how if you go out badly dressed they laugh with you and not at you, if your car breaks down they stop and help you, if you need sugar the neighbor gives it to you, if you catch a taxi and don't have enough money, the driver tells you it's no problem. These are all the good things the Revolution has led to. The Revolution is a badly developed concept. It could have been something idyllic, the most fantastic thing in the world, but along the way it got twisted, and human errors were committed. But on the other hand, it's created a good human being: the average Cuban. That's its greatest achievement—not health and education, like so many people say, because that's over, that's already gone to hell."

I met up with Gerardo again a couple of days after the fight to go to Guanabocoa, where we were going to attend a Santeria ceremony in which an ex-classmate of his, who was becoming a *babalawo* (a priest), would carry out his first *toque de santos* (a musical religious ceremony). On the way we drove through Centro Habana, and he took a detour onto Calle Animas because he wanted to show me the place where he'd had Giro stuffed. I asked him why he'd done it, and his reply seemed to say much about what people are living through on this island that is so difficult to explain, so contradictory, so liberating and so suffocating: "Well, because the things you love, you want them with you forever. I came to really be fond of that rooster, and so I want him with me, even though he's dead."

MI AMIGO MANUEL

BY PATRICIA ENGEL

Four o'clock on a Sunday morning in September 2015. Manuel and I walk along Calle 12, through the dark tree-lined corridors of Vedado. We keep to the middle of the street, where moonlight glows on the pavement. We are a pair of shadows among the silhouettes of stray cats and sleeping dogs until we reach Zapata and we come across more bodies like ours, ambling between broken streetlights, all headed in the direction of the Plaza de la Revolución.

We, like all the others, locals and pilgrims from around the world, are on our way to see Pope Francis. In fact, Manuel and I have already seen him. Yesterday we were riding in his taxi around Miramar and came to a road closure where we saw dozens of people standing at the intersection. We got out to take a look and within a minute, the holy caravan was at our feet: the pontiff standing atop a white roofless jeep, waving to all, close enough for us to reach out and touch the edge of his white cape.

Manuel doesn't believe in God. He doesn't believe in much

of anything except work, which he does for about fifteen hours a day, with only Sunday for rest. He's taken me to see countless churches around Havana and its outskirts, yet he always waits for me outside. I tell him what my grandmother used to tell my father, and he, in turn, told me as a child: whenever you set foot in a church for the first time, say a prayer and make a wish and it will come true. But Manuel doesn't believe in wishes either. He's forty-six years old. He does not believe in wanting what is out of one's reach. He has never been on an airplane or a train or traveled beyond the western half of Cuba. Once, in the early days of our friendship, I asked him if he'd ever thought about leaving the island, as so many others have. He shook his head without hesitation. "No," he said. "Never." It wasn't about love for his country, though. Not a shred of patriotism or nostalgia, he insisted. In his case, it was because he could never leave his mother. And his mother, he knew, could live nowhere but Cuba.

———

Manuel and I met through a friend of a friend. Like so many things I found to be worthwhile on this island, one only comes upon them by personal recommendation, a secret, trusted referral. I'd said only that I was returning to Cuba for the second time and needed to find someone with a car who was willing to drive me where I wanted to go and not ask me too many questions. Perhaps I was defensive, given that on my first trip to Cuba, in January 2013, I'd been detained at the airport for extensive questioning.

The guard who questioned me was friendly. I dared ask him why the security staff had identified only me as suspicious off an entire charter flight from Miami. He said it was the fact that I was not Cuban or Cuban American, yet my government had given me permission to be here and fly direct. Also, I spoke

Spanish fluently; if not identified as foreign by my documents, I would have passed undetected. I explained that I was a writer doing research for a novel. I showed him my paperwork and even an itinerary I'd sketched out. He smiled. "Will you make Cuba look good in your book?"

"I'll write the truth about what I see."

He nodded.

"You can go," he said. "But be careful. Maybe you think you don't attract attention, but everyone, the ones who matter, I mean, knows that you're here. Understand?"

When I returned to Cuba that July, Manuel and I arranged to meet in my hotel lobby. I found him standing by the entrance, in jeans and a collared shirt, light eyed and smelling of cigarettes. We shook hands and I followed him out to his car, parked around the corner. A tiny white Korean Daewoo Tico, which he explained belonged to his girlfriend, who had inherited it from Russians who left it behind after the Soviets pulled out of Cuba in the nineties. The air-conditioning didn't work and the windows were permanently rolled down. We started on our way along the streets of Centro Habana, dusty wind blowing in my face. Manuel never wore sunglasses despite the harsh sunlight. I warned him it would lead to cataracts. But he cared more about protecting his skin from the sun, covering his left driving arm with a nylon sleeve. So he wouldn't get too dark, he said. I turned to him. "You mean, like me?"

I am Colombian. What they call trigueña, falling firmly within the spectrum of mestizaje. But I quickly found that in Cuba I was simply considered dark, not prieta but dark enough for people to feel they could remark upon my complexion openly, saying it was okay that I wasn't pearl skinned because my hair was straight or that I had a nice nose, as if to offer consolation. But if I stood around outside too long without the cover of shade, it wouldn't be long before a complete stranger would come up to me and warn, as if I were in grave danger, "Niña, get out of that prickly sun before you get even darker!"

An older couple that I met bragged to me that their daughter was blond, as if that would be her ticket in life. When I went to a drugstore in a hotel to buy a Band-Aid for a blister on my heel, the saleswoman also offered me a tube of skin-bleaching cream.

Manuel would come for me every morning. I'd already done the bit of walking Havana to death. I'd seen all the recommended tourist sights. I'd been to all the museums and gotten lost in different neighborhoods. I wanted to cover more ground, and that was why I needed Manuel and his car. I found that I also liked being in his company. He reminded me of my older brother. A quiet, calm, responsible presence. Our conversation was easy and respectful, and I appreciated it even more when I started noticing that when I was on my own, sitting down for a bite to eat or a drink at a café or restaurant or even a hotel bar as I scribbled in my notebook, foreign men, mostly Europeans or Canadians, would often approach me, mistaking me for a jinetera.

The streets that are on the pope's official motorcade route have been freshly paved, sidewalks repaired, building façades newly painted in bright hues, as if the decades of neglect that preceded this visit had never happened. But beyond the papal map, the roads remain forgotten, crumbling with neglect. The government knows where to direct the eye, Manuel says. The Vatican delegation will see only beauty, Havana wearing its best party dress, all made up, while the real Havana is kept in the shadows, out of sight.

We walk the edge of Cementerio Colón and have to do a huge loop up Hidalgo to Tulipan because the streets have been blocked off. Of the crowds we joined along Zapata, many have dropped out, not expecting to have to walk so much. With the last pope's visit, Avenida Paseo was wide open and everyone walked straight up to arrive at the plaza for the Mass. But this morning, still in predawn darkness, the streets are closed and Manuel says this convoluted, labyrinthine passage is just another government manipulation, a ploy to thin the crowd of the faithful, to show that this pope, with his renegade peace-loving rhetoric, can't pack in an audience as large as any of Fidel's.

As we cross the avenue at Carlos Manuel de Céspedes, I stand in the middle of the crossroads watching the first peek of sunrise beyond the edge of the hill. This is the same road we always take back to the city after Manuel waits for me, sometimes for hours, to emerge from the airport, after the security questioning, after my luggage has been searched, among the swell of Cubans waiting for their loved ones to return from abroad. Manuel doesn't have any family overseas. His father, who left his mother when he was young, died in Las Vegas, but they had already been estranged for decades. He had a second family, and Manuel doesn't speak to them, either. He has a cousin in Argentina, but he left years ago and has never been in touch. Manuel's never even been inside the airport. He only ever goes there, he says, to wait for me.

Manuel and I stand in the middle of the road. Desolate except for the police ushering people through, pointing them to the back roads, Ermita to Ayestaran, in the direction of the plaza.

Despite the commotion, I feel a strange stillness. We can see clear down to the massive memorial to José Martí. I look at Manuel to see if he feels it too.

Since I met him, Manuel had been telling me that his days of driving the Tico were numbered. He and his cousin were in the process of restoring a 1952 Chevrolet so that Manuel could drive it as a shared taxi for locals. His cousin had worked for years on cargo ships to save money to buy the car part by part. The deal would be that Manuel would drive it all week long and pay his cousin a daily fee of thirty CUC for the privilege of operating it. The almendrón was years in the making, and when I returned to Cuba for yet another research trip the following April, Manuel came to meet me at the airport in his new car, which he introduced, with both pride and a tinge of embarrassment, as El Frankenstein.

Its shell was unmistakably Chevy, painted a thick matte black because Manuel said they didn't yet have enough money to pay for a gloss. Its interior was the original red leather, and the dash had been cobbled together in bits imported from a dealer in California. The engine was from a Kia and it ran surprisingly smoothly. As we drove back to the capital Manuel explained to me that he was doing la ruta now, driving popular commuter paths, picking and dropping off paying customers. He started each day at seven in the morning and didn't end until around ten at night. It took him about eight hours to simply make enough to pay his cousin his agreed daily operating fee. Everything he made from that point on, usually around ten or fifteen CUC, Manuel got to keep for himself.

"What about the Tico?" I asked.

He told me the car and the girlfriend were gone. I'd met her once or twice. Cassandra was her name. She wasn't especially friendly, but Manuel spoke so highly of her that I considered her amazing, too. She'd been an economist but left her job at the bank when she figured she could earn the same if not more just driving around people from her neighborhood. But Manuel said lately she hardly left the house. Not to work. Not to see friends. She was in a real depression, which he said happened about twice a year, lasting four or five months each time, that culminated in fits of rage. She'd thrown him out, so he went back to live with his mom. Then she'd begged for him to come back, so he did. Then she'd thrown him out again. Now, Manuel said, he was done.

Over the dozen or so trips I made to Cuba during those years, sometimes he asked me about my life, but always in a careful, discreet way that gave me an out if I didn't feel like answering. He asked me if I was married and then, why not? He asked me if I had a boyfriend. Sometimes I did and sometimes I didn't. Manuel planned on never getting married. He'd briefly considered it with his girlfriend, but now he was totally against the idea. But even then, in their best days together, they'd never wanted children.

"I would never bring another life onto this island," he said. "Me, I didn't have the choice. But if I had, I would have never asked to be born here. This island is a prison. This life is a purgatory. Every single child born here, especially of the new generations, thinks of nothing but escape."

Manuel and I find a small clearing in the center of Plaza de la Revolución. He and his mother have told me about all the times it was mandatory to come here to take in one of Fidel's seemingly endless speeches, standing for hours and hours, in the sun and in the darkness, with his voice booming across the ministry buildings faced with the likenesses of Che Guevara and Camilo

Cienfuegos. Manuel's mother, a devout Catholic, had wanted to come with us. She's seventy-three but is used to walking all day since she still works as a hairdresser, meeting clients in their homes, from Habana Vieja to Nuevo Vedado to La Lisa, all by foot or maybe with the help of an almendrón. But this morning she was tired, so Manuel left her at home. A good thing, too, he says, because with all the detours they made us take to get here, she would have surely had to give up and go back home.

The sun is up and the sky is a pastel blue, cloud covered but bright. We still have two hours until the Mass is due to begin. We sit on the warm and sticky pavement. The empty spaces in the plaza fill with large groups from Mexico, Venezuela, Panama, and Poland. Some are praying, singing songs; others are just laughing, telling stories or jokes between them. Manuel didn't want to come today. He hadn't gone to see Pope John Paul II or Pope Benedict when they each came to town. He thought it was all a big show and hated how each pontiff met privately with Fidel. I'd told him that with the changes announced last December, this visit was something historic. When we met a few years ago, neither of us could have imagined the changes that were on the horizon, Raúl Castro and Barack Obama pledging to begin a new era of relations between Cuba and the United States.

Manuel is skeptical, like so many others. I've never tried to convert him with optimism. I'd planned to come to the Mass on my own, since none of my Cuban friends were interested, either, lamenting the traffic and that the plaza itself filled them with dread. But I considered it another page in my research. At the last minute, Manuel said he would come, too.

"I'm warning you," he said, "I don't know any of the prayers."

"That's okay. A lot of people don't."

"I just want to hear what the guy has to say, you know? He seems like a good guy, this pope."

Manuel's brother died when he was eleven and Manuel thir-
teen. In those days, they lived in Alamar. His father, who was
a military man, had been given an apartment, what they called
a cajón, in a building facing the sea. He took me there to see
it once. We parked at the corner, where some guys had tied an
angry cock to a low tree. I stepped a bit closer to get a better
look and the cock lunged at me, its enormous, sharp talons dig-
ging into the dirt.

"You'd better step away," one of the guys warned me. "It will
tear off one of your fingers."

Manuel took in the narrow road. He used to play here, he
said. One day, when Manuel's brother went out, some older kids
dared him to jump onto the back of a moving bus. The boy did
as they said, but he got caught on a rail, fell to the street, and got
tripped up in the wheels and run over. He died in the children's
hospital. We pass it often when we are driving past Habana Vieja
toward Vedado on the Malecón.

"That's where my brother left us," Manuel says whenever we
pass it.

We've been to Cementerio Colón together many times. I
like to get lost in its serpentine roads. We've seen all the fa-
mous graves, spent hours with the hundred-year-old man who
guards the statue of Amelia La Milagrosa. We've been robbed
by security guards there, caught in rainstorms, and left flowers
at the grave of a friend's relative after thieves robbed the tomb
for its bones for use in rituals. We both know the cemetery well
by now, but it wasn't until yesterday, when I said, "Manuel, let's
take a ride in the cemetery," that Manuel took me to a far corner
of the property against one of the back walls where the burial
plots are more modest and less adorned. He parked the almen-

drón, pointed to a single flat raised tomb, and said, "That's my brother. Nothing of him left but bones."

━━━

I spend my days with Manuel. He lends me a cell phone since mine doesn't work here. He gets me Wi-Fi cards, introduces me to his friends, takes me home to visit with his mother. And he comes with me wherever I want to go, from Matanzas to Varadero, Mariel, or Viñales; he is at my side as we visit Santería altars to meet with babalawos; and he takes me across the bay to Regla to visit the church that overlooks the harbor.

But at the end of the day, when sunset has already folded into the waters of the Straits of Florida off the Malecón, Manuel and I say good-bye and I go out with other friends, mostly non-Cubans who, because of their work or their relationships, live here now. They invite me for drinks at their houses, take me to parties, restaurants, bars filled with foreigners and the moneyed Cuban class with government connections. We go to nightclubs where Cubans wait on line outside and foreigners walk right in. We go to embassy parties, cultural festivals, and private musical performances. I often invite Manuel to come along, but he always declines. He doesn't like to go out, not even to dance or to see a movie. Instead, he prefers to remain working until his eyelids fall, demanding sleep, and wake up early, before night turns to day, to drive la ruta again.

In the mornings, when Manuel comes for me, I tell him about my nights.

"It's like when I leave you, you go to another Cuba," he says. "It's a place I've never seen."

The past six or seven times I've returned to Cuba, I've brought Manuel the one thing I know he really wants, what seems to be worth more to him than gold: chocolate. I watched the first time he tasted a Hershey bar. It was so new and special, he looked deeply moved by the experience. I'd brought him a whole selection of supermarket delights. Kit Kats, Snickers, Butterfingers. He shared them with his mother.

"Never in my life have I tasted anything like this," she said, savoring the last bits of a Milky Way.

I bring them bagfuls every time I go back, and they dig into them with childish delight. I also bring his mother cosmetics, perfume samples, and hand creams. Luxuries, she tells me, she could never find here. For Manuel, I bring books or DVDs. I've discovered his favorites are true crime. He loves them and then lends them to friends. He gives me gifts, too. Reggaeton CDs, which he knows I love, or burned DVDs of the latest popular Cuban films. Once his mother tried to give me her best piece of antique bone china, but I insisted it would probably get confiscated at the airport, so she relented. I spend a few hours with her every time I come to Havana. We sit together in the small living room of her apartment in Vedado, where she and Manuel sleep in twin beds on opposite sides of the single small bedroom. A family of cats lives on the tin roof just below their bedroom window. She knows I like cats and lets me sit there to watch them, the mother and father cat fussing over the four tiny kittens, as she tells me stories of her girlhood in the campo, where her father had cattle and you didn't need government permission to slaughter a cow; before the Revolution and before her husband brought her to Havana. Sometimes Manuel's mother pulls out old photographs of herself to show me she was once young and beautiful.

"You can't believe it when you look at what's become of my face," she tells me, running her fingers over her cheeks and her lips. "All that beauty turned out to be good for nothing."

One day, Manuel and I planned to leave early to drive out to Pinar del Río. I bought us some chicken sandwiches from a hotel lobby restaurant to take with us for lunch on the road. We'd made it just beyond the limits of Jaimanitas when the car broke down and Manuel had to pull over to the side of the road. He opened up the hood while I waited, then sent me across the street to a bar to ask for some water to cool the engine down. When the car got moving again we decided to turn back to Havana and stopped near Parque de la Fraternidad to take refuge from a sudden rainstorm. I pulled out the sandwiches and gave one to Manuel. He looked at it curiously and turned it around in his hands. I realized he didn't know what to do about the tinfoil it had been wrapped in, so I showed him how to peel it back. He stared at it, fascinated. He'd never seen tinfoil before. And he'd never seen the whole wheat bread the sandwich was made with. He ate it slowly, marveling at the taste and texture, then decided to put half away to share with his mother because he was sure she'd never tasted anything like it, either, so different from the bland, stiff white bread they sold in the local bodegas. He wanted to save the foil, too, and asked me for mine when I was done with my sandwich. He flattened and smoothed it out carefully, touching it as if it were silk.

Vans and trucks full of Red Cross medics line the periphery of the plaza, though Manuel says they're likely not real medics but undercover police keeping tabs on the pope's audience, ready to subdue any potential protest or dissident activity. I'm skeptical until I approach one of the vans in search of a Band-Aid for a bleeding toe and the medics give me blank stares.

One of them finally says, "We don't have anything like that here."

"Do you have any sort of bandages at all?" I ask, showing them my bloody foot.

They shrug. "Maybe if you buy an ice cream down the road, they will give you a napkin and you can use that to clean up the blood."

"Are you really medics?" I ask.

Again, they shrug. "Why do you ask?"

The pope appears seemingly out of nowhere. Once again atop an open-sided white jeep, he cruises around the edges of the plaza, waving to the audience, picking up and blessing a baby, before heading to the altar at the far end, beyond the ministry buildings. The front rows have seating reserved for the government officials, ambassadors, even members of the FARC delegation, who are in the midst of their Havana peace negotiations. Everyone else, including us, is beyond the barrier, standing or sitting on the pavement, leaning on one another under the hot morning sun.

The Mass begins. Manuel watches intently.

———

A few years ago, I was walking along the beach near my home in Miami when I felt the tide push something to my feet. I looked down and saw what looked like a strand of wooden beads over my toes. I picked it up and saw that it was a rosary; at its center, on the bead that would have been the first glorious mystery, was a carved wooden heart imprinted with the face of Pope John

Paul II. Things wash up all over Florida shores, from wooden planks and plastic bottles to dead bodies and car parts. I have seen bones wash up on the sand. Pieces of clothing. I have seen rafters touch ground on Florida shores and cry out in ecstatic joy, and I have seen others caught by the coast guard before they touched American soil, who were therefore immediately taken into custody and set for deportation. Something told me to hold on to the rosary. I put it in my pocket and took it home.

A year or so later, I made a new friend, a recently arrived Cuban. He spoke no English. He'd arrived to the United States by crossing the Mexico border on foot. He told me about his upbringing as a child of proud Communist parents, a proud young pionero, through the struggles of the Special Period. He told me about his hunger. The things his family had to do for food. His disillusion. And ultimately, his defection.

I showed him the rosary I had found on the beach. He recognized it immediately. "Those were the rosaries they gave out when the pope came to Havana," he said. His mother had one just like it. "They were thick and rough edged because they were handmade."

I thought of how the owner of those wooden beads had brought them from Cuba with them, likely by boat, intending to land in Florida. The beads were lost at sea. I wondered about the person who'd had enough faith to carry those beads with them on their journey. I wondered if that person's life had been lost in the waves, too.

When I found that I would be back in Cuba precisely when the new pope would be visiting, I decided that I would go to the plaza to see him, not just out of my own intellectual curiosity, my writer's spirit, which propels me to be a witness, but also in remembrance of that person who owned that lost rosary, wherever their life and soul may have left them.

Sometimes I accompany Manuel on la ruta. He likes to start on the base of Avenida 23, near the Malecón, and ride high into the hills, or sometimes we just take Linea, picking up and dropping off people until we're nearly in Playa. I sit in the front seat next to Manuel, leaving room for another passenger to my right. In the back, three more passengers are legally permitted, but occasionally Manuel lets a fourth squeeze in, usually a small child. Passengers are mostly silent as they ride. University students sit with their earphones tucked in, the volume loud enough for the rest of us to hear the buzz of their Cubatón music. When it's time for their stop, a passenger nudges Manuel in the shoulder or simply says, "Chofe, aquí," and Manuel pulls over. They hand him their coins, usually not more than fifty cents' worth. Maybe another passenger will climb in at that stop. And the almendrón continues on its way. Up and down the avenues. Picking up and dropping off. The endless ruta.

One day we pick up a trio of young girls dressed provocatively. Two of the girls give instructions to the third on how to behave when they meet their dates at the hotel. Their dates, I am able to gather, are German.

"It doesn't matter if you can't understand a word he says," one girl advises. "Just look at him as if he's speaking to your soul. They *love* that."

We drop them off near Parque Central. I watch as they walk toward the hotel, fat tour buses and hordes of foreigners standing out front.

Later we pick up a pair of santeras dressed in white, heads covered, colored beads layered around their necks. They ask Manuel if they can hire him for the hour. He agrees and we take them to the forest in the hills above the Río Almendares and park along a ridge. When the ladies get out of the car, I notice for the first time the canvas sack they've brought with them, and when they step in front of the almendrón and make their way down the slope of soil to the river's edge, the fabric of their bag moves from within. Manuel and I watch from the car as the ladies find a place near the water, pull fruit and a live chicken from their sack, and with a quick, almost invisible movement, leave the animal dead, bleeding from the neck, the blood dripping into a bowl at their feet.

Sometimes we pick up non-Cubans, usually Europeans who've been in Cuba awhile and already know how to navigate the shared cab system. One day we pick up an Italian man. He must be in his midsixties. With him is a Cuban girl who can't be older than seventeen. In the rearview mirror I see him kiss her neck while she looks bored and stares out the window. An older woman sitting on the man's other side closes her eyes as if to pray or at least not to be complicit, until we leave the man and the girl on the corner of Neptuno.

One day Manuel and I drive out to El Rincón to visit the church of San Lázaro. We head down the dusty road past shacks and lonely skinny horses and stacks of beaten sugarcane. Outside the church property, we are surrounded by beggars and vendors of candles and wooden saints. I expect that Manuel will want to wait for me outside, as he usually does, as I go in and look around, lighting a candle or two at one of the altars. But this time Manuel says he will go inside with me. We walk together into the large white church. We part and wander separately from altar to altar, where people have left mounds of flowers for Lázaro of the parable, and at another altar for Our Lady of

Charity. I go outside to the fountain of holy water where people missing limbs rub water into their skin and cross themselves with its drops.

Beside the church is the lazaretto where lepers still live, exiled from society. A few dogs roam the church grounds. A group of caretakers taking their lunch in the shade tell me those dogs were abandoned here and adopted by the church. The small cream-colored one is named Belén, because last Christmas she was found as a puppy abandoned in the crèche, curled asleep beside the baby Jesus. I tell them it's sweet that they care for the dogs here, but one of the caretakers tells me the dogs are only allowed to roam when supervised. Otherwise they are locked in a garden for their safety.

"People are capable of terrible things," one caretaker tells me. "It wasn't so long ago that many found their only meals in dogs."

I have heard this many times before. I have also heard it vehemently denied.

One day Manuel and I were driving through Buenavista when we saw two men skinning a dead dog hanging from a beam that had been suspended over an alleyway. Manuel stopped the car to ask the men what they were doing.

"Don't ask questions you don't want the answer to," one man responded.

The other man laughed. "Want a bite?"

My favorite part of the church of San Lázaro is the small house that holds the ex-votos, proof of prayers answered offered in gratitude to the saint. Knitted baby booties, photos of families reunited. Olympic trophies, boxing championship medals. I wander among the glass cases holding the prayer memorabilia and see Manuel doing the same, reading the letters written by the faithful in gratitude to San Lázaro for granting their petitions.

One of the reasons Manuel doesn't believe in God or the orishas or anything considered divine is because he says he has been so close to it all—he's sat in countless church services with his mother and gone to plenty of toques de santos with people from his neighborhood—yet he never feels anything.

"I always stand there waiting for something to happen, waiting to be moved by the music or the prayers or the ceremony, and nothing happens. I don't feel anything."

At the pope's Mass in the Plaza de la Revolución, we listen to music, the echoes of prayers like a fortress around us; watch the consecration, enveloped by a communion of silence. The pope leaves the crowds with words encouraging peace and courage and freedom. He tells the crowd never to give up hope.

Once Manuel and I were driving along the Malecón in the direction of Cubanacán, where I was to meet a friend for lunch. Few cars were on the road that morning, but I noticed a pelican walking, dazed and disoriented, across the avenue. Manuel swerved so as not to hit the bird. I turned in my seat to see if the pelican had made it across to the sidewalk. Manuel said pelicans rarely appeared on that stretch of the Malecón. He saw my look of concern. He knew me well by then—how I would save scraps from my lunches to offer stray dogs and how I wouldn't hesitate to bend over and pet stray cats. As soon as he found a place to turn, he looped back to the same spot on the Malecón in search of the pelican. We found a small white van parked in the same place, its back doors open, and the driver had already scooped up the bird and loaded him in.

We tried to stop the man. I was so stunned I could barely find the words to explain why the pelican should be free. The man simply looked at me and said the pelican was *his* now. Manuel tried to reason with him, but the man quickly slammed the doors shut, climbed back in his van, and drove off.

I thought about the pelican all day. At lunch at my friends' house, they served juicy chicken breast procured from a government connection, far better than the meatless thighs only occasionally available with the government ration card. I told them about the pelican. They laughed. They didn't think the man had taken it to eat it.

"Pelicans give very bad meat," they said. "Maybe he took it to sell for brujería. Or maybe to sell to a foreigner as a pet."

They teased me for caring so much about things that had nothing to do with me.

"You have to learn to look away," they said. "One can't be sentimental in Cuba and survive."

We are part of the exodus leaving the plaza that Sunday morning. The roads are still blocked and there is no public transport. We will have to walk just as we came. But my feet are raw with blisters, my hips stiff from hours walking, standing, and sitting on pavement. The sun is high, blazing. The masses disperse and Manuel leads the way, finding a shortcut through parks and uphill across Avenida Salvador Allende until we land on Zapata and I spot an unoccupied cocotaxi and call it over. I ask the driver to take us back to Paseo and he says he will, for seven CUC. I agree and climb into the backseat of his scooter-rickshaw, but Manuel hesitates, arguing that it's too much for such a short distance. I tell him I will pay for it, and besides, this is the only ride around,

and if we don't take it we will have to walk all the way back, and
look at my bloody heels and toes. Manuel gets in reluctantly. He
has never been in a cocotaxi, he says. They're for tourists.

In a few minutes we arrive on Paseo and again, Manuel tries
to get the driver to agree to a more reasonable fare.

"It's not right that you're exploiting people just because they're
tired from having walked miles to see the pope."

The driver laughs in his face. "I'll do what I want."

"I drive a taxi myself," Manuel says. "I know what it costs to
drive people. The ride you just gave us shouldn't cost more than
two CUC."

"What do you know? What kind of car do you drive?"

"An almendrón," Manuel says.

Again the driver laughs. "You drive a garbage taxi and you're
trying to tell me what *I* should charge?"

I see the shame wash over Manuel's face.

"Come on," I say. "Let's go."

I pay the driver, but Manuel still wants him to know he has
no conscience. He's robbing people. "That's not right," Manuel
says. "You're a thief."

Another cocotaxi pulls up and the two drivers greet each
other.

"What's going on?" the friend asks our driver.

"Nothing, asere. This almendrón jockey thinks he knows
everything."

"Ha," says the friend. "If you ever see me driving an almen-
drón, kill me."

Manuel and I get on our way. He's angry like I've never seen
him. Angrier than when we got robbed by the security guards of
Cementerio Colón. Angrier than the day he got bumped from
behind by another almendrón and the Chevy was taken out of

commission for a month. Angrier than the last time Cassandra kicked him out and made him leave his DVD player behind.

"We had a beautiful morning," he says, lighting himself a cigarette, "and that shameless guy has to ruin it. It's the story of our island. It's the reason we've become just a hole in the ocean."

Months later, Havana prepares for a visit from the American president.

Once again, one can follow the planned motorcade route by the visible restoration of particular corridors. Quinta Avenida all the way to Cubanacán. A friend lives in a small building just off the main avenue and the government has sent workers to repaint and replaster the broken balconies—requests the residents have been making for years, all but ignored until it was determined Obama might glance in that direction when being driven to his quarters at the embassy residence.

The only differences Manuel has noted since the official changes were announced in December 2014 are that there are now many more Americans visiting the island. So Cuba has changed for *them*, he says. But for ordinary Cubans, Manuel insists, nothing has changed at all.

It's true, now there are Wi-Fi hotspots in public parks and on street corners. I was surprised, one day back home, to receive an e-mail from none other than Manuel, who wrote that he didn't know anyone else with an e-mail address and that's why he was writing to me. But that was the first and last e-mail he wrote. Everyone he knows, he says, is easier to reach by phone or by just driving over to their home.

Now, Cuba prepares for the arrival of Obama. For the first

time in all my years visiting, I see the American president's face silk-screened on T-shirts and the American flag hanging high outside the U.S. embassy.

Manuel just shakes his head at any mention of it, waving his hand through the air as if swatting a fly.

"Popes and presidents. They come and they see Cuba, then they leave and they forget us," he says. "But for us, nothing changes. Here we are. Here we will always be. *En la misma Cuba, la misma ruta, la misma lucha de siempre.*" The same Cuba, the same *ruta,* the same struggle as always.

THE OTHER SHORE

BY JON LEE ANDERSON

The primary school my daughters attended in Havana was called the Eliseo Reyes, named after a Cuban guerrilla who died fighting alongside Che Guevara in Bolivia. Over the door of the entrance to the school was a sign that read: "Muerte a los Traidores" (Death to Traitors). Every weekday morning, the children were gathered by their teachers in the school's front garden, where they uttered the obligatory oath: "Pioneers for Communism, we will be like Che."

There was an inescapable paradox in the situation. My daughters Bella and Rosie were not Communists, and moreover, they were half American, thanks to me, but nonetheless I had brought them, their British mother, Erica, and their younger brother, Máximo, to live in Havana so that I could research a biography of Che.

It was the early nineties, and Cuba was in a state of seemingly inexorable collapse. The Soviet Union had recently disintegrated, and with it had vanished the generous subsidies that had kept

Fidel Castro's Revolution alive for the previous three decades. Fidel had dubbed Cuba's crisis the Special Period in Time of Peace. It was a time of extraordinary austerity and penury. Accustomed to fairly high levels of material comfort, Cubans were faced with inadequacies of just about everything, from food to medicine. There was insufficient fuel to produce electricity, and so there were rolling blackouts, all over the island, sometimes lasting twelve hours a day or more. Oxen had replaced tractors in the countryside and Chinese bicycles had replaced cars in the cities. Queues for the few city buses lasted for hours. People walked and hitched rides where they could. Many were not eating enough.

We, on the other hand, were foreigners with hard currency and privileged access to the array of coveted items available in the Soviet-style Diplomercado, a drab shop with a paltry selection of overpriced imported foodstuffs that were, nonetheless, beyond the reach of most Cubans. Next to the Diplomercado was the walled diplomatic compound of the former Soviet Union, with several apartment blocks for the diplomats and their families. At the center of the compound was the embassy itself, a strange windowless edifice that rose some fifteen or so stories before bulging out into a box with wraparound polarized windows. It resembled an air traffic control tower, or a robot with its arms amputated, and was the tallest building in Havana. The Russians themselves were almost invisible; their greatest evident legacy, after all the years as the *madre patria* of global socialism, was the rusting Ladas and Moskvitches that jerked fitfully along the roads and broke down everywhere, belching black smoke from their exhaust pipes.

While the majority of Cubans adhered to the expected public displays of stoicism and revolutionary fealty—such as the one that took place every morning in the Eliseo Reyes schoolyard—

most of them were simultaneously engaged in a personal quest to secure enough food to feed themselves and their families, even if it meant stealing or hustling. These were mutually exclusive pursuits, for the most part, and posed a dramatic dilemma for people across the island, forcing them to live a schizophrenic existence that became known as *el doble cara*—literally, two-facedness.

Having granted us permission to live in Cuba, the relevant government agency tasked with dealing with diplomats and "foreign technicians" allocated us a house to rent in a seaside residential neighborhood of western Havana known as El Náutico. The house was a fifties-built two-story, three-bedroom villa that sat cheek to jowl with several others on a short block that ended at the seaside. The three houses that lay between us and Náutico's own little corniche along the rocky shoreline were occupied by Cuban families. They were severely dilapidated. Most of our neighbors had originally come from elsewhere in Cuba and had been given their homes by the government after their original owners fled into exile years before, leaving them vacant. But few of them had the means to maintain their homes, which were falling apart. Náutico's houses were made of cement, and because of their proximity to the sea, *el salitre,* the salty sea air, had chewed away the façades of some of them right down to their corroding rebar.

Our assigned home was falling apart, too. It had been left unoccupied for a couple of years since its last occupants—Bulgarians, apparently—had left Cuba when the Cold War ended. Cuba's government promised to have the house repaired and painted so that we could live there. In the meantime, we lived a couple of miles away in the residential district of Miramar, in a small apartment building overlooking another stretch of the rocky shoreline—the formation known as *diente de perro,* dog's tooth—that skirts much of Havana. The strand in front of our apartment was a place of encounter for lovers, who conducted their business on one of the several concrete benches that had been placed there, and the occasional white-garbed Santería initiates, who came at dawn to throw flowers and other offerings into the sea as part of their purification rite.

The government workers' brigade that was dispatched to whip our house in Náutico into shape consisted of three elderly men, and they worked very, very, very slowly. One of the reasons for their slowness, I soon learned, was that they were hungry. Each day they traveled to Náutico from their own homes in one of Havana's far-flung peripheries. Because of the shortage of fuel and the scarcity of passenger buses, this journey, which should have been no more than a thirty-minute run, was taking as much as three hours. Once they got to Náutico, the first thing they did was to go to the local *comedor popular,* a kind of soup kitchen for state employees, that was supposed to provide them with lunch, to see if it had food for the day. If there was none, they would turn around and return to their homes. This happened around twice a week. And when there was food, it was very often little more than *chícharos*—split peas—or sometimes rice and beans, never meat, and it was clearly inadequate.

Once I discovered the reasons for the lack of progress on our house, I began going to the Diplomercado every weekday morning, buying food, and taking it to the workers before they had given up for the day. I usually brought them pork sandwiches and the canned malt drink that Cubans love—men in particular, because they believe it enhances their sexual energy. The men were grateful and began coming to work more consistently than before. I would often stick around to chat with them. One of them, Mederos, regaled me with tales of his time serving as a soldier in Angola a decade or so earlier. Cuba's military expedition to Angola was one of its proudest moments, in which

Fidel Castro airlifted thousands of Cuban soldiers to assist the embattled Marxist Angolan regime, which had come to power after the end of Portuguese colonial rule, only to come under siege from guerrilla armies that were armed and financed by the American CIA and South Africa's white apartheid regime. The Cubans had helped the Angolans prevail by winning a crucial battle against the South Africans, weakening the apartheid regime and leading to the negotiations that led to Nelson Mandela's release from prison and the country's return to democracy and black-majority rule. Whatever they thought about their own government and some of its errors, most Cubans were rightly proud of the achievements of their adventure in Angola in the name of revolutionary solidarity.

Mederos was an unswerving Fidelista, and despite the penuries of his own life, he saw everything he did within the context of his revolutionary commitment. His current job—painting the house of a strange Yanqui who was writing about Che, something he had been ordered to do by the Party—was not something he questioned. I admired Mederos for his sense of duty and his ceaseless ordeal traveling to and from my house, and although I knew it was a double-edged sword to provide him and his comrades with their daily food, I enjoyed the rapport we struck up. While many Cubans were wary of outsiders and limited their conversations to brief informational exchanges, Mederos's patriotic garrulousness was a refreshing source of friendly banter, as well as a window into the world that the Cubans inhabited.

Eventually, the job was done. Painting our house in the old-school manner that Mederos's crew had employed—one pains-

takingly slow brushstroke at a time—had taken no less than
seven months to complete. Along the way, things in Cuba being
as they were, we had also found ourselves employing an ever-
increasing number of people to help us negotiate daily life. These
included two women in their fifties, Marta and Carmen, our
neighbors in the apartment building where we had been liv-
ing, whom I had put to work transcribing and typing up tape-
recorded interviews for me. Carmen was a poet, while Marta
was a retired counterintelligence agent who had once infiltrated
the CIA before her cover was blown and then been forced to re-
turn to Cuba. Another woman, Lisette, in her thirties, helped us
look after Máximo, who was just a few months old when we ar-
rived. Lisette had been abroad only once in her life, to Ukraine,
a reward for having outperformed her fellow workers in a Cuban
factory where she had been employed.

In Náutico, our staff expanded to include a gardener to tend
to our tiny strip of garden, where we planted banana trees and
hibiscus bushes; a jack-of-all-trades handyman for things that
went wrong, which they invariably did; and a mechanic named
Gilberto, whom we called *el hombre de los brazos fuertes*—the man
with the strong arms—because he was muscular, and whom we
kept on permanent retainer because the secondhand Lada I had
bought from the departing second secretary of the Indian em-
bassy was a useless vehicle, constantly breaking down. We also
hired a housekeeper, Sofía, who had been the nanny for Che
Guevara's kids and now became ours. And we hired another
woman, Aleidita, as well. Aleidita was a retired government sec-
retary, who helped Sofía by acting as an extra pair of hands with
our children. And there were more. (I once calculated that in
the end, no fewer than forty-two Cubans, including the depen-
dents of our employees or helpers-on-retainer, depended on our
financial largesse.)

Despite all the backup personnel, some things in Cuba were never entirely normal. Our home in Náutico was like-new: its walls inside and out had been freshly painted and its terrazzo floors polished, but as soon as we moved in, we discovered that it had no running water. Havana had severe water shortages, and most of our neighbors received only an hour or two of water every day, anyway, but our house didn't even get that. It was a dry house. This posed a conundrum. The notion that we would have no running water in our house had simply never occurred to me.

I asked our new next-door neighbors, Rodolfo and Annie, about the water situation and learned that they didn't have any, either. They got by on water borrowed from more fortunate neighbors. Once or twice a week, Rodolfo and Annie came and went from that neighbor's house with buckets and filled up an old oil barrel they had acquired; just enough for them to get through with the basic necessities of cooking, cleaning, and bathing. Since I had access to dollars, Rodolfo suggested, why didn't I pay for a *pipa*—a state cistern truck—to supply us with water? It was soon arranged, and before long, in exchange for a single but highly coveted U.S. dollar bill, we had weekly visits from Nestor, an amiable man, who appeared religiously in front of our house every Friday to unfurl a hose from his truck, its cistern labeled with the logo and title of his employers, the Cuban Atomic Energy Commission. Nestor ran a long black leaky hose from his truck through our house into the kitchen, where there was a well in our kitchen floor, and pumped it full of water. During this noisy proceeding, our children jumped up and down delightedly, chanting, "*la pipa, la pipa,*" over and over again.

As a gesture of friendship, I asked Nestor to fill Rodolfo and Annie's cistern, too. They did their best to reciprocate by letting

us know, via whispers over our shared rear garden wall, when-
ever black-market fish or pork was available in the neighbor-
hood. In those days, Cubans were only legally able to obtain
their foodstuffs through the government rationing system. Each
head of family had a rationing booklet that entitled them to cer-
tain amounts of basics per week—food products as well as cook-
ing oil, soap, washing powder, and so forth. In the halcyon days
when everything was paid for by the Russians, this meant that
food was plentiful, and most Cubans had grown accustomed to
eating well and regularly. But in the Special Period, there was
simply not enough food available in the rationing system. Cu-
bans who could fish did so furtively, floating out to sea in truck
inner tubes with an oar and some fishing line, in the hope of
catching something they could later sell on *la bolsa negra,* the
black market, in order to get enough money to buy whatever they
needed on *la bolsa negra.*

In Náutico, the chief black marketeer was a shapely Russian
woman with violet-dyed hair, who could often be seen posing
sexily in her open doorway. *La bolsa negra* had, in fact, been
started during Cuba's years as a Soviet client state, as Russians
posted to the island made money on the side by selling contra-
band items to the Cubans. As a result, most of the Cubans I met
held the Russians in contempt, and they referred to them as *los
bolos,* because they were often drunk.

The Cubans also despised the Russians because of their
strong body odor, an unfortunate result of their habit of sticking
to a fatty Russian diet in spite of Cuba's sweat-inducing tropical
climate. Cubans, by contrast, were obsessive about their personal
hygiene and, however hard up they were, always strove to be
scrupulously clean. (It was also sadly true that many young Cu-
ban women prostituted themselves with foreigners in exchange
for a few bars of soap, or a bottle of shampoo.)

Most of the other Americans living in Havana were political fugitives of one sort or another. They included a number of former Black Panthers who had, years before, hijacked airplanes to get there, and who had stayed on under the protection of Cuba's government. I met one of them, William Lee Brent, who lived near us in Miramar. He had once been Eldridge Cleaver's bodyguard, but now, he taught primary school. Robert Vesco, the fugitive American financier, was another Havana resident. He, his wife, and their two sons, who attended Havana's international school alongside the children of expatriate diplomats, were known as the Adams family, but everyone knew who they really were. There was also a pair of renegade former CIA agents, Frank Terpil and Philip Agee, who had offered their respective services to Cuba's Revolution in exchange for sanctuary.

And there was Ron. Ron was a thin American man in his midfifties, a sixties-era radical from California who had come to Cuba because he saw it as the "last best place" for someone like him. He had come to work for the Revolution and to live like a Cuban, and that was what he had been doing since he arrived a few years before. He had participated as a cane cutter in several *zafras*—sugarcane harvests—despite his age, and periodically traveled back to the United States to give laudatory public talks about the Revolution. As a gesture of its gratitude, the Cuban government had given Ron residency in Cuba, signed him up on their rationing system so that he could have food, given him a Chinese "Flying Pigeon" bicycle so he could get around, and had also allocated him a small house where he could live virtually rent free. Ron had made strenuous additional efforts to prove his revolutionary mettle. A couple of years earlier, in an act of protest against the 1991 American invasion of Iraq during the

First Gulf War, he had gone so far as to burn his U.S. passport in front of the U.S. Interests Section, for the benefit of CNN's cameras.

After a year or so, Ron's Cuban handlers had summoned him and gently advised him to go back to the Interests Section and beg for a new passport. They reminded him that his greatest value to Cuba was in being able to travel and spread the word about the virtues of its socialist revolution. They told him: "Ron, you're of little use to us if you can't leave the island." Meekly, Ron had complied. He recalled ruefully how, when he presented himself at the Interests Section, the American official who had received him had been cool but polite. When he eventually received his new passport—notably, valid for a year only—the official had laconically asked Ron to "please try to avoid burning it." With his passport, Ron began traveling again.

By this time, Fidel had undertaken new emergency measures to ameliorate Cuba's worsening economic predicament. In order to combat the growing influence of the black marketeers and emergence of a counterrevolutionary underclass, he legalized the dollar as the de facto currency of choice in *la bolsa negra;* initiated a policy to promote foreign tourism to the island; and authorized a number of small private business initiatives, such as family-run restaurants, called *paladares,* and beauty salons. He also authorized some Cuban state agencies to establish joint ventures with foreign capitalist partners. And he okayed the creation of a national network of dollar stores where Cubans who received remittances, or who worked in tourism and were given small amounts of dollars each month as *estímulos,* could buy imported products. It was enough to allow them to buy a few bars of soap, a bottle of shampoo, a liter bottle of vegetable oil, perhaps, or other small things. It was not much, but it was the first real relief made available for many Cubans since the Soviet collapse in 1991.

As Cubans' living situations improved and as increasing numbers of tourists began to arrive—mostly Latin Americans and Europeans—Ron found life on the island more and more frustrating. He regarded himself as a "revolutionary internationalist," and had come to share Cubans' socialist reality by living and working alongside them. But as the Cubans he had come to help turned to private enterprise as the key to relief for their misfortunes, he turned sour. We had become friends, and he had gotten into the habit of dropping by our house in Náutico on his bike for dinner or a glass of rum once or twice a week. He often vented about the island's growing contradictions, and once he arrived in a terrible rage because earlier that same day he had been approached by Cubans who thought he was a tourist and tried to hustle him for dollars.

El jineterismo, the hustle that all foreigners in Havana were subjected to by streetwise Cubans, either trying to sell them black market cigars or rum, or to pimp them girls, was something I was accustomed to, but not Ron. He took it as a personal affront to his revolutionary self-image, and it was not long before he left Cuba and went to live on a socialist cooperative farm in rural Denmark, where daily existence seemed more in concert with his deeply felt principles.

Ron's departure from Cuba was only one of many. In the summer of 1994, as many as thirty-five thousand Cubans fled the island on improvised rafts and boats. *La crisis de los balseros,* as the extended drama became known, capped months of mounting tensions in Havana's poorer neighborhoods. There was a series of hijackings and attempted hijackings of boats by Cubans seeking to escape to the United States across the Strait of Florida.

The mood had darkened considerably after an incident in which a tugboat belonging to Cuba's coast guard had rammed a boat attempting to head out to sea, causing it to sink and drowning dozens of people. Finally, on August 5, a popular uprising broke out on Havana's seaside promenade, the Malecón. In *el maleconazo*, as it became known, thousands of angry men and boys gathered, throwing rocks and bricks and shouting antigovernment epithets.

It was an unprecedented situation that looked as if it might spin out of control, and Fidel dealt with it with aplomb by personally going to the site, wading into the crowd, and asking the protestors to stop what they were doing. Incredibly, they did as he asked, and, once calm had returned to Havana's streets, Fidel went on state television and told the nation that if anyone wished to leave the island, they were free to do so.

For the next three weeks, thousands of Cubans took Fidel at his word and set out from Cuba's coasts on improvised rafts and boats. Entire families left and, in some cases, drowned or were eaten by sharks as their precarious craft broke up in the waves. The U.S. Coast Guard and private yachts and other vessels rescued many of the refugees, but untold hundreds died. Our next-door neighbor, Rodolfo, was among those who left.

Early one evening I was at home when a great commotion came from the Náutico seashore. I rushed there to see what was going on. Most of our neighbors were already there. Sofía carried Máximo in her arms, while Rosie and Bella clung to me as we observed the drama taking place. A truck with two peasant families had pulled up to the seashore and the men had unloaded a rickety raft they had built. As the evening sky descended over the sea and distant lightning bolts heralded a coming storm, they placed their raft on the water and, one by one, helped their women and children onto the raft. Some of our neighbors began crying and beseeching them not to go, telling them they were headed into certain danger. The rafters did not reply, or speak, and silently began pushing away from the shore. At the last minute, a woman on the raft with a young boy, about four years old, thrust her child toward a woman on the shore, who held out her arms. The boy fell into the water but a man hauled him out and he was delivered, shivering with cold and emotion, into the hands of the woman on land. After more shouting and chaos, his mother asked to be returned, and the raft came and let her ashore, where she gathered up her son, weeping. Then the raft, with the rest of its passengers, nearly twenty people, including many children, pushed away and headed out to the darkening sea.

The crowd on the Náutico shoreline stayed, watching in shocked silence until the night sky had enveloped the raft.

A few days later, I looked over Rosie's shoulder as she drew pictures with crayons. She was about four years old at the time, the same age, roughly, as the boy who had plunged off the raft. Normally Rosie drew princesses and other fairy tale creatures, but this time, I noticed her picture consisted of a square with three podlike creatures assembled on it, side by side. "What are those?" I asked Rosie, genuinely curious. *"Balseros,"* she replied matter-of-factly, and went back to her drawing.

After three years in Cuba, we left for a new life in Spain. The children's nanny, Aleidita, emigrated herself not long after we left. Sofía, who was a Cuban cane cutter's daughter and a true child of the Revolution—a Fidelista through and through—also expressed her wish to join us in Spain. We began the necessary paperwork, but Sofía sadly died of a sudden heart attack within a few months of our departure from Cuba.

Our former neighbor Rodolfo survived his sea crossing and went on to make a new life for himself in Miami. His wife, Annie, who had decided not to join him on his maritime adventure, remained behind in Náutico with their little boy, Rodolfito, and it was not long before she had a live-in boyfriend. Rodolfo dutifully sent regular cash remittances to Annie, but in his absence, his son began calling the new man in the house "Papá."

Over the years, I have returned to Cuba many times to witness the evolving dramas of its revolutionary life. I watched carefully from afar as Fidel hosted Pope John Paul II, played baseball with his new best friend, Hugo Chávez, and launched a "battle of ideas" to instill socialist fervor in a new generation of Cuban youth. He was indefatigable, until he fell seriously ill. He recovered but remained in delicate health. After being replaced in his duties by his younger brother, Raúl, Fidel spent the last decade of his life on the sidelines, alternately grouchy and reflective about the shape of things as illustrated in a string of letters he had published in the official Communist Party daily, *Granma,* and in the occasional public interventions.

Fidel's coterie of loyalists dwindled as some passed away and others fell out of favor. There were also those who fell out of faith. Most kept their silence, but some fled to Florida—as two generations of exiles had done before—and wrote tell-all books. These included one of Fidel's own daughters and a trusted former bodyguard. Others returned. A friend's son who had fled Cuba on a Windsurfer during the rafters crisis came back, years later, transmogrified into a middle-class doctor with his own private practice in the United States. We ate lunch one day with his elderly parents at a new private restaurant on the Malecón. Seated at a table nearby was a famous Cuban rap artist with his entourage of friends and pretty girls, who were all wearing colorful sports apparel and gold jewelry, eating lobster, and drinking wine. With private enterprise beginning to flourish after being authorized a few years earlier by Raúl, Cuba was beginning to change.

On the day the U.S. embassy was reopened after a closure that had lasted for more than fifty years and the then secretary of state John Kerry came to oversee the hoisting of the flag, Cuban residents of the adjacent apartment blocks cheered and waved. One of them, a man in his late fifties, told me nostalgically of how as boys he and his friends had dived into the water off the Malecón for pennies, thrown for them by the embassy's marine guards. Nearly an entire lifetime had gone by, but now the Americans were back.

The restoration of U.S. and Cuban relations in 2014 and Barack Obama's historic trip to Havana two years later were extraordinary milestones in an ongoing epic. My arrival in Cuba to study Che and the Revolution had once been a source of bemusement and disbelief to many Cubans. Twenty years later, the American president himself stood in Revolutionary Square paying his respects, and all around Havana, American and Cuban flags fluttered alongside one another. Unlikely as it was, it seemed to be the end of a long estrangement.

Cuba's story has no definitive conclusion, of course, but with Fidel's death at the age of ninety in November 2016, just a few months after Obama's visit, it felt as if the Revolution he had sustained for a half century with equal measures of obstinacy, guile, and charisma had died with him. In post-Fidel Cuba, the talk was no longer of revolution but of business deals.

After years of neglect following our departure, our house in Náutico has been repainted and is once again inhabited, but the houses around it look as beat up as ever. On a recent visit with my daughter Rosie, who is now a young woman in her midtwenties, I took her to the old neighborhood. We walked past our house to the spot by the seashore, where the rafters had fled when she was a little girl. Rosie pointed to the ground. It was littered with used condoms. The departure point for desperate Cubans escaping into lives of exile was now a rendezvous for a new generation of Cuban lovers.

SECRET CUBA

BY MAURICIO VICENT

TRANSLATED BY CECILIA MOLINARI

Singer Ibrahim Ferrer's official biography states that in 1996, when he was called upon at his home on Indio Street to participate in the Buena Vista Social Club album, which would garner Compay Segundo, Rubén González, and other eminent Cuban musicians international fame, Ibrahim was making a living shining shoes. He was on the brink of his seventieth birthday, and like many of his Vieja Trova colleagues, at that stage of his life he'd already thrown in the towel and survived as best he could in a Havana devastated by the Special Period's austerity. The power outages on the island had reached fourteen hours a day, tractors on farms had been replaced by four hundred thousand oxen, and, in the absence of public transportation, the government had distributed one million Chinese bicycles so the country wouldn't be at a standstill, while on TV and in the plazas Fidel Castro ended his speeches with the slogan "Socialism or Death."

The country had plunged into its deepest shortages after the collapse of the socialist bloc, and while popular vegetable gardens flourished on Quinta Avenue and chicks were distributed to the people so that they could raise them and turn them into food, as an individual lifeline each person was also allowed to seek self-employment in hundreds of fields, such as shoe shiner or manicurist, continuing down to absurd options like button coverer, clown, or spark plug cleaner.

While Ibrahim shined shoes, on busy San Rafael Street some of the new personal manicurists set up shops in the middle of the sidewalk with tables and chairs to serve the public. It was the worst part of the crisis: TV shows featured recipes such as minced banana peels or grapefruit steaks; on summer nights, people dragged their mattresses out into the street to cool off and sleep through the power outages; a homemade deodorant made of baking soda and milk of magnesia was invented. Reality was so stark, there was no way to escape it. It was just too heavy.

Back then, when two or more Cubans ran into each other in a line or at a party, it was hard for them not to talk about "how bad things are." It was every day, every hour, and everywhere, so much so that one of the San Rafael Street manicurists, who'd had enough of people using their nail-fixing time as a means of catharsis, had placed a sign on her table with a warning: "Talking about *things* is strictly forbidden." To fend off negative energy, next to this phrase, the woman had drawn the number 33 and a turkey vulture, which Cubans call *aura tiñosa*.

Ibrahim knew all too well what that woman meant by the symbols on her sign, given that his livelihood derived from another activity of his, which couldn't appear in any biography: he was a number runner for *la bolita, charada* being the most popular of them, a numbers game brought to Cuba from China, where numbers are associated with figures of animals, people, or things. *La bolita*, like all gambling, had been forbidden after the Revolution's triumph. Nevertheless, Ibrahim was a charming number runner and he had many clandestine clients in the Los Sitios neighborhood, where both his beautiful voice and number running expertise—which included writing down numbers according to his clients' experiences or dreams—were much appreciated.

The San Rafael Street manicurist had written down, as a spell, the number 33 and drawn the vulture, the figure equivalent to that number in the numbers game, which Cubans use to designate any evil that clings to you or suddenly befalls you—bad news, a union meeting, unresolved paperwork. If you dreamed that you were walking across a cane field barefoot and were bitten by a snake, you unquestionably had to bet on 21, the serpent, or maybe 8, death, or 83, tragedy. If, however, you imagined that the neighbor's wife across the street escaped her husband and spent the night partying with you, the number was 58, adultery, although you could also bet on a *parlé* with 66, or go for a *candado* with the two previous numbers and 12, hooker or bad woman.

Obviously, if as you left your house you stepped on dog shit, or a pigeon crapped on you, or you had any such accident, there was no question: 7, excrement—which was also the number for Yemayá, the orisha owner of the sea in one of the two main Afro-Cuban religions, the Rule of Ocha, which is also called Santeria. However, just in case, it was a good idea to also bet something on 38, money, because everyone knew that stepping on a piece of shit brings luck and personal development.

The *charada,* according to Cuban poet Gastón Baquero, is the illogical linkage of apparently logical things that happen to us during the day and especially at night, while we sleep, and in that cartography of dreams you travel through the fantasy you've experienced and guess at what you're about to experience, or what you have inside and don't know yet. Baquero said that these enjambments were not the result of ignorance; on the con-

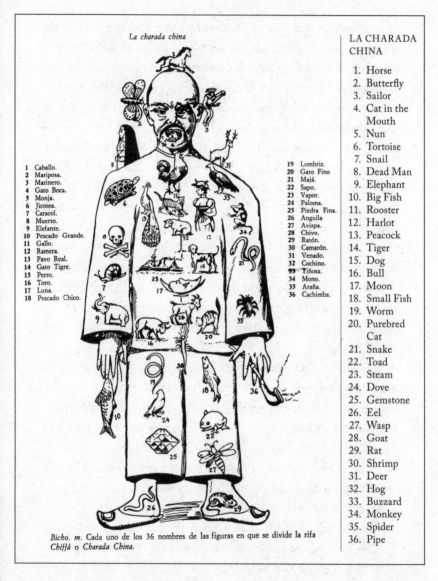

La charada china

LA CHARADA CHINA

Bicho. m. Cada uno de los 36 nombres de las figuras en que se divide la rifa *Chiffá* o *Charada China.*

trary, they were completely poetic and one of the most obvious expressions of the inexhaustible "magicifying" skill of the Cuban people, understanding this to be the ability to transform the surrounding world into something magical, a power that was the source of both strength and resistance in Cuba, like *choteo* (mockery)—when people make fun and light of what they can't deal with—or the belief that if a woman cleanses herself with mountain herbs or offers a goat to Changó, ruler of thunder and virility, equivalent to Siete Rayos (Seven Lightning Bolts) in the other main branch of the Afro-Cuban religion, Rule of the Palo Monte, or Mayombe, she can tie down her womanizing husband.

When old Estrella, in a La Aurora tenement, told Ibrahim Ferrer that dead Prudencio, a Haitian who had been appearing in her dreams for more than forty years, had come down to see her the previous night and had whispered in her ear that she should bet on 22, the toad, but that in addition to betting twenty pesos on that fixed number, she was also going to bet another twenty on 31, the deer, the Buena Vista Social Club singer thought this made perfect sense because he knew all too well that Prudencio had been a light-skinned black man and in *charada* the 31 not only meant deer, but also betrayal and *mulato*.

If the man who is awake is nothing and only the sleeping one is lucid, as Baquero argued, everything made overwhelming sense when Estrella woke up in the morning at the bunkhouse she called home and told her neighbor: "Listen up, Martillo, check out what happened to me last night, because at one point I saw Prudencio at a distance and every time I see that black man it means something, and I'm telling you, I'm sure if I do a good job at interpreting what happened, I could become rich: I was at carnival when I felt someone calling me and inviting me to dance, the drums were beating at full volume and I could hear at a distance a *corneta china* and people seemed crazy, and then a fist and knife fight broke out and I hid beneath a table thinking they were going to kill me." After that story, Estrella and Martillo would sit in the doorway and begin to rewind and search for the hidden connections: "Hey, Martillo, if Prudencio appeared, I'm sure I have to bet on 64, which is large death and silent death, and not on 8, which is also death, but that death talks and Prudencio didn't speak to me in the dream." And after that first conclusion, they'd both continue going over it all, because there was no coincidence at play and everyone knew that the dead and the *fumbes,* or Santeria spirits, communicate with people through dreams, revealing ways to help them improve their situation or warning them of dangers.

From then on, what takes place is an endless game of chess because, as noted by ethnologist Lydia Cabrera, everything, absolutely everything—dignitaries, animals, trades, moods, people, Catholic saints and orishas, weekdays, trees, and bushes—can be translated into numbers, and Cubans believe that the connections between these numbers and things are traced with a drawing pen from the great beyond without us even realizing it, and that's why we must sit down and think it through to discover them. "So, tell me, Martillo, isn't it true that in addition to large death, I should bet on 76, the ballerina, because during the dream I didn't stop dancing until the fight broke out, and also on 50, the police, because if there was a brawl and knives the police must have surely followed, and the fact remains, Martillo, that if people looked crazy it could be because there was a lot of beer and they'd had a lot to drink at the carnival, so the right number is 49, the drunk, and if I hid beneath a table and made it my home and shelter, I should bet ten pesos on 7, the snail, because I turned into a snail . . ."

It's understandable that, following this shattering logic, Sunday, November 27, 2016, was a bad day for the *bolita* bankers in Cuba. None other than Fidel Castro had died the night of the twenty-fifth, and the next day, November 26, people overwhelmingly bet on the numbers that represented or could represent the Cuban leader, starting with 1, the horse, given that this was what Fidel's followers and adversaries called him.

They had no luck. However, the following day, Estrella and others like her, dream and *charada* scientists, hit it big in the numbers game: the winning numbers were 55, the father; 54, flowers; and 2, *mariposa*, or the butterfly, which in addition to being an insect was the name of Cuba's national flower. "I won twenty-two thousand pesos, son, almost one thousand dollars for a bet of no more than sixty. And it was just a matter of deciphering the dream," said the woman, convinced that Prudencio was the one who had once again blessed her.

Back in the nineties, when Ibrahim wrote down the list of numbers for his neighbors at Los Sitios, the *bolita* was played by using the last numbers of the Venezuelan lotteries Táchira and Zulia (which were drawn on alternate days), so people followed the Venezuelan results on their shortwave radios. The last digits of the first three winning numbers were the valid ones, so, for example, if Táchira had drawn 34,537, 7,062, and 11,905 on Wednesday, the relevant numbers for that day were 37, 62, and 5.

There are one hundred numbers at play in *charada*, but the combinations are practically endless because they can be played as fixed numbers, running numbers, in *parlé* (a combination of two numbers), or in *candado* (three at a time). Betting one peso on fixed number 37, the black hen or witchcraft, can get you a seventy-five-peso prize. If you chose the *parlé* of 37 with 62, marriage, you get one thousand pesos for each peso you bet, and if you're in luck and you chose to go with a *candado* using the previous two numbers and 23, vapor, the prize equals three thousand pesos. The same ratio is used if instead of pesos you bet dollars or convertible pesos (at the exchange rate of one to twenty-five).

Naturally, on special days such as December 17, the feast day

of San Lázaro, which is syncretized with Babalú Ayé, the most
beloved and miracle-working orisha of the Yoruba pantheon,
bankers limit the amount of money you can bet on number 17,
since, in the event that it were called, it could bankrupt the bank.

For some time now, thanks to communication improvements
and more leeway with DirecTV's clandestine antennas—which
Cubans call "the channels"—the *bolita* is no longer ruled by the
Venezuelan lottery, but rather by the one in Miami, more specif-
ically the Cash 3 and Play 4, the two games drawn daily, one at
2:00 P.M. and the other at 8:00 P.M., which is the important one.
Barely five minutes later, in the tenements in La California and
Mil Condones, or in the entire neighborhood of Jesús María,
come the buzzing from balcony to balcony and the questions:
"Hey, Cacha, what telephone number was called out?" "Evaristo,
what riddle did they use this time to kill us off?"

Although gambling in general, and *charada* in particular,
has been illegal since the triumph of the Revolution, there's a
high tolerance for it. In Cuba, the *bolita* is a national sport, but
that doesn't mean people aren't careful not to give themselves
away. The *bolita* is played from east to west, in big and small
towns, in the cities and on the farms, and it is played by the
rich and the poor, from the most downtrodden Cubans to the
new wealthy class of young women with homes in Miramar,
who despite their refined taste know all about how the 35 is a
spider, the 40 a priest, and the 10 a large fish. But no one brags
about it.

At the apex of the *bolita* is the banker, the moneyman, the
one few know, and he must be a solvent and trustworthy person
because he's in charge of supplying the cash on the following
day for the winning bets. Beneath the banker is an entire well-
compartmentalized, Gothic scaffolding, with the number run-
ners who go house to house during the day writing down people's

numbers and picking up their pesos, which they later deliver to higher-ranked collectors, who then go to the big guy, the banker. Many of these links don't even know each other. There are small, medium, and large banks, which can have several partners, but they're all ruled by the same law—trust—given that the following day they must pay up even if the number drawn was 63, the murderer, the day after a well-reported crime had shocked Havana.

The *charada* vice entered the island together with the first ships arriving in Cuba in the mid-nineteenth century carrying Cantonese and Macanese people, and with it came the entire magical world of symbols, hexagrams, fire dragons, red moons, elephants with golden trunks, and *I Ching* readings, an entire poetic and ancient philosophy that crossed paths on the island with another culture no less fantastic, that of the Yorubas, Congos, and Araráas of Africa, who traveled to the New World on slave ships together with their pantheon of deities: Osain, ruler of nature and all mountain herbs and plants that have magical powers; Oya, the queen of the cemetery; Elegua, the road opener; Obatalá, owner of all heads.

In a short time frame, four great races met on this Greater Antilles island. The first to arrive, the pre-Colombian Indians, traveled on canoes from the continental lands of the Amazon and the Yucatán and from other Caribbean islands. The Siboney and above all the Taíno left their food and some words—including the word *Cuba*—in addition to tobacco and its spellbinding smoke, used to communicate with the gods. Then came the Spaniards, devoted to the cross, playing cards, and the guitar; the black Africans, worshippers of the mountain's herbs and sticks and uniquely connected to the forces of nature; and the Chinese, with their lottery, opium pipes, and fiery spells.

In a classic essay, "The Human Factors of Cubanidad," the

Cuban ethnologist Fernando Ortiz compared Cuban culture and its formation with an *ajiaco,* the most genuine local stew, made of various types of legumes and pieces of different types of meat. Throughout half a millennium, Cuba was an open casserole in which a dense and sedimented sauce with copious dressing was thickened. "This unique and primitive spelaean dish consisted of placing on the hearth a casserole filled with boiling water and adding to it vegetables, herbs, and roots, which the woman grew on her parcel of land according to the seasons, as well as the meat of all types of vermin, quadrupeds, birds, reptiles, fish, and seafood, which the man caught in his predatory runs across the mountains and coast," explained Ortiz. "Anything edible ended up in the casserole, uncleaned meats that were sometimes already rotting, unpeeled vegetables often with worms that gave them more substance. Everything was cooked together and seasoned with strong shots of pepper, which masked all the insipidness with the exciting crowning of its spiciness. That pot provided, time and again, everything they wanted to eat; the leftovers remained in the same container for the following meal. The next day, the *ajiaco* was awakened to a new boiling point; water was added to the pot, as well as other viands and little animals, and it was boiled once again with more pepper. And so, day after day, the uncleaned casserole, with its stock-filled bottom."

Cuba, an open casserole, a pot cooking on the fire of the tropics and beaten by the hurricanes, where the four bloodlines blended together with their superstitions, customs, rhythms, traditions, and legends, with their heroes and traitors and their universes filled with myths, such as that of the light of Yara, which floats in eastern Cuba—to this day the Baracoa *guajiros* claim it is the spirit of Chief Hatuey, who was burned at the stake for rebelling against the Spaniards and who once in a while comes out and walks across the fields.

Also in that stew are the four races' unique ways of conceiving time and reality, their fears, their profound beliefs, and their differences—since among the Africans there were Yoruba, Mandingo, Bantu, and Carabalí, all as different from each other as a Castilian from an Andalusian—and their ways of understanding the world and defending themselves from power and their ability to invent stories and turn the image of a saint or the root of a ceiba tree into magic. All of this over time blended together and became one root and one culture, Indian, black, white, and yellow, like the famous Chinese *charada* man, who had thirty-six tattoos on his body of birds, cats, peacocks, prostitutes, ships, wasps, diamonds, monkeys, and sailors, next to their corresponding numbers.

Only by accepting the rolling boil of this miscegenation is it possible to comprehend the figure of the incredible Wifredo Lam, son of a Chinese man and a black woman, who with his brushes dragged into surrealism his entire heritage and a world of dreams and masks filled with supernatural beings, simultaneously human, animal, and vegetable. Or the worlds of José Lezama Lima, Alejo Carpentier, Guillermo Cabrera Infante, or Nicolás Guillén. Or to understand the reason why, years ago, an ex-minister of Cuba's foreign affairs department planted himself in the home of a famous Afro-Cuban priest, follower of the Rule of Palo Monte, and sacrificed roosters and rams in a unique ceremony before a *nganga* carrying gunpowder, machetes, and bones of the dead, in order to enter the political bureau of Cuba's Communist Party, atheism's temple; or why some old Catholic women who go to church every day in Cuba place a small jet stone in their grandson's cradle to protect him; or why, when opening a bottle of rum, even the most skeptical Marxist pours one out for the saints; or why even the police, whom Ibrahim Ferrer avoided while collecting bets in the neighborhood, placed a bet on 4 on Saint Barbara's Day.

In 1974, Gastón Baquero said that playing *charada*, and following all the rules, obeying the superstitions, was a way of philosophizing. "Moreover, it's a way of having faith in transcendental things, in the tremendous mystery of the universe and the presence of man in it. It's poetry for poeticizing the surrounding reality, changing it, subjecting it to the laws of magic." He continued: "It's moving for a few hours into the realm of that which is wonderful and abstract. It is traveling to the world of the unknown, no matter what. That's how Columbus discovered the New World and how the Americans reached the moon."

Hand in hand with the *charada* are the Afro-Cuban religions and the belief that everything has a solution, even the worst health problems or persecution by the authorities, if you treat the saints properly and carefully choose the mountain herbs for your cleansing rituals and the animals to offer the orishas. Any Santeria practitioner, or *santero,* knows that the owner of the Palo Caballero (a magical stick used in Santeria practice) is Changó, who is found in bay cedars and has the power to do everything because he can both keep you from falling off a horse and protect you from witchcraft and bad influences; therefore, you must always carry in your pocket a little stem from this plant, which serves as a *detente bala.* There's also esparto grass, used for footbaths or when a possession is being disputed—its fibers are tied into a knot and bound to a trunk and the interested party tightens it each day until he's exhausted his adversary. Additionally, ginger and lemongrass can age Oggún, master of iron and guard of warriors, who in Mayombe is Zarabanda, absolute owner of the vast stretches of land that border the mountain and ruler also of keys, chains, and prisons, whose numbers are the combination of 3 and 7, and whose days are Tuesdays, Wednesdays, and the fourth day of every month, according to Natalia Bolívar Aróstegui, Lydia Cabrera's disciple and author of a reference book, *Los orishas en Cuba* (The Orishas in Cuba), which paradoxically is one of the biggest bestsellers published in revolutionary Cuba.

Natalia is a descendent of the liberator Simón Bolívar and belongs to a distinguished Havana family, but at a young age was initiated in the Palo rituals and now lives in an apartment in Miramar filled with the spirits of important people, where filmmakers, academics, doctors, and painters seek out her advice, as do simple people from the marginal neighborhood of Coco Solo, where witchcraft and spiritual malevolence are commonplace.

Natalia explains that in Cuba, regardless of their class or rank, everyone gets cabalistic, turning to numbers and witchcraft. Unlike the Europeans, especially the French—and specifically scholars, whose understanding of reality is square and who don't accept as real whatever doesn't fit in that square—in Cuba, and in the Caribbean, and generally in the Americas, for a boy to be born with a pig's tail due to a family curse seems to be the most natural thing in the world. That's why in these lands *One Hundred Years of Solitude* is a deeply sensible and realistic novel, just as everyone knows that the saints have the same tastes as people and that's why they are grateful to receive tobacco, rum, goat meat, perfumes, honey and other sweets, or a violin to play some music and shake their bodies in religious ceremonies, and there's also no problem believing that the dead can speak and that the orishas communicate through people they choose as horses to come down to earth at a *bembé* (orisha religious fiesta). Have you never seen an old and thick *mulata* dance while completely possessed during a *tambor* (drum circle), jumping around like a teenager and totally uninhibited when her personality is actually quite the opposite? Natalia can vouch for it all.

As she recalls, in 1957, when a group of university students with whom she sympathized decided to bring Fulgencio Batista to justice in the Presidential Palace, they didn't take into account that the dictator's priests had warned him, after consulting Orula, that in his path was the number 93, revolution, and that's why Batista had built a secret door in his office, through which he escaped from the armed group as they charged up the palace's stairs ready to kill him. It is also said, and hardly anyone questions this, that Fidel Castro himself, during a trip to Africa, did what he had to do to get the protection of the spirits and deities living in the mountains of Yorubaland, and that's why, during that trip, for the first time since Sierra Maestra, he took off his olive-green uniform and appeared on TV dressed in white from head to toe. It's also said that once a renowned *santera* approached him and said, "Commander, you have nothing to worry about because you will die whenever you desire it," and the fact remains that he died on November 25, 2016, after stating in Parliament that he was tired, and it was precisely on November 25, sixty years earlier, that Castro embarked on the *Granma* yacht in Mexico and headed to Cuba to begin the armed battle.

Natalia explains that, on another front, but with the same reasoning, a good *palero*, or shaman, can help align the stars and tend to any demand, such as the long-suffering employee at a state institution who wants to "cool down" his boss to stop him from breathing down his neck—well, there are spells that help the enemy lose his or her way. And then there's the office colleague who's the target of rumors and criticism and, to end the issue and shut the rumor mill's mouth, turns to a *mayombero*, also a shaman, who will procure two roots from the plant named *apasote*, or wormseed—also used as an antiparasitic and to pass gas—and a white-cloth-covered rod, and a lizard's tongue, and a bottle of moonshine, and will ask the interested party to bring something that belongs to his or her adversary. And what of the jealous woman who goes to the *ngangulero*'s house and begs him to work his magic so that her husband can no longer get it up with another woman, and regardless of what the *palero* may ask her to bring, she will bring it, no matter what—a pair of stained boxers, seven black candles, the sweat of a horse, or the bones of an insane dead person from the Calabazar cemetery, once again 68, the graveyard?

The magic of the *bolita* and the African religions and their pantheon, which the slaves syncretized with the Catholic book of saints when they came to the Americas, in addition to being practical and offering home remedies, has another great advantage: it's an incredibly powerful psychological weapon for facing life, since relying on its inspiration makes it easier to resist, and no matter how bad it gets, you can always win a *parlé*, or obtain dark favors from the deities living in the mountain. And here the *charada* and the saints unite under another resistance mechanism, which Cubans rely on—the *choteo* (joking around or mockery), studied by philosopher and journalist Jorge Mañach in his memorable essay "Investigating the *Choteo*."

Mañach explained back in 1928 that making light of serious things was essential to Cubans, that this "disrespectful habit" was based on the "aversion to all authority," and that usually the mockery was a subterfuge employed by the weak against the powerful, equivalent to an act of dodging. Mañach said, "Not all authorities are lawful and desirable, and that's why mockery has always been a resource for the oppressed—regardless of the nature of the oppression." On par with the Cuban people's greatest afflictions, he argued, chronic mockery had been one of their great defenses:

It has served as a buffer during adversity, a dock to resist political pressures that are too cumbersome, and an outlet for all types of impatience. In other words, for us, it has been an

incredibly effective decongestant. Since its operation consists
of belittling the importance of things, in other words, stop-
ping them from affecting us too much, the *choteo* emerges in
every situation where the local spirit is embittered by a false
or unwieldy authority.

When facing an uncompromising bureaucrat who's screw-
ing you over at a window and someone from the middle of the
line says, "Forgive him, it looks like he isn't getting any from his
woman," and the room bursts into laughter, that simple act of
insubordination also holds something magical, like betting on
45, the shark or president, because in the blink of an eye, the
tension is dissolved.

According to Mañach, there are two types of *choteos*, "a quick
and healthy *choteo*, basically following vices or failures of atten-
tion derived from the same local psychology," which is what
happens when, for example, during a performance in Havana's
Gran Teatro, a tenor's voice cracks and someone in the audience
automatically stands up and yells out, "Hey, you'll be singing
for one less person, 'cause I'm outta here." And another type of
choteo, which is more "profound and skeptical," originating "from
a true failure of authority," where the *choteador*, or joker, comi-
cally loathes "every principle of conduct and every disciplinary
demand: of absolute veracity, punctuality, conscientiousness, of
the ritual and ceremonious, of the methodical," since what he
or she is defending is their independence, just as when you play
the *bolita* you are completely free and powerful the instant you
translate your dreams into a number.

Originally, the *charada* bankers managed the numbers as
they pleased, without being affiliated with any other lottery. At
a certain time in the morning, "they hung it out," meaning they
randomly picked any number and hung it from the roof of their

home, suspended by a cord tied to a ring. Some banks, generously and to encourage bets, gave the players a hint during the day in the shape of a cabalistic verse or riddle: if, for example, they said, "A very serious lady who pays heed to no one," the nod could be to 5, the nun; "an elephant that walks on tiled roofs but breaks no tiles" didn't refer to the mastodon but rather would point to 4, the cat. Lydia Cabrera, in her book dedicated to Ochún, which is syncretized with Our Lady of Charity, or *la Virgen de la Caridad del Cobre*, Cuba's patron saint, quotes another one of these tricky riddles that someone with Estrella's experience wouldn't find difficult to solve, "A bird that bites and leaves." The dead, like birds, fly; and the dead, arriving through their own will or sent by a witch, bite, hurt, put a spell on a live being, and leave. The number then would be 8, which in *charada* is not only the dead but also the tiger, the table, the pumpkin, and on and on.

TROPICANA REDUX

BY FRANCISCO GOLDMAN

t was like returning to a lushly primeval mythical island—or like Peter Pan returning to Never Never Land—entering the grounds of the Tropicana nightclub in Marianao, a popular borough of Havana, for the first time in a quarter of a century. In the ensuing years I'd only occasionally thought about my time in this place, it was so anomalous to the rest of my life, but now everything I saw was vivid with fresh recognition, the towering royal palms, fruit trees, jungle plants; the eight nude female dancers sculpted in marble, known as the neoclassical Fountain of Muses; the elegantly spare, red-trimmed glass and concrete architecture of the main complex; and in front of the entrance on its own little island, the statue by Rita Longa of a slender ballerina en pointe, swaying from the waist up like the stem of a water lily in a current, arms held gracefully out, which has become the Tropicana's emblematic image. Our tattered old taxi stopped at the reception guard-booth in the drive. I left my wife, Jovi, with the driver and stepped into a room whose walls were

adorned with enlarged black-and-white photographs of some of
the Tropicana's past star performers. Now, though I didn't know
the name of anybody I should ask for, I had to explain what I
wanted to the man sitting behind the desk. I'd last been here in
1993, when I'd written an article on the Tropicana for *Harper's
Bazaar,* the women's fashion magazine. I'd spent about ten days
hanging around the club, going to shows and rehearsals. Now
I wanted to write a new piece, about the current Tropicana in
these changed times, and I also wanted to find some of the danc-
ers I'd gotten to know back then, listen to their perspectives on
the passing of time, in their own lives as dancers and in Cuba
generally. Maybe someone at the Tropicana could help me to
contact some of those people.

The man behind the desk looked at me skeptically and said,
"They must all be dead by now."

I wondered if that was a comment on how visibly I'd aged in
twenty-five years, though, of course, he hadn't known me back
then. He was about forty, at most, I guessed. "Some of them
were teenagers back then," I said. "They're only in their forties
now younger than you."

I was feeling a bit of pressure. I had only three days left in
Havana to do whatever reporting I was going to be able to do
here for this piece. He made a phone call. I studied the photo-
graphs on the wall: glittering skimpy costumes, legs, arms, hips,
nalgas, fabulous headpieces, portraits of legendary divas, one of
an almond-eyed woman with a thoughtful-looking, sensuous
expression. I was a little disconcerted to be having an awed crush
on a photograph and told myself that was the most beautiful
face I'd ever seen in my life. The man behind the desk, on the
telephone, was more or less faithfully describing my request to
somebody, though his caustic tone of voice didn't seem to prom-
ise that he would help my cause very much.

He passed me the phone so that I could speak to a woman from the administration office named Sandra. I explained myself again, and told her I'd brought photocopies of my old magazine article and lots of snapshots I'd taken back then. Sandra said she would meet us by the entrance—I told her that Jovi, who'd been waiting in the taxi, would be coming, too. Our taxi driver, a man with a heavy, narrow-eyed Slavic face, agreed to wait, but no more than twenty minutes, he said.

It was my photographs that really did it. They'd all been taken with those Kodak disposable cameras; the mobile phone digital camera era was still some years off. Sandra, a warm, hearty woman, sat alongside me in her office, going through them one by one, images of rehearsals and shows, of dancers backstage and some in their own homes, and sometimes she exclaimed in recognition. "These photographs are precious," she said. "You should do something with them; the people here have to see them. That was a golden era at the Tropicana." When I'd been there in 1993, the titular director was the legendary Tomás Morales, but the choreographer of the troupe and of the show who I got to know was the also-legendary Santiago Alfonso—such words as *legendary, mythical, immortal,* and *diva* are part of the essential and unavoidable Tropicana vocabulary. I'd originally tried to renew my contacts with the Tropicana through Santiago Alfonso. When I'd phoned him from Mexico City and told him my plans—he didn't have any memory of me, of course—he'd spoken as if he'd be happy to meet and help me out, and I'd expected to be able to quickly get to work. But now, here in Cuba, I'd already wasted two days chasing Santiago on the phone. After telling me several times to phone back, he'd growlingly asked how much I was going to pay and told me that his lawyer had advised that he shouldn't speak to me unless I paid. This is just for an anthology that's being published in New York

and Spain, I explained. Various writers, I told him, would be
writing about various aspects of life in Cuba, and I—Santiago
roared at me, "And you think the world needs you to tell it about
the Tropicana?" "Of course not, it's just that—" I'm pretty sure
I just began to giggle, with nerves but also because I found his
antagonistic onslaught really funny. Frankly, I could even un-
derstand his wanting to be paid for granting an interview and
providing information; it even occurred to me that it was sur-
prising that request didn't come up more often. But I didn't have
a budget to pay Santiago Alfonso. And he wasn't going to help
me. That's why I'd come directly to the Tropicana that day, with-
out knowing who to ask for there.

I was fortunate to have found Sandra. She phoned the cur-
rent director-choreographer, Armando Pérez, who is known as
El Jimagua, "The Twin"; his twin brother, Alberto, has also been
a member of the Tropicana family for decades, both starting out
as dancers. The possibility of my being able to write a new piece
on the Tropicana hinged on this one telephone call. If it didn't
work, Jovi and I would just be having a short vacation in Cuba—
not a terrible prospect, of course. After all, it was here in Havana
where, on the Malecón three years before, I'd proposed mar-
riage. But the weather was rainy, windy, and cold, the coldest
January week, people were saying, that they could remember.
Because of the waves surging over the sea wall, the Malecón
was closed to pedestrians and traffic. There were going to be
no quick trips to a beach or afternoon breaks by the swimming
pool. Havana Vieja's former charm has pretty much been spoiled
by the hordes of American and European cruise ship tourists
crowding its old streets, driving restaurant prices so high that
even a plate of rice and beans with a fried egg on top now costs
the equivalent of twelve dollars. The highlight of our days so far
had been going to a little food stall run by a boisterous group

of women on a Vedado side street, where the customers paid in Cuban pesos and you carried your plate of delicious *congri* and roast chicken across the street into a little park. I could tell that Sandra was giving an enthusiastic pitch on my behalf. Then I heard her say, as if repeating instructions, "Okay, so they can see the show, but they can't sit at the director's table." And after she hung up, she told us to come at eight the next night to the performers' entrance behind the Tropicana. El Jimagua would talk to us before the show.

On the way out, before returning to our taxi, we stole a quick look around. Here was the indoor theater, Los Arcos de Cristal, the Crystal Arcades, a modernist classic by Cuban architect Max Borges, constructed in 1951, which fits into its bowered setting like a tropical glade. Borges went into exile after the Revolution, had a long if quiet architectural career—compared to his significant one in Cuba—in Washington, D.C., and Virginia, where he died in 2009. I went down through the open lobby to find Bajo las Estrellas, the famous Paradise Under the Stars, where the show takes place almost nightly, unless bad weather forces it inside: rows of tables face the stage, which is ensconced among trees, a wall of verdant foliage laced with delicate-looking metal catwalks and bridges where at night, in colorfully blazing and popping lights, female dancers wearing soaring headpieces hover high above the audience. Back in the pre-Revolution glory days, that stage had featured the greatest stars of Cuban music: Rita Montaner, Bola de Nieve, Olga Guillot, Benny Moré, Celia Cruz. It welcomed international performers, too: even Nat King Cole performed there. The nightly audience included infamous mafiosos and nearly every movie star of that era that you can think of, from Ava Gardner to Marlon Brando. Even if after the Revolution the celebrities in the audience were more along the lines of Soviet cosmonaut Yuri Gagarin or, very occasionally,

Fidel himself, the Tropicana has remained one of Havana's gaud-
iest, most effervescent and talent-rich nightly spectacles. Now it
was midday; everything was quiet. At the back of the stage was
the sculpture of geometric tubes from atop which, I now remem-
bered, the star soloist Lupe Guzmán used to launch her famous
swan dive at the climax of one of the show's most iconic num-
bers. Before we'd left the wonderful Sandra upstairs, I'd asked if
she knew how to contact Lupe, who was in several of the snap-
shots she'd looked through and who was prominently featured in
the *Harper's Bazaar* article, too, in a photo with her then teenage
daughter, Lianette Beltrán, who was already a sought-out model,
both women leaning upper torsos, heads, and golden Rapunzel
manes out through the windows of an old fifties-model automo-
bile. Even back then, when she was still performing, Lupe was
regarded as one of the Tropicana's all-time greats. Sandra wasn't
sure where she was now—maybe in Miami, where her daughter
had moved decades before to pursue her modeling and acting
career. Santiago Alfonso would have known, but his *gruñonismo*
had made me feel too intimidated to ask.

Our taxi driver had been waiting for about an hour. Of course,
we agreed to pay more. Supposedly few "ordinary Cubans"—
meaning nearly all Cubans living in Cuba—ever go to the
Tropicana to see the show because the ticket prices, which have
provided the Cuban government with desperately needed tour-
ist dollars, are too exorbitant. But our taxi driver had saved his
money in order to bring his wife for their recent anniversary.
Times are relatively good for Havana taxi drivers nowadays, with
so many tourists from the United States and elsewhere pouring
in, ever since Raúl Castro and Barack Obama respectively de-
cided to open up the island and relax travel restrictions. For his
wife, the taxi driver told us, it had been a dream come true to see
in person the cabaret she'd heard of all her life and had glimpsed

on television and in movies. "The bodies of those dancers," he told us, "are a heart attack."

———

I don't remember anymore how it was that the invitation to go to Cuba and write about the Tropicana came about. In college I'd taken a translation course from the astonishingly young, already-celebrated translator Suzanne Jill Levine—I remember my crush on her as practically a sickness—and apart from her translation of those memorable opening pages of Guillermo Cabrera Infante's *Tres tristes tigres*—"Showtime! *Señores y señoras*. Ladies and gentlemen. And a very good evening to you all, ladies and gentlemen. *Muy buenas noches, damas y caballeros*. Tropicana! the MOST fabulous nightclub in the WORLD . . ."—I don't think I had any particular awareness of the Tropicana or had even wondered if it still existed, much less thought that I wanted to go there. I was living in Mexico City with my girlfriend, Tina, who was half Cuban, when, out of the blue, came the invitation to go to Havana and do a piece on the Tropicana for *Harper's Bazaar*. The idea for the piece itself had come from Enrique Badulescu, a Mexican who was a rising star in fashion photography. I could easily fly from Mexico to Cuba and circumvent U.S. travel restrictions if I was sure to ask the Cubans not to stamp my passport. Tina's mother, Margarita, along with her mother's parents, older siblings, and some of their small children, had fled Cuba to the United States—to New York and New Jersey—after Fidel Castro's revolution made its sharp turn toward communism. Her mother had married an Englishman she met in New York City, so Tina and her own siblings had been born and raised in London. I knew Tina was dying to visit Cuba for the first time in her life, and so it was for her, especially, that I seized this opportunity to go.

What ensued was really one of the strangest, most fun, and most utterly unexpected experiences of my life. For nearly two weeks, I became a sort of Toulouse-Lautrec of the Tropicana, granted the most improbable access to rehearsals, classes, and backstage during shows, even allowed to wander in and out of the dressing rooms. To this day I don't understand how that actually happened. Tina, meanwhile, went off into Havana to have her own adventures. She would long cherish the experience, but it wasn't always easy; she had the features of a dark-skinned young Cuban beauty at a time when Havana had become a destination for sex tourism from Europe. I remember her furious exasperation that she couldn't even go down to the cafeteria in our hotel for a sandwich without some old German wrenching his lips into leering kisses aimed in her direction. Cuba was enduring the notorious hardships of the Special Period, when the Soviet Union's collapse had left it isolated and without its main source of economic support. Things were so bad, I remember, that on Cuban television there were cooking shows that were teaching people how to bread grapefruit rinds in order to fry them like veal or chicken, assuming grapefruit rinds were even available. One day, as we stood on the muddy street behind the Tropicana complex, outside the staff and performers' entrance during a break from classes and rehearsals, blond, curly-haired, very soft-spoken Toni Suárez, then the company's regisseur, or dance master, asked me if I'd noticed that you never saw any cats in Havana anymore. Before, you used to see cats everywhere, he said, but now you didn't see any, because people had eaten them all. (At least now, in 2017, Havana is a city of cats again.) Toni had explained to me that the Tropicana's iconic headpieces, known simply as *gorros*, or hats—as in the "star *gorro*" or the "rooster *gorro*" or the twenty-three-pound "chandelier *gorro*"— were so big because of the trees. "The hats are bigger here than at any other cabaret because there's no roof, and so there's no limit," he told me. "If the hats were smaller, the women would look smaller; you wouldn't see their splendor. So the hats have grown immense as we've looked for ways to make the women complement, or compete with, this setting." It was Toni who told me that he considered Lupe Guzmán, then forty, whom he'd known for thirty-four years, the "most charismatic" dancer the Tropicana had ever had. I'd become pretty friendly with Lupe back then, enough so that she'd invited me back to her home, which, despite her star status, was a modest apartment in a fairly utilitarian apartment block. Probably the woman I'd been friendliest with was Maria Elena, a willowy *mulata* with a warm and tender demeanor whose husband, Miguel, a handsome, slight man who worked as a welder, had encountered her on the street one day and invited her for an ice cream at Coppelia. At her audition for the Tropicana, Santiago Alfonso had noticed her among the hundreds of girls trying out to be selected as a potential *figurante*—the company is divided into a few soloists and larger contingents of dancers and *figurantes*, as the statuesque women who wear the *gorros* are called—and told her to go and try on a *tanga*; it was the first time she'd ever worn a bikini in her life. Alfonso put her through dance steps and flexibility tests, and told her she had fifteen days to lose twenty pounds. She succeeded, and was thrown immediately into dance classes and rehearsals. Now she'd even traveled to Europe to perform with the company. Every day she bicycled back from her small bungalow, where she lived with her mother-in-law and Miguel, and every night when she returned Miguel, without fail, had a warm bath waiting for her.

My favorite memories include attending the daily dance classes, Santiago Alfonso prowling the hot, sweaty room, constantly taking drags from his cigarettes, shouting instructions, while in a corner drummers banged furiously on their drums. I loved being backstage during the shows, amid the dingy warren of dressing and costume rooms. I even went out onto the catwalks, though, of course, not far enough so that the audience would have seen me. I remember waiting on one of those catwalks with one of the *figurantes*, slightly older, more womanly than my still-girlish friend Maria Elena. She was in her sparse spangled costume, her enormous *gorro* set down alongside her, sitting in a crouch as both of us smoked and quietly talked. When it was time for her to go on, I remember with what spectacular grace and strength her body unfolded upward and towered over me as she lifted her *gorro* onto her head, and the rhythmic, queenly walk with which her long beautiful legs and hips propelled her farther out onto the catwalk, out through tree branches above the illuminated stage.

———

We had trouble hailing a taxi from Playa, where we were staying in a friend's apartment, and arrived a little late at the backstage entrance, on that muddy, residence-lined, unlit street which, as soon as we arrived and I saw it again after so many years, looked so familiar and unchanged. It turned out that Armando Pérez hadn't arrived yet. He was at a benefit performance in a Havana theater with some of his dancers. He'd either forgotten about our appointment or had forgotten about the benefit when he'd made it. We had no choice but to wait, which was in its own way enjoyable and, for me, a bit nostalgic. Sporadically, young dancers filed in out of the dark as if out of the past, only now some of them wore hoodies, along with sweaters, sweatpants, and jeans, some eating ice cream cones from the little parlor just around the corner. But most of the troupe was already inside, preparing for the show after their long day of classes and rehearsals. A few musicians arrived, too, and other performers, singers, and acrobats. Everyone had to open their bags and musical instrument cases atop the table inside the entrance to be inspected by the guard.

A few people were huddled outside in the darkness attending to a young man from Croatia. He wore eyeglasses and a wool sweater tucked inside his belted pants. His voice was pleading and earnest. He'd met a Tropicana dancer, he said, the night before, and she'd told him to come here to the performers' entrance and to ask for her before the show. He knew her name, but the two people attending to him, who did seem to want to help, perhaps a stagehand and a makeup or costume woman, didn't recognize the name. The Croatian was unable to describe her any more specifically than to say that she was dark. "How dark?" the stagehand, beginning to sound annoyed, asked. "Black like I am, or lighter skinned?" "Black," said the Croatian, sounding plaintive. I remembered, from 1993, frequently hearing that a common ruse among Cuban *jineteras*, women who sold sex to tourists in exchange for money or even in exchange for such coveted goods as Calvin Klein underwear or a night out in a restaurant or club, was to tell men that they were Tropicana dancers. It's a reputation that has clung to the cabaret's female dancers from the scandalous old pre-Revolution days and may even have been mythical back then; the Tropicana dancers I'd seen, who spent at least twelve hours a day at the cabaret complex, in classes, in rehearsals, in the shows, from early afternoon on, virtually every day and night of the week, didn't have time to be out and about at night trying to meet men, never mind in order to solicit dates for money. It was obvious the ruse was still a staple of Havana sex tourism now. The Cubans finally grew impatient and lost interest in the Croatian; their voices, which had sounded kind before, turned curt, and they went back in-side, and that Croatian, his romantic or erotic fantasy shattered, trudged off alone into the night, perhaps to try to meet another Tropicana dancer.

Finally somebody came out to get us, and we were led in-side and up some stairs to a back office and handed over to the company's current regisseur, Lourdes Hernández Domínguez, who told us to sit down. She was a bit frantic, though, because she didn't know if Armando Pérez and the dancers he'd taken with him would make it back in time for that night's opening number, in which case she was going to have to assemble a dif-ferent corps of dancers; on her mobile phone, she was trying to keep up with their movements. It was going to be tight; they were just now, she told Jovi and me, receiving an encore ovation in the theater where the benefit was being held. Lourdes had spent twelve years of her life as a Tropicana dancer and had now risen to a position just beneath Pérez. She was, I guessed, in her fifties, a handsome, sturdy black woman, with syrupy dark eyes that were steady and attentive, who answered questions carefully and warmed to the conversation as it progressed. As had hap-pened the day before with Sandra, Lourdes was especially taken with my stack of twenty-four-year-old snapshots. She recog-nized most of the dancers. This one was living in Italy now, she told me, and this one, too—she'd opened her own dance school in Italy; and this one was in Miami; this one, poor woman, had gone mad—I'm pretty sure it was the same woman I'd smoked a cigarette with on the catwalk that long-ago night. Tender Maria Elena, she thought, was in Monterrey, Mexico, where she'd also opened a dance school. A lot of former Tropicana dancers did that when they got settled abroad. Who better to teach any and all of the dance styles of the Latin American Caribbean? The male dancer standing next to her in my photograph had died of cancer, barely forty. I was in that snapshot too, in my midthirties and looking even younger than that, hair curly and totally black, my unlined face beaming with happiness. Lourdes's dance master predecessor, Toni Suárez, so trim back when I'd known him, had grown obese, she told me, and had died of a heart attack. Lupe Guzmán, she thought, was living in Mexico now, though she often came back to Havana.

"They all leave," said Lourdes gruffly. Though plenty, like herself, stay, too. Veteran Tropicana dancers, women in their forties and fifties, she told me, had recently formed a new dance troupe of their own that had been putting on well-received shows.

And she spoke of her own time as a dancer. "All the famous personalities who visit Cuba come here to the Tropicana," she told me. She'd performed in front of Salvador Allende *and* Pinochet, at different times, of course; in front of Brezhnev, too, and, in 1974, for Fidel, when he brought the winners of the 1974 World Boxing Championships, which Cuba was hosting that year, up onstage with him.

"I was a *jovencita,* so young, when I began here," Lourdes remembered. "Life just goes by; time went by; when you're enjoying yourself you don't even notice that it's passing. I satisfied all my wishes here." Lourdes married an athlete, a Cuban judo champ. After she retired as a Tropicana dancer, she worked as a dance teacher and choreographer for some of the other companies and cabarets and television dance shows in Havana. Cabaret hasn't just been essential to Cuba's tourist industry, but is a tradition-rich popular art form that expresses a part of Cuban identity. If Afro-Cuban dance and music are perhaps Cuba's most glorious and influential contributions to the Americas and to the world, the Tropicana, since its founding in 1939, has been a major showcase and laboratory for both. Cuban sensuality and eroticism are essential expressions of that identity, of course, something perhaps missed or misunderstood by people who wonder how the otherwise often puritanical Communist ideology of the Revolution could have permitted such a supposedly licentious and seemingly superficial place as the Tropicana to survive. When Lourdes explained that the Tropicana was a part of Cuba's "idiosyncrasy"—a word that always seems to come up when talking to Cubans about the Tropicana—that's what she was referring to.

Now Lourdes was in charge of training and rehearsing Tropicana dancers who are as young as she was when she joined the company. Students from Cuba's elite ballet, modern, and folkloric dance schools, from its schools for gymnasts and acrobats, increasingly even from its athletic academies, audition for the school, in which the Tropicana prepares its own revolving companies—the one that performs at the cabaret, which includes over a hundred dancers and performers, and other, smaller companies that tour the world. That course lasts ten months; after the first three months, though, many are cut. The Tropicana in Havana puts on a show every night, 365 shows a year. The dancers come in around two in the afternoon for their first classes, which are followed by rehearsals, and the show goes on at ten at night. The Tropicana becomes a dancer's life. It has to, there's no other way.

Lourdes said that it's harder now with young dancers. So much in Cuba has changed and is changing. "They're looking for other things. Sometimes they're less devoted to the art than we were." It's her job to teach them to be "disciplined artists, and to be ready to put on a show every night. You've got to be ready to bring it every day. It's our food, after all. Whether it rains, or if there are winds, we have to maintain our quality. You have to give yourself to it completely."

Backstage, in one of the open-air corridors between the

dressing rooms, the twenty-three-pound chandelier *gorros* are set out in a long rack. Twenty-four years after I last saw them, they've kept their featured role in the show, which will be beginning in minutes. Seeing those enormous hats of glittering crystals, I smile as if running into an old friend.

"Señores y señoras . . . Welcome to PARADISE under the STARS . . ." and the show begins. Jovi and I have a guest table to ourselves, overlooking the stage and the packed audience, with one of the small platforms on which dancers and singers perform positioned right in front of us. The stage is now even more brightly and colorfully illuminated, more high tech, inevitably, than it was when I was last here. But now, as then, there's the opening act, one of the show's most spectacular, as the flanks of the stage and towering trees fill with women dazzlingly costumed, and for the next two hours or so, the spectacle overloads your perceptions with beauty, movement, music, color, exuberant eroticism, and dance dance dance, with spangled bikinis, gold lamé boots, flowing and ruffled Caribbean dresses, bikinis and long gauzy capes, perfectly toned smooth torsos and limbs, long thighs, rounded backsides, all those different styles of glowing *gorros* climbing toward the stars; the chandelier *gorros* worn by women in black minituxes for an elegant number that evokes Gershwin or Ellington; singers in evening gowns; mambos, cha cha chas, guarachas, boleros; Afro-Cuban modern dance. An older male singer in a loose white suit climbs onto the platform in front of us to perform, and afterward, as he steps off it, the beads of sweat on his brow shining in the lights, he gives us the loveliest Louis Armstrong smile. There are several astonishing acrobatic numbers, too; the young husband of one of

the female acrobats arrives to sit at our table only for the dura-
tion of her number; during our brief conversation, he tells us
that he's a university professor. What impresses me most is how
fresh and joyful the show feels, a product not just of the beauty
of the dancers and of their costumes and the music, but also of
their precision and skill, all those exuberant steps and gestures
perfectly in sync, nothing wasted. The crowd seems to absolutely
love it. The Afro-Cuban centerpiece of the show, with its rous-
ing drumming, depicts a slave rebellion and a love triangle; at
the climax, the light-skinned soloist flees the slave master who
desires to possess her by taking her famous swan dive off the
top of the stage's sculpture of twisting arcs, which, back when
Lupe Guzmán used to do it, was a symbolic suicidal leap into the
void. Now it ends differently, with that night's soloist—her name
is Sojuila—leaping into the arms of her beautiful and muscular
slave lover, so that they can escape together.

That is one of the ways in which Armando Pérez, El Jima-
gua, had renovated and put his own stamp on the show. After
all, he told Jovi and me, that number is a part of a cabaret dance
spectacular, so why should it be sad? Why shouldn't love tri-
umph? "Sadness, I decided, was not invited."

It was the next afternoon, and we were watching the re-
hearsal being run by Lourdes on the Tropicana stage while we
sat with Armando at a table. While the young dancers onstage,
wearing sweats and shorts and T-shirts and workout leotards,
were led by Lourdes through their paces, others sat in the front
rows watching, quietly talking, or immersed in the small screens
of their phones.

Armando is a lanky, cheerful, handsome man who really
does look at least a decade younger than his sixty-four years.
As the director of the Tropicana cabaret, he sits atop a rich line
of predecessors and tradition that he clearly reveres and feels

deeply connected to. Back in 1941, only two years after the Brazilian Victor de Correa had purchased the six-acre tropical garden to establish his Tropicana casino and cabaret, he'd hired the Russian-born American ballet dancer and choreographer of the Ballet Russe de Monte Carlo, David Lichine, to collaborate with the Cuban choreographer Julio Richards to create an Afro-Cuban ballet, *Congo Pantera*, featuring singers Rita Montaner and Bola de Nieve, and introducing drummers on platforms in the trees, mixed with a Busby Berkeley sense of spectacle. It was Montaner who brought the legendary Rodney (Roderico Neyra)—Cabrera Infante gives him a shout-out on the first page of *Tres tristes tigres*—a small man from an impoverished background who was afflicted with leprosy, into the company after saving him from being sent to a leprosarium. Rodney would be the Tropicana choreographer for years, after the nightclub's ownership had passed in 1949 from de Correa to the also-revered Martin Fox, its last capitalist owner. Rodney can be understood as the personification of what Ned Sublette meant when, in his landmark book *The Music of Cuba*, he wrote that "whatever happened on stage happened better in the barrio"—he was a master of bringing the latter to the former. Rodney founded the satellite dance company of young, mostly unschooled female performers that became known as "Las Mulatas de Rodney" and later as "Las Mulatas de Fuego," who, after he sent them to Mexico, became an international sensation, shattering racial and sexual taboos, brown-skinned women dancing mambos in bikinis—in photographs they are jaw-droppingly gorgeous, sassy looking, and sexy—and featuring the young guaracha singer Celia Cruz. When, as a young boy, Armando Pérez saw Gene Kelly in *Singin' in the Rain,* he knew wanted to be a dancer. He and his twin brother studied at the Vocational School of Modern Dance, beginning their careers as dancers on television. Once they joined the Tropicana, they trained and performed under the guidance of Santiago Alfonso, whom Armando describes as "touched by God." Studying under Santiago, he said, instilled "demanding discipline and rigor, and he formed you as an artist."

More than once Armando abruptly paused in our conversation to call out instructions to Lourdes and the dancers on the stage, now rehearsing in the velvety shadows of the giant trees and of twilight. "The new one is separating her feet too much," he shouted, and a moment later, "She's doing it wrong, have her open up so that the heel turns outward!"

I kept stealing glances at the rehearsal, finding, just as I had twenty-four years before, that the young dancers' lithe athleticism was even more apparent, and that the grace with which they executed even the simplest arm and hand gestures, the light, quick, and precise synchronicity of their steps, was even more beautiful and transfixing to watch in the intimacy and simplicity of a rehearsal than amid the full-blown show.

"When she does her demi-plié," Armando called out, "turn the heel, so you can see the line of the foot better." Returning to the subject of his own years as a Tropicana dancer, he said, "All I had to do was dance and the people would applaud me, and that was my thing. And then I'd wake up the next day and come here and I wouldn't leave. It absorbs your whole life. You lose your friends, your relationships." He remembers with special fondness the preparations for the inauguration of a new show, the intense rehearsals conducted before that night's show and after it that continued until dawn. He and his twin brother were dancers for seventeen years, and famously performed with a pair of female dancers who were also twins, Mery and Ketty, who now live in Tampa. "It abuses your body, the muscles and bones wear out," said Armando of his long dancing career. In the mornings all his joints ache (mine do, too, I told him). "Movement makes you live," he said. He never wanted to stop dancing, but now he channels his own desire to dance into the dances he choreographs and directs. He is always thinking of new moves and dances, and of tweaking and perfecting the existing ones.

"Life is constant learning," he said. From the new generations, he learns new rhythms, many that come from the United States, and incorporates them. Armando also spoke about that Cuban idiosyncrasy that he finds at the heart of Cuban cabaret, which he defines as joy, dance, rhythm, the cultural catharsis of Caribbean carnival wedded to a kind of vaudeville. You take a bel canto "'O Sole Mio," he explained, and arrange it to bachata, and it becomes universal in a new way. "The Cuban woman," he said, "is still the symbol of the spectacle, the sensuality of Cuban women, down to the rhythm and musicality of the way they walk." He tells the story of how close this Cuban world of the lavish cabaret came to disappearing in the early years after the Revolution. Two of the great casino cabarets, the San Souci and the Montmartre, had already been razed when the bulldozers came for the Tropicana. But the Tropicana was saved, Armando recounted, by a young militant named Miliki, who like his mother before him worked at the nightclub, in the kitchen: Miliki went out to confront the bulldozers wearing his *milicia* uniform. It wasn't only his understanding of what the cabaret meant to Cuban popular culture, but his own sense of belonging that Miliki was defending, said Armando. He got a chance to give his arguments to Raúl Castro. For many years after, Miliki was the Tropicana's administrator.

It's that sense of belonging, said Armando, that the young dancers most lack now, and that it is his greatest challenge to try to instill in them and make them commit to. Every dancer, he said, is a distinct individual, of course, but they've been affected by the way the times have changed. Most were born in the Special Period. They grew up in an era of great uncertainty on the island—just as so much remains uncertain now—and of "lost values." Armando said that "the idea of the Revolution shaping *el hombre nuevo o la mujer nueva* [the new man or the new woman]" had lost the meaning it held before.

Was he saying that he tried to reawaken in them a sense of belonging to the Revolution? I asked.

"Oh, no, no, no," said Armando. "I want to make them love this place, and to give themselves over to this life. Getting them to love this place, and to feel that they belong to it, that's the hardest challenge, but we do manage to achieve it."

The show is soon to begin. But before we leave, we return to say good-bye to Lourdes in her office, where she is sitting at her desk going over the cast roster for the night's show. One of the young dancers, Anaelys Martin, happens to be there, and we get a chance to talk to her for a moment. She tells us about the stages of her long education in dance, the first classes when she was four, her early schooling in the Casa de Cultura, entering the Escuela Nacional de Art when she was twelve, the Vocational School of Modern Dance at fifteen, three more years in the School of Stage Arts, studying dance and ballet.

Lourdes interjects to explain that Anaelys's finishing training in that last school was in the repertoire and techniques of what we'd talked about the other day, Cubanidad, those idiosyncrasies that are expressed, she said, "so gesturally." Lourdes said that back then, "I could see her talent. It doesn't take a lot of work to notice somebody who lives to dance."

Anaelys auditioned for all the companies, for television, for the Tropicana and the other cabarets. She was accepted into the Tropicana's school. It was her dream to one day be a Tropicana dancer, but she didn't feel ready. "I was still just a big girl," she said. She spent six years dancing at the Havana Parisien cabaret as a soloist before entering the Tropicana over a year ago. Now she's twenty-five. "This place steals your life," she says. "Your social life is here." She said, "I thought I'd learned everything," but in the daily classes at the Tropicana, whether in ballet or contemporary or folkloric dance, she finds herself constantly learning. "It's technique, it's a way of feeling; here you have to dance in a way that's *larger*."

Lupe Guzmán turned out to be easy to find. Armando hadn't known how to contact her, either, and had suggested I ask Santiago Alfonso, but even if I'd wanted to try that, our time in Havana was up. But it turns out that all you have to do is type in *Lupe Guzmán* and *Tropicana* on Facebook, and she pops right up. Once I'd returned to Mexico City, I went to see Lupe in the apartment she shares with her daughter Lianette and her four-year-old granddaughter, Mimi—she's already a model, too, featured in Mexican advertisements for Huggies—in Colonia Napoles. She said that she and her daughter have an apartment in Miami, too; she also still has her apartment in Havana and returns whenever she can, but now, she said, it is her devotion to her granddaughter that rules her life.

Her hair is still blond; she may no longer be as lithe as she used to be, her face a bit more lined—whose isn't?—but she's still very recognizably Lupe, both high strung and effusively warm at the same time. Lupe performed until she was forty-eight. It wasn't until one night in 2001, when she went out onstage to dance and suddenly found that she couldn't move, her sciatic pain was so strong, that her career ended. She would never perform her signature dive or even dance onstage again; she was forced to retire. She begins to cry, nearly to sob, as she recounts those days when she had to accept that her legendary dancing career was finally over. She's had two operations for herniated discs. After she stopped dancing, she told me, she fell into a long and severe depression. "I was very sad, for a year I did nothing, I was always crying." But Santiago Alfonso—Lupe refers to him as "a luminous being"—never left her alone. He'd told her that she could still have a career as a teacher, that she'd be a wonderful dance teacher. "But I didn't want to be a teacher," said Lupe. "I wanted to be a dancer." She credits him with pulling her out of her depression, doting on her—if anyone knew how to nurture a true diva, Santiago did—and convincing her that she could have a wonderful life as a dance teacher in his own dance company, where she soon became the regisseur. And she enjoyed it. *"Fue bien bonita la experiencia"* (It was a lovely experience). Until she held the newborn Mimi in her arms for the first time and thought, Here it all ends; from now on I'm going to go wherever my daughter goes, and I'm going to be the super *abuela*.

The Tropicana was her life, though. "If I could die and be born again," said Lupe, "I'd want to do it all over again, I wouldn't change anything." She was a ballerina in the ballet company of Camagüey when she heard that the Tropicana was looking for a classically trained dancer. It had been the dream of her life to dance there, and she entered the company as a soloist in 1973. She made friends for life, lived through beautiful and sometimes trying times with them. "We were a big family. You always spent more time in the Tropicana than in your own home. When we'd go out, we'd all go out together, to see the other shows." Once Lupe recalled a hurricane closed down the Tropicana for a week, and what a special time that was, when the whole company, including directors and kitchen staff, came to work every day anyway to help repair the damage, cleaning away downed trees and branches. She told me about the time when Fidel came to a show, and how she got to stand next to him onstage, and how she took hold of his beard, which she says was as soft as the hair on a baby's head, and held his hand, the softest, finest hand, she effused, that she's ever held. She showed me an extraordinary photo that she keeps in her phone, of Tropicana dancers in lamé costumes and shiny bathing-cap-like headpieces, all tightly crowded around Fidel, Lupe standing the closest, her large dark eyes beaming up at him.

At one point Lupe asked me if I was going to pay her for our interview. I was again struck by what a sensible request that is and by a sense of surprise that I don't hear it more often. Leave it to a culture new to capitalism to realize that time should be economically valued, too. But what will happen to journalism and all the other interview-driven forms if it catches on? Well, at least I had brought Lupe a little box of chocolates.

And, of course, we talked about her famous leap, which was called *el vuelo del pájaro* (the flight of the bird). "I'd always been a dancer who took risks, and who was in the air all the time." But no leap was more memorable than one she performed in Italy once, on television. The traveling Tropicana company was performing in a circus tent there. A long pole with a ladder on the side held the tent up at its highest point. Santiago suggested that during the show she perform the leap from midway up. But one day a crew from Italy's RAI television came to the show, along with some Italian ballet dancers, and Lupe began to climb the pole for her leap and just kept climbing, past the four-meter mark where she was supposed to stop. She heard Santiago shouting below, "Lupe, stop!" but she kept going. She'd nearly reached the top when she stopped and looked down and saw that everyone looked very small. *"Díos mio,"* she said to herself, "what did I do?" She'd climbed nearly seven meters, some twenty-two feet. She heard the drums and the music and threw herself into the air, and then she heard the applause.

SODOM'S BOOKSTORE

BY RUBÉN GALLO
TRANSLATED BY LISA CARTER

Eliezer was one of the first people I met in Cuba. It was 2002, and a Princeton professor by the name of Peter Johnston—the epitome of a WASP: very white, tall, thin, serious, with blue eyes that stared intently ahead, expressionless—had invited me to accompany a group of students to the island. Peter had been traveling to Havana for years and knew many of its writers. He took me to Antón Arrufat's house; to Reina María Rodríguez's rooftop; to visit a young novelist who had just won a prize for his novel *El paseante cándido*. "That Peter knows everyone. Word has it he's CIA," a friend would later confess.

"You've got to meet Eliezer—he's the best bookseller in Havana," Peter Johnston said one day.

We took a taxi to El Vedado, got out in front of the Coppelia ice cream parlor, and walked until we reached an entrance on L Street bordered by four simple pillars. We knocked, and a voice from inside shouted: "It's open!"

Upon entering, we found ourselves in someone's living room: there were lace curtains, dusty and lit up by a neon sign; porcelain figurines—angels and shepherds; and, in the middle of the room, an older couple sitting in rocking chairs, watching one of those big old cabinet television sets. They must have been about sixty. She was in a bathrobe; he was wearing shorts and a muscle shirt that rose up to show his hairy belly.

"Eliezer?" Peter asked, getting straight to the point as always, wasting no time on useless pleasantries.

We must have come to the wrong place, I thought. Weren't we coming to see a bookseller? This was an old couple's home, and it smelled musty.

The man paid no attention to us and remained fixed on the TV, but his wife replied without looking at us: "In the back, down there, see," pointing to a door at the far end of the room. The image on-screen was blurry, in black and white, of a news anchor.

We crossed the living room, passing between the old couple and the television, came to the door, and walked into a bedroom. There, sitting on a chair, surrounded by piles of books stacked on the floor—some of the heaps reached as high as the ceiling—was Eliezer, a very handsome young man, about thirty years old, with thin, dark eyes and classic Arab features. Must be of Lebanese descent, like so many Cubans, I thought. His gaze was intense, his smile mischievous.

"Peter," Eliezer said, as if he had been expecting us. "I got a first edition of *Paradiso* for you."

"We already have it," Peter replied drily.

"I also got a real gem for you," Eliezer went on as he rummaged through one of the piles. "Wait until you see this."

He pulled out a book seemingly at random and passed it to Peter. I was amazed the tower of books hadn't come down with it.

"Look at this gem. You won't find another copy in Cuba, or anywhere else in the world most likely. It's the album from Saddam Hussein's visit to Havana in 1979. Wait until you see this picture. Look: Saddam with Fidel and Raúl. Can you imagine? Take it . . ."

Eliezer was asthmatic and would run out of breath halfway through a sentence: he paused to inhale, and the constant interruptions lent a breathy, mysterious quality to the conversation: "Look at this . . . eeegh . . . Can you imagine . . . eeegh . . . that dictator . . . eeegh . . . here in Havana?"

"How much?" Peter asked.

"For you . . . fifty dollars. I'm giving it away."

"Fine," Peter said. "And have you got any material on churches? I'm interested in documents about Protestant churches in Cuba—pamphlets, fliers—for the Ephemera Collection at Princeton."

"Not right now, but I'll get some for you. What I do have is this. Look: *Los siete contra Tebas,* the banned book by Antón Arrufat. An autographed copy."

"We already have it," Peter said.

"This is the essay that won the Casa de las Américas Prize this year. It sold out, but if you see here—"

"I'm only interested in Protestant church pamphlets."

I listened to the conversation and the haggling while contemplating, in amazement, the piles of books all around me. There wasn't a single bookshelf or a single cabinet in the entire room, just towers of novels, books of poetry and essays. How many? A thousand? Two thousand? A lot, in any event. And Eliezer seemed to know the inventory of these insane depths by heart: he could find a book and pull it out of a stack in a matter of seconds.

"I'll come back tomorrow for those Protestant pamphlets," Peter said.

"Come whenever you like . . . eeegh . . . You know I'm always here."

We walked back through the living room, the old couple still in exactly the same place, their eyes still glued to the TV. "Revolution is construction," a voice announced over images of workers pouring concrete.

Out in the street, as we walked back to the Hotel Habana Libre, Peter told me about Eliezer. He had been studying history at the University of Havana, but his studies were interrupted during the Special Period, when there was also no power at the university and no food in the student cafeterias. It was during those desperate times, when everyone had to invent some way to survive, that he began to sell books, first on a sidewalk in the El Vedado district and then in the Plaza de Armas. He did so well that, within a few months, he was able to rent a room from the old couple to receive customers somewhere a little more discreet, because at the time it was illegal to run a business.

A clandestine bookstore! I recalled how Eliezer had kept his voice low and would glance at the door as he showed us his treasures. I also remembered how, upon arriving at the airport, the customs agents had checked every one of my books and written DOCS on my baggage tag: they were looking for book smugglers, the way customs agents in other countries pursue drug smugglers. Books instead of drugs: one of the many peculiarities of this island, a paradise for bibliophiles.

The next day at the breakfast buffet, a hotel employee handed me a note from Peter. As was his custom, he had written it on Princeton letterhead:

I forgot to tell you that, for legal reasons, it is ABSO-
LUTELY FORBIDDEN to ride in three-wheeled vehicles.
They are extremely DANGEROUS and university insurance
does not cover accidents that occur while in them.

Three-wheeled vehicles? It took me a minute to understand
that Peter was referring to cocotaxis, those yellow motorcycles
with a Pac-Man-shaped cab, which were the most entertain-
ing, efficient way to get around Havana: they race along the
Malecón, transporting fair-haired tourists, long hair blowing in
the breeze. Oh, Peter! I thought.

I left the hotel, flagged down a cocotaxi, and asked the driver
to take me through the streets of Centro Habana. He was a
strapping twenty-five-year-old, with muscular brown arms,
sculpted in the gym of life. Like so many Cubans, he radiated
sexual energy. He told me that he drove a cocotaxi three days a
week and a regular taxi the other three days.

"Which do you like better? The cocotaxi or the regular?"

"I prefer the regular taxi."

"Why is that?"

"With a regular taxi, if a tourist gets in, I can take him wher-
ever he wants to go, anywhere."

"Anywhere?"

"I'm here to make the tourist happy. You get me?"

As he spoke, I stared at the black curls escaping from his
helmet and the shapely biceps that flexed every time he turned
the handlebars to change direction.

"And if I were to tell you to take me to Camagüey?" I asked.

"To Camagüey? Well, that's far . . . really far. We'd have to
come to an agreement. Here, take my phone number."

I noted his number—William was his name—as he sped us

along the Paseo del Prado. In two minutes we were in front of Trocadero No. 162, one of those mythical addresses in the history of literature, like Boulevard Haussmann No. 102, or the corner of Río Guadalquivir and Reforma in Mexico City.

Trocadero: I had always imagined the street in an elegant section of Havana, like its Parisian namesake, which has a view of the Seine and is flanked by the mansions where so many of Proust's friends lived. But the Cuban Trocadero was a dusty street in Centro Habana, full of crumbling buildings, with mountains of garbage on the sidewalk and shirtless kids sitting in doorways. It looked more like Africa than Paris.

José Lezama Lima's home was now a small museum: three rooms that housed the writer's furniture, paintings, photographs, and part of his library, locked away in sealed bookcases.

"May I consult the books? I'm actually writing about Lezama and Proust," I said to an employee in a government uniform.

"Well, you can't exactly consult them, no. You can, however, see them through the glass. The bookcases are sealed and can't be opened."

"Do you know if Lezama had Proust's novel in his library?"

"Well, what we've got here are Lezama's novels and the books he read, but not all of them. Some of them are at the National Library."

So poor, this Lezama Museum! Especially in comparison to museums like the Louvre and the Metropolitan, those transnational storehouses of first-world culture, with their luxury buildings, with armies of employees and million-dollar budgets. And yet this little and lonely museum—with its three employees in khaki uniforms and cats prowling the courtyard—seemed somehow more authentic. You could feel Lezama's spirit here.

The employees watched with curiosity as I studied the titles sealed away in the bookcases. No Proust. When I was done, the girl who sold tickets—in the same khaki uniform—asked:

"Where are you from?"

After leaving the Lezama Museum, I spent hours wandering through Centro Habana, dodging piles of rubble, motorcycles, and taxis. "Oyeee, oyeee" could be heard everywhere, and—as always happens whenever I walk through this neighborhood—I felt immeasurably happy to be surrounded by blacks and *mulatas*, old women sitting on stoops, and *jineteros* hustling boys, girls, cigars, pirated music, and almost everything else.

I walked back to the hotel, all along the Malecón, passing by Maceo Park and the Hotel Nacional de Cuba. By the time I got to La Rampa, I had decided to pay another visit to Eliezer and went through the ritual I had learned from Peter: I knocked on the door, said hello to the old couple, walked through the living room, past the television, until I reached the door at the end. Eliezer walked up to me with a bright white smile and held out a hand as he said: "Look what I've got for you. First edition of Virgilio Piñera's short stories, published in Buenos Aires. It's the only copy anywhere in Havana. And not only that: look at this dedication. 'To my friend Gombrowicz, with admiration from your Cuban disciple. Buenos Aires, May 1954.' It's dangerous for me to have a treasure like this here: someone might steal it. You take it."

The price—two hundred dollars—was more than I had left for the rest of my trip, but Eliezer didn't give up. He opened two folding chairs that were propped in a corner; we sat down, and he continued to propose treasures.

"Look here," he said. "It's a book of poetry by a lost Ori-

genista. Have you read María Zambrano? You can't get any-
thing of hers in Cuba, but I've got a novel that came out in
Mexico. And look at this: the speech Carpentier gave at the Pi-
oneers' first youth congress in '63. Can you imagine? Not even
the Fundación Alejo Carpentier has a copy. A friend brought it
to me, an old guy who knew Carpentier, went to the event with
him, and kept one of the handouts. The great Neo-Baroque
novelist speaking to a bunch of twelve-year-olds. Do you think
they understood a word he said?"

Eliezer's little room was a library of Babel that seemed to
contain the entire canon of Cuban literature. You only had to
mention an author from the island—Julián del Casal, Gertrudis
Gómez de Avellaneda, Lydia Cabrera—and, as if by magic, he
would pull out a copy that also had a whole story around it: a
first edition, signed by the author, a bookplate from a famous
collection, a banned work, an avant-garde journal published in a
far-off province . . .

Among the thousands of tomes, there were a few treasures:
books by Guillermo Cabrera Infante, Reinaldo Arenas, Severo
Sarduy, and other exiled writers. "I don't show this to anyone,"
he would say as he surreptitiously pulled a book out from under
a chair or behind a curtain. "Look at this treasure: *Pájaros de
la playa*, Sarduy's posthumous novel about his illness. Did you
know he died of AIDS? A friend brought me this from Spain. I
don't know how he got it through customs. If they'd caught him,
they'd have arrested him. Can you imagine? It's the story of an
island full of terminal patients, young men aged by disease . . .
the bomb. This book, it's a criticism of the UMAP* camps and

---

* Editor's note: UMAP is an initialism for the Unidades Militares de
Apoyo a la Producción, or Military Units to Aid Production, a euphemis-

what the government did to gay men in the eighties: lock them up. If they ever find me with this, they'll lock me up, too."

Apart from being Babelic, Eliezer's bookstore was also monothematic: every single book about Cuba was there, but nothing else. There wasn't a single foreign author, unless it was a Hemingway or a Humboldt who had written about the island. Carlos Fuentes? From the look on Eliezer's face, I suspected he had never even heard of him. Borges? "No, never had a book by Borges here . . ." Vargas Llosa? "A year ago someone brought me a copy of *Conversación en la catedral,* but, being a banned book, it didn't last long. I sold it for a mint. Have you ever seen *Fresa y chocolate*? In the sixties, we Cubans could recite the first page of *Conversación* by heart: it was a form of protest."

We were chatting like this when I heard a door close behind me. Eliezer stood up.

"Well, look at that. I didn't think I'd ever see you here again," he said to the visitor.

As I turned to see who had come in, I came face-to-face with a six-foot-five blond, with a gymnast's body and a pair of impressive biceps, who looked like he had just stepped off the page of *Vogue Italia* or *International Male*. Bronzed skin, long hair, blue eyes, and muscles everywhere. Was he Swedish? Norwegian? Danish? A Nordic athlete? A Scandinavian bodybuilder?

"You speak Spanish?" I asked.

"*Sí,*" the Viking replied. "Michael," he said, offering his hand.

"And where are you from, Michael?"

"I'm from Granma."

---

tic name the Cuban government gave to work camps from 1965 to 1969, where homosexuals and all those who did not fit within the revolutionary parameters were detained.

Granma?

In the region of Oriente, over five hundred miles away, is the beach where Fidel Castro disembarked before heading into the Sierra Maestra mountain range: he arrived on board a yacht called *Granma,* which he had bought from an American in Mexico, and after the Revolution, the province was named after it, as were the official newspaper and many other things in Cuba. The American had chosen that name in honor of his grandma. And so the yacht—which is on display at the Museum of the Revolution— the newspaper, the province, and even this Viking continue, to this day, to honor that little old lady who, unbeknownst to her, became the grandmother of the Cuban Revolution. How many great things had been given to this island by that anonymous grandma?

"From Granma? But you look Swedish. Is your family Scandinavian?" I asked, expecting a story about Communist parents who had come to Cuba to support the Revolution.

"Huh? Swedish? No. I'm from Granma. My family is from Granma."

Maykel—I later learned that's how his name was spelled— had a hick accent and when he spoke he filled the room with fresh country air.

"From Granma, but I moved here for work."

"What do you do?"

"I'm a baker," Maykel said.

Maykel was wearing a tight sleeveless white T-shirt that delineated every muscle in his back. The very spectacle of that body—freckled shoulders, triceps, long arms—made me dizzy.

Eliezer had observed our interaction in silence, his smile dripping with irony. How did he know Maykel? This baker did not look like a bookworm.

"Tell me about Granma," I said. "What's life like there?"

"Well . . . I live in the country there. It's not like here in Havana. It's different."

Maykel told me that he had left Granma because of a girlfriend; she was so jealous that one day she found him talking with the neighbor and went crazy. She went into the kitchen for a knife and threatened him, screamed that she would kill them both, but then, no, she would kill herself, and Maykel had to tackle her to get the knife and stop her from slitting her wrists. She made such a scene that the police came and nearly arrested all three of them. The girlfriend was a lost cause, so he decided to move to Havana.

"I didn't do anything wrong. I was chatting with the neighbor. But my girlfriend doesn't understand. *Muchacho,* the problem is that there in Granma, everyone stares at me. It's not my fault; it's just the way it is. I go out, and people stare, and the girl loses it. That's why I came to Havana."

"And people here don't stare at you?" I asked.

"Well, yeah. They stare here, too. But at least no one's monitoring my every move."

"What do you mean, people stare?" I insisted.

"Just that. If we were to go out now, you'd see: people stare at me."

"Let's go see what that's like. A *guajiro* peasant from Granma walking around El Vedado, and people staring at him," Eliezer said with the same enthusiasm as when he talked about books. "A baker from Granma strutting down La Rampa. We have to see that."

Maykel smiled in amusement at Eliezer's words.

The three of us left the room—the old couple was still glued to their TV—and headed out into the street. Night was falling and the sky had clouded over with birds heading to roost in the trees of El Vedado. Just before we reached La Rampa, as we walked past the Cine Yara, Maykel said: "Walk behind me so you can see how people stare."

Eliezer and I let Maykel walk a few steps ahead. He moved as if he were a runway model, strutting through the crowds: cute couples on their way to the movies, office workers waiting for the bus, students on their way to Coppelia for ice cream. Maykel wiggled hips and shoulders, but—despite his handsome, muscular physique—there was something awkward about the way he moved. He was much sexier when he stood still and said nothing. When he walked, he looked like a robot, a bad actor bumbling across the stage. Maykel paraded to the corner, then stopped and turned around.

"Did you see how people stared?" he asked with pride.

But in fact—poor Maykel!—no one had even looked at him. The streets were teeming with sexy, athletic, seductive bodies; amid all that beauty, Maykel had passed unnoticed.

The following day—my last before returning to New York—I went back to visit Eliezer.

"I got you another book by Severo Sarduy," he said upon seeing me. "Look: erotic sonnets that hide pornographic scenes. Do you know how it begins? *'Omítemela más.'* Can you imagine? Omission becomes a synonym of penetration. Take it . . . you'd be doing me a favor. Can you imagine if the police found this here?"

"And Maykel?" I asked.

"The baker from Granma is probably out *jineteando,* chasing after foreigners," he said with his impish smile. "That's what the entire province lives off: *jineterismo,* hustling."

I told him it was my last night in Havana and said, "Let me

take you out for dinner. Peter recommended a family-run *pala-dar* nearby."

Eliezer grew serious and replied, "I don't go to restaurants with foreigners."

"What, do you think I'm going to rape you? We're going to dinner, not to a brothel."

"I've never been to a restaurant. On principle."

"Principle? I don't know what you're thinking, but I'm inviting you because I like you, I like talking to you. We'd continue the conversation over a glass of wine and a plate of *croquetas*. The *paladar*'s nearby, up on a rooftop filled with shaded plants. We'll sit outside, and you can tell me more about Maykel and your books."

"I never eat at night," Eliezer said, his expression unchanged. "And I'm not going to a restaurant."

There was no way to convince him.

I gave him a hug and said good-bye. That night, as I ate alone at the Hotel Habana Libre restaurant—an enormous room with a socialist vibe, full of pasty tourists and waiters dressed in black bow ties—I thought of Eliezer a few blocks away, eating all alone in his little book-filled room, as the old couple sat, still glued to their television.

After that trip, I lost touch with Eliezer for several years. Back then, there were still no cell phones or e-mail on the island; you disconnected from friends when you left, until your next trip. When I finally got back to Havana—in 2005 or 2006?—I figured he had probably moved houses, or, like so many Cubans I had met on that first trip, might be living in Miami by now.

I asked after Eliezer when I met with Antón Arrufat.

"Didn't you hear?" he asked in surprise. "*Chico,* they nearly put him in jail."

"What did he do?"

"Nothing. He didn't do anything. But they accused him of illicit gain—you know it's forbidden to do business in this country. They took him to trial, but us writers helped him out: we went to testify that no, he wasn't doing business, he was offering a library service to help novelists, exchanging books and supporting Cuban culture. I went with Reina and Jorge Ángel, and a few others, and we signed a statement to get him out."

"What's he doing now?"

"What's he doing? The same as always: selling books and telling stories. He makes me dizzy. I haven't seen him since the trial. The other day, I walked by the store but didn't go in: every time I see him, he pulls out a stack of books for me to sign because autographed copies are worth more. I hate seeing him at book launches; he shows up with three or four of those *guajiro* peasants that are always around him, and they buy up the whole edition—down to the last copy. To top it all off, they buy them in local currency and sell them in dollars. Last year, I had given away all my copies of *Entre él y yo.* I had to go buy one from him and it cost me an arm and a leg."

"Do you know a friend of his by the name of Maykel, from Granma?"

"From Granma? No, *chico,* I don't. Why? Should I?"

That night I went to visit Eliezer. Everything was exactly the same—the house, the old couple watching TV, the little room in back full of books, although he seemed to have acquired many more in the past few years. There used to only be piles of books along the walls and now they were everywhere: in the middle of the room, on the chairs, in the hallways.

Eliezer greeted me as if we'd seen one another the day before:

"Look at this: it's a bomb. *Fuera del juego* by Herberto Padilla. Do you know the story? They put him in jail, he had to write a statement of self-criticism, and a whole commotion erupted around the world. This edition is from Miami and contains blurbs from all sorts of people. If they find me with this, they'll jail me for sure."

Eliezer didn't seem particularly traumatized by his encounter with the Cuban justice system. He was even talking about expanding the bookstore: "I'm looking for a bigger place. I can't fit everything in here anymore. I told the old couple I need another room, that they should rent me their bedroom. They're always in the living room—they can just sleep there and give me their room for my books. But they don't want to. As soon as I find something bigger, I'll move. I'm going to put up bookshelves and have it all organized."

"And Maykel?"

"Maykel had a kid but is still hustling around Central Park. His woman lost it. She called him a fag and yelled at him. He told her he did it for her and their son, and there was this whole uproar. Can you imagine? Whoring to support his kid."

"So he doesn't come around here?"

"He hasn't. But you've got to meet this other guy, newly arrived from Holguín. He's like Maykel: blond, blue-eyed, looks like a movie star. He's got a bicycle taxi, but that's just an excuse to ride tourists. He comes by every evening. Drop by tomorrow around seven and I'll introduce you."

"Another time. I leave for Santiago tomorrow."

I realized that Eliezer's world, like Freud's unconscious mind, was timeless. Eliezer wasn't fazed in the slightest by announcements of arrivals and departures, news of international flights and travel plans, because he lived in a static world that never changed. All that marked the passage of time were his

books, piling up over the weeks and years: grains of sand in a big
Havana hourglass. What would happen when the last grain fell?

After that trip, it was years—nearly a decade—before I returned
to Havana again, and during that time so much happened: Fidel
Castro fell ill and withdrew from politics; Raúl rose to the presi-
dency; private property was legalized and so were *cuentapropistas*,
those small-scale entrepreneurs; Mariela Castro campaigned for
LGBT rights.

When I arrived in March 2014, I noticed changes the minute
I got into a taxi at the airport. I recalled how, on my first trip,
before I'd learned the hand signals, I had been careless enough
to ask the driver—a lovely, candid woman in her thirties—what
she thought of Fidel Castro.

"Shhh!" she hushed me. The rearview mirror revealed the
panic in her eyes. "Don't say his name. Do this," she said, using
her right hand to stroke a long, imaginary beard, then changed
the subject and asked me about life in New York.

But that was then. This time, my taxi driver was a plump,
chatty man. Once we had left the airport, I asked: "So, how are
things going with Raúl?"

"Raúl?" he growled. "That piece of shit? He just fucked the
country more than we were fucked already," he said as a prelude
to launching into a list of complaints that was also a review of
the last fifty years of Cuban history. "Angola?" he demanded.
"We went over to Angola to fight, and now that they've got cash,
do you think those ungrateful black bastards remember Cuba?
Not so much as a thank you. Do you know how many of us went
over there? We went to do a job and to fight for those bastards
who are now oil millionaires and don't even remember socialism.

Angola! Then we had to get through the Special Period. And the Russians, who were supposedly our best friends? Do you think the Russians sent a dime? No! We're practically dying of hunger and it's as if we don't exist, after their missiles nearly get us caught up in a world war. Do you think they remember that?"

There was no stopping the monologue that seemed to cover it all—from Sierra Maestra to the alliance with Venezuela—and lasted until we reached the hotel.

"Okay," the driver said, putting an end to his diatribe as he took the twenty-five Cuban convertible pesos I handed him as I got out.

Things were noticeably different around the Hotel Habana Libre, too. The surrounding streets had filled with small businesses: cafés, music stores, souvenir shops, and restaurants that offered food from around the world, everything from Italian to Iranian. The sidewalk in front of the hotel looked like a small bazaar filled with customers of every nationality: Germans and Brazilians, French and Mexicans, Italians and Argentines, all bartering with taxi drivers and getting on and off Transtur buses.

The only thing that hadn't changed in all those years was Antón Arrufat: he was still living in the same apartment on Trocadero and was still as sharp as ever. We headed out to one of the many new restaurants that had opened in Centro Habana, and he told me the latest gossip over dinner.

"Did you hear about Eliezer?" he asked.

"No. What happened?"

"With the new laws, he got himself an entrepreneur's license so his bookstore is now legit."

"He must be happy."

"Happy? Says he doesn't sell nearly as much now; what tourists wanted was the thrill of buying from a clandestine bookstore. Now that it's legal, no one comes. At least that's what he says."

"I'll go see him tomorrow. And I won't stop buying books from him."

"You'll see the house is quite different."

"Do you still have to walk through the old couple's living room?"

"The old couple? *Chico,* they died years ago. Rumor has it that Eliezer killed them to get the house."

"Do you believe that? How could he? They were so fat and he was so thin."

"He killed them like this . . ."

Antón's face assumed a naughty-boy look as he brought his two palms in front of my face and clapped an imaginary object between them.

"He asphyxiated them . . . with the dust from his books."

I went to see Eliezer the following day. The front porch was now crowded with bookshelves and tables at the entrance, displaying neat stacks of the Cuban Revolution's bestsellers: biographies of Che, speeches by Fidel, the works of Eduardo Galeano, accounts of the 26th of July Movement. The door to the living room was open, and I peeked in to confirm that the old couple really was gone. The interior was unrecognizable: gone was the furniture, the television, the figurines, the lace curtains. Books had taken over everywhere: there were mountains of them all over the place, barely enough room to get around—a bibliographic metastasis.

I tried to remember where the old couple had sat to watch TV, but it seemed impossible that this insalubrious storeroom had ever been a home. There was dust—and *churre,* the Cuban term for grime—everywhere. Clearly no one had cleaned in years. Books lay open on the floor, covers ripped off or crumpled under the weight of other books. And from it all, there exuded a pungent, acrid stench.

"Well, look who's here," Eliezer said, coming out from among the mounds of books, using his arms to keep his balance, as if sliding down the side of a cliff.

He was the same, or near enough. No longer the handsome thirty-year-old, he was still thin and trim, sporting the mischievous look I knew so well.

"I've got a new book for you, about all that's happening in this country. It's called *Al otro lado del espejo* and it caused quite a stir: it tells the whole story, about *jineteros*, prostitution, the *guajiros* who come to Havana from the provinces to chase tourists," he said, as if picking up a conversation we'd started the day before.

"Nice to see you," I said. "You haven't changed. But the house has. What happened to the old couple?"

"Poor things passed away," he said, and I thought I caught an ironic glint in his eyes.

Apart from books, the house was also now full of dogs. I had seen three or four lying in the entrance as I came in. I thought they were strays, until I saw a tiny one come out from between the stacks, following Eliezer, and then three more sleeping among the piles. They were runty and mangy, and smelled horrible. The stench permeated everything, including Eliezer. The tiny dog began to bark, sharp yips that didn't stop until Eliezer shouted, "Nachi! Enough! Shut up!" as he lifted her up in his arms.

"*Compañero*, you wouldn't have any medical texts, would you?" asked a young student who had come in to browse.

"No, we don't sell those here," Eliezer replied curtly.

"And that radio, how much is it?"

Eliezer was now also selling old radios; models from the forties and fifties were on display on a table next to speeches by Fidel.

"They sell in dollars. Thirty each."

"Thirty dollars!" the student repeated, aghast.

"They're more than fifty years old," Eliezer said, but the student was already out the door and didn't hear him.

"Naaachi!" Eliezer said in that voice people often use when talking to babies, high pitched and childlike, as he rocked the dog in his arms. "I know you're jealous, but I have to speak to customers." Then, to me: "Do you know why she's called Nachi? There are two of them, both puppies I picked up when they were abandoned. This one is Nachi, which is China transposed. Do you know why? China is Raúl Castro's nickname. Her sister is Elfid, which is Fidel transposed. You see? Two female dogs named after the two brothers. Do you know how I got them? Before the old couple died, they rented a room to a *jinetera*. After they got sick, I didn't want any trouble with the police, so I threw her out. Can you imagine? They accuse me of being a pimp and throw me in jail. She left behind two puppies in the wardrobe. She hid them there so the old couple wouldn't find them. And then she was just going to leave them there to die. You see how mean people can be? I found them and thought: I don't want the same thing to happen to them that has happened to us under the Castros."

A dogfight had erupted at my feet: a black one leaped on the back of a white one, biting her, as a gray one tried unsuccessfully to get into the game. The three tousled and nipped.

"Let me show you something," Eliezer said, lifting Nachi way up.

"Isn't that right, Nachi?" Eliezer said, his lips practically against the dog's snout, as if about to kiss her, speaking in such a piercing voice that it made him sound like a kid having a tantrum. "You'll never snitch on me, right, Nachi?"

Nachi—who was up above Eliezer's head—raised her snout to the ceiling and, as Eliezer continued to ask, "Isn't that right, Nachi?" let out a long, deep howl, as if responding to her master's exhortations with that sharp, interminable complaint, her desperate wail filling the bookstore.

"You'll never snitch on me, right, Nachi?" Eliezer repeated as the dog howled louder and louder. Some of the other dogs had woken from their slumber and joined in her melancholy yowl. Wooow wooow wooow wooow. Wooow wooow wooow wooow. A cacophony of dogs howled and barked around Eliezer as he continued to ask, "Isn't that right, Nachi?" and glanced down in amusement at this canine circus, which lasted for several minutes, ending only when he brought his arms down and set Nachi on the floor.

"Did you see that?" he asked. "For me, taking in strays is a form of resistance. Can you imagine if State Security found out that my dogs are named Nachi and Elfid? What I'm doing is exposing how bad the people have it, so bad that we live like dogs. I live like my dogs: I sleep on the books like they do—over there, look, on that table by the entrance—and I eat what they eat. Whatever I earn, I spend on food for them and to pay the *guajiros* who help out. What I'm doing is showing the mess that this country is in, while they try to hide it. Look, let me show you something. Come."

Eliezer plunged into the mountains of books that filled what had once been the old couple's living room. I followed him, both of us treading over mounds of paper, advancing slowly as we stepped on copies of *La historia me absolverá,* Raúl's speeches, *El socialismo y el hombre nuevo,* all of which seemed to have been strategically placed under our feet. We finally reached the room at the back, where I had visited Eliezer the first time I came. He opened the door, and the room was unrecognizable: it was now roofless—up above you could see the blue Caribbean sky—and at my feet, lit up by rays of sunshine, was a pile of rubble: bricks, plaster, and cement.

"What happened?" I asked.

"The roof *capsized*," Eliezer said with his impish smile.

I saw Eliezer regularly over the few months I was there. I would stop to say hello whenever I went by the Hotel Habana Libre or Coppelia. Well, not always. Only when I had a free afternoon, because one needs hours to visit that world of books and dogs and *guajiros*. Sometimes, out of curiosity, I would look at my watch upon leaving and discover that I had just spent four hours in there.

On every visit, I noticed slight, barely perceptible changes: one day a new dog would appear and the off-key concert of barking would become even more cacophonous; another day I would be met by a helper I'd never seen before, some young man newly arrived from Holguín or Camagüey, Santiago or Guantánamo; sometimes I would notice how much taller the mountains of books had grown; other times I spotted new cracks spidering up the bookstore walls. One day, exhausted by the heat of summer and the noise on La Rampa, I asked Eliezer to take me into the back room, now a roofless patio, just to get away from the mounds of books and packs of dogs for a few minutes. I noticed something different as we walked in: there was no more rubble on the floor; everything seemed tidier; you could see more of the sky.

"Did you notice?" he asked. "A couple of black guys stole my roof."

"But the roof fell down. You told me it had *capsized*," I replied.

"But the beams were still there, wooden beams. So one day, a couple of black guys come along and tell me they can sell them to buy concrete to put up a new roof. I said okay. In a single morning, they took out all the beams: took them down and carried them out as if they were pencils, up on their shoulders as if they didn't weigh a thing. They never came back, and I was left with no roof and no beams. You can't trust anyone in this country, much less the blacks."

As we chatted, Eliezer's new helper had come over. He was about twenty-five, short, athletic, with a face like a thug. His skin was tanned by the sun, and he was wearing the same uniform that all bookstore helpers wore: a sleeveless white T-shirt that left his shoulders and arms bare.

"Ever since the blacks stole my roof, he's been my bodyguard," Eliezer said, pointing to the young man who stood watching us with arms crossed. "He's a police officer, but since they pay him a pittance, he comes here every afternoon and I pay him to look out for me."

"Police? He looks like a nice guy, though."

"Nice guy?" Eliezer laughed. "Reinier, show him."

Reinier looked around and with a magic wave lifted the bottom of his T-shirt to reveal a muscular belly and a gun tucked into his waistband. I barely caught the glimmer of metal: he immediately pulled his shirt back down and looked mischievously at us.

It was the first time I had ever seen a gun in Cuba.

"With a police officer from Sancti Spíritus here at the bookstore, we're safe. Plus, if you could only see," Eliezer whispered in my ear, loud enough that Reinier could hear, "what a way he's got with the foreigners. Yesterday, an Italian took him home and started to scream when he took out his gun. *Pericoloso, pericoloso,* he screamed, as if he were about to be killed. Later he loved it and kept cooing, *il fucile, il fucile.* Isn't that right?"

"Ey," Reinier smiled at us.

"Speaking of foreigners," Eliezer said, "have I got a gem for you: the first gay art exhibit in Cuba. They had to print the catalog abroad, and they shut the whole exhibit down after only two weeks. Wait until you see this. Hey," he said to Reinier, "go get it for me."

"The cookie one?" Reinier asked.

The catalog for the *Sex and the City* exhibit, curated by Píter Ortega, is a thin white pamphlet, printed in color on glossy paper, that includes the typical homoerotic photos and kitschy paintings that appear in gay art shows around the world. After several pages of inoffensive nudes, toward the end, is the work that unleashed the censors' ire: a photographic series called *La galleta*, or "The cookie." It shows a group of muscular, dark-skinned young males, without a stitch on, gathered in a circle, like a football huddle. The first photo shows them stroking biceps and triceps; the second one, kissing; in the third photo, one of them is holding a very common brand of cookie, a thin, round biscuit, in his hand; the fourth shows one of them holding his penis above the cookie; and the fifth captures the instant a whitish spurt drenches the biscuit. In the last image, one of the men—green eyes, pert nose—devours the soggy pastry.

"How about that cookie!" Eliezer said. "There was no way those photos could be printed here in Cuba: no printer would dare risk being arrested for pornography. That's when the Norwegian ambassador stepped in and had them printed abroad, in his country. Then when the show opened, all hell broke loose!

As you can imagine, all of the fags in Havana wanted to see this famous cookie, and the gallery became one big gay pride space. But the party didn't last. Within a few days, the police ordered the show closed. The catalogs sold out; this is the only one left in Cuba. Take it. It's dangerous for me to have it here. More so now that State Security has come by."

"State Security came to see you? Why? You've got your entrepreneur's license."

"They came to ask me about the Spaniard who was killed. Because he used to come here . . ."

"A Spaniard was killed?"

"Didn't you hear? Now, that was a ruckus. They nearly arrested me because he'd been here the day before he was murdered."

"Tell me what happened."

"He was a millionaire from Spain, owned all kinds of companies over there, and loved Cuba. He'd been coming here on vacation for years, would spend months at a time. Then, about two years ago, he retired and bought a house, a big huge mansion in El Vedado. He would come by the bookstore in his car and stay for hours talking about books and eyeing the *guajiros* while his driver waited outside. To see him you'd think he was a saint, but in actual fact he had a thing for criminals, the lowest of the low. He'd head out to the parks, and El Chivo beach, all the worst places at night. Then, yeah, one day they found him stabbed to death in the shadows of Centro Habana. So here is my advice to you: avoid the dark spots. Best to stay in the well-lit spots."

"The dark spots?"

"When they investigated the murder, they found out that he used to come here all the time, had been here the day before he was killed. So they came to interrogate me, thinking I must be his lover or partner in lust. They didn't believe me when I said he just came here to buy books, and I was never with him, never went into the dark spots with him. Since they didn't believe me, I had to go to court and testify. The good thing is, they found the guy who killed him and haven't been back here since. But they've got their eye on me and could come at any time. On the bright side, I've got a police officer to watch over me. Isn't that right, Reinier?"

"Ey," Reinier said with his little grin.

"Just imagine if the police come and find another police officer. I'd say, 'Why are you here to see me if a police officer's already here?'"

Reinier crossed his arms, as if posing.

"Be careful out there," Eliezer said to me. "Someone's killing gay men. A few months ago, they found Tony Díaz, a famous theater director, knifed to death in his own home. They say it was a robbery, but I don't believe it. As a foreigner, you need to be careful . . ."

"Anyhow, Eliezer: it's late. Besides, it's time for me to take a walk in the dark spots," I said before giving him a hug and heading out to stroll down La Rampa.

A few days later, as I was preparing my class—a seminar on urban culture in Cuba for a group of Princeton students at a café in El Vedado, I had an idea. What if I took the students to the bookstore and asked Eliezer to give them a lecture? Eliezer loved to talk, and the kids could have a firsthand experience of the Cuban baroque.

I arrived at the bookstore one day in February with a group of fifteen American twentysomethings. The night before, I had asked Eliezer to clear a path through the mountains of books, so the students could congregate in the back of the house, in the roofless room. The students piled out of the van—wearing shorts, T-shirts, and running shoes—and, following Eliezer's instructions, crossed the living room in single file, passing between piles of books, into the hallway.

"Careful: don't step on the pregnant dog!" Eliezer shouted.

Between two stacks, I noticed a dog the same color as the floor, sound asleep, not fussed in the slightest by shoes passing dangerously close to her head. The fifteen students zigzagged between the mountains of books, stepping on copies Eliezer had placed strategically on the only path through this bibliographic jungle: *La agricultura en Cuba,* by Fidel Castro; *Diarios de guerra,* by Raúl Castro; the speech by Comandante Ernesto Guevara at a ceremony to mark the second anniversary of the Union of Young Communists. As each student walked by, the books were subject to yet another stomp that broke their spines, ripped covers off, undid their stitching, and scattered pages all over the house. The university convoy left a battleground in its wake, printed cadavers and moribund tomes attracting the dogs' attention. Nachi walked over to one wounded notebook, sniffed it, lifted her leg, and emptied her bladder on the mess of papers.

Out in the roofless room, the students gathered around Eliezer. Nachi had followed him in and lay down at his feet. Reinier leaned against the doorjamb, as if guarding the entrance, adopting his usual cross-armed pose.

"I took a vow of poverty," Eliezer said, "and live here with these books. I sleep on that table you saw by the entrance. There's no bathroom or kitchen. It's a form of protest against our leaders—who live in their mansions with their gardens and pools, and hold obscene dinner parties—to show what has happened to the people. It's also a way to protect myself: when State

Security has come, when the police have come, they walk in and see this clutter, and think surely no political activity can go on in this dump. Then they see me and think I'm crazy, and they leave me alone. Although that's dangerous, too: they could cart me off to an insane asylum, commit me against my will. All they need is for the neighbors to sign a paper saying I'm nuts and, since they hate me, it would be a piece of cake. But that hasn't happened yet. There's a reason behind everything you see here. Why are there no bookshelves? You might think it's 'cause I'm messy, but that's not it. If I had shelves, and the books were organized by author or title, and State Security were to come here one day, they'd arrest me for possessing banned books. This way, they can come and they'll never know what I've got, never find all of the books by exiles and dissidents. And since everything smells of dog, they're not going to want to dirty their hands digging through these piles. This is a country that has wanted to control everything, but they'll never be able to control this bookstore. Chaos has been my protector."

"What kind of classification system," a short plump girl began, "do you use?"

Eliezer looked at her with his impish smile. He brought his index finger to his temple and tapped several times.

"The entire classification system is here in my head. Nothing's written down. I don't use a computer, or a phone, or a cell phone, or any technology. The only way to speak to me, to know whether I've got a book, is to come here. That's another form of protest. You've all heard of Yoani Sánchez, the dissident, with her blogs and her Internet accounts and all that? One day she came here wanting to write about the bookstore and to present me as a dissident. I told her she was wrong, that I worked for State Security—because she's the one who works for them—and she left in a huff. Can you imagine? She puts me up on her blog as a dissident, and the next day Security comes and shuts me down."

"Could I ask you, sir," a pale reed of a girl with long legs began, "why there are no women in your bookstore? You're male, your assistant is male, and the customers I've seen are male. It's like an all-male world."

"Of course, it's a male world. I can't hire women, for all kinds of reasons. First, if they see a woman working here, they'll say she's a whore and arrest me for being a pimp. Second, you can't trust women. Third, have you seen how big the piles of books are? I need people to help me pick up a pile, move it, carry it from room to room, and a woman can't do that. That's why the guys that work here have to be strong, like the police officer watching over us," Eliezer said, looking at Reinier.

Reinier still had that little smile on his face.

"I want to know," the blondest of the blondes began, "why the Afro-Cuban community isn't represented here at your bookstore."

"You want to know why there are no blacks? Imagine if State Security were to come one day and find me with a house full of blacks. Can you imagine? That's why I don't hire blacks: to protect myself. Better to have this blond policeman here."

"In your opinion," a Puerto Rican, the brightest student of them all, began, "how will the reestablishment of diplomatic relations between Cuba and the United States, as announced by presidents Castro and Obama, affect your bookstore?"

"I need to prepare to receive the number of people who'll be coming to the bookstore. Once the documentary comes out—a kid from the film school came here last year—it's going to be a problem: I don't have enough space for everyone who'll come. I need to get a whole army to fix the place up. Here in this room, I want to have an art gallery and also a space to screen the documentary, but that's going to cost a lot of money. I've got to redo the roof and repair the other rooms. This won't be just a bookstore: it'll be a cultural center."

"Tell us more about the documentary," I said to Eliezer.

"Nothing, just one day this kid showed up and said he wants to film me, with my books and my dogs. He came with his camera and wandered around. I was afraid he might be State Security, but then I saw he really did know about making a movie, so I let him film me. He wanted me on-screen with Nachi, so she made her acting debut. Like this, see."

Eliezer lifted Nachi up high, and the dog began to howl, her snout pointing to the sky, as Eliezer repeated the same scene as before, saying, "You'll never snitch on me, right, Nachi?" And Nachi howled as if she could imagine the persecution.

Wooow wooow wooow wooow, Nachi bawled.

"Can I take photos?" a freckled redhead asked me, holding up her iPhone.

"When he saw this," Eliezer continued, "he said this thing Nachi and I do is a performance. Can you imagine? A performance? I said no, it wasn't a performance but a *perro*formance— get it, with my dog, my *perro*? He loved it, said he'd put it in his documentary. I thought that was a great name. Look, I even printed some flyers. Hey," he called to Reinier. "Find me a couple of those leaflets we printed."

Reinier plunged into the mountains of books and came back with a few sheets of paper in hand. Eliezer passed them out to the students: each page bore a photo of him carrying Nachi, followed by the line "Librería *Perro*formance" and the address.

"When the documentary airs," Eliezer went on, "people from

all over the world will come, and State Security won't be able to do a thing about it. With so many foreigners in the gallery, I'll be well protected."

"Do you have any banned books?" the short chubby girl asked.

"Raúl Castro recently declared that there are no banned books in Cuba. 'We have never banned a single book in this country,'" Eliezer mimicked Raúl in a shrill voice. "Can you believe it? They used to jail you for playing the Rolling Stones record, let alone reading dissidents and counterrevolutionaries. But I take precautions. That's why Reinaldo Arenas's books are hidden well away. I'm the only one who knows where they are. Not even my policeman knows. Ever since I was robbed, I don't trust anyone."

"You were robbed?" I asked.

"There was this *guajiro* from Holguín working here. I helped him out, gave him a job, and one day, when I took my pregnant dog to the vet, the ungrateful bastard disappeared with five Reinaldo Arenas novels. You can't trust anyone anymore, not even the *guajiros*. Can you believe it? Someone brought me those books from Spain. They cost a fortune, and he knew it. He thought he'd be able to sell them in the Plaza de Armas. And you know what? His name was Alejandro. When I discovered he'd stolen from me, I remembered that Alejandro was the code name Fidel used when he was hiding out in the Sierra Maestra. I thought, Shit! It's as if Fidel has come back to fuck me all over again in 2015. The kid didn't think I'd report him, didn't think I'd tell the police because the books were banned, but he was wrong. I just had to think very carefully about what to report so as not to get in trouble, and to keep them from locking him up, because if they threw him in jail he'd for sure rat on me. So that's what I did, and they found him, and brought my books back, and now I'm the only one who knows where they are."

"But the books are banned, so why did the police give them back?" asked the Puerto Rican student.

"Because that's their modus operandi," Eliezer replied.

Every time I went to the bookstore, it seemed as though the helpers had changed: sometimes it was Reinier; other times a tall *guajiro*, with sunburnt skin, who rarely spoke but was fascinated by every little thing ("From Mexico!" he said once. "Shit! From Mexico! Mexico!"); still other times I'd find some down-and-out, smelly, marginal types sitting out on one of the low walls, guys who would never speak to customers.

"You're going to love this," Eliezer said with an exceptionally impish smile one day when I had been walking around El Vedado with Antón Arrufat and we stopped in the bookstore to browse.

Eliezer didn't plunge into the bookish mountains this time, didn't pull out a banned novel or a catalog from a censored exhibit: he went into the living room and came back out with a good-looking young man. He looked like Tintin, thin, with a boyish face. He couldn't have been more than twenty-five.

As an introduction, Eliezer said, "This Leonardo DiCaprio is from Bayamo and newly arrived in Havana. He has a girlfriend and a son, and you wouldn't believe what a hit he is with the foreigners. Ever since he started working here, the store is overrun by Spaniards and Italians. The bad thing is they don't always buy books: they want to buy him, but he's not for sale."

"Alberto," the young man said in a steady voice as he shook my hand.

Antón was watching all of this. He would pretend to look out into the street or at the books, but he was taking sidelong glances at Alberto.

"If this young man were to come to my house every afternoon, and sit for me for a couple of hours, oh, how I could write! I'd be done with my novel within two months," Antón said under his breath as he continued to look out at the street.

A glint flashed in Eliezer's eyes, the way it did whenever he found something amusing. Alberto, on the other hand, didn't seem to notice and began to tidy the books on the table.

"If you could see the way his girlfriend watches his every move," Eliezer said. "She calls him all the time, and if he doesn't answer because he's with a customer or carrying a pile of books, she gets mad and throws a fit when he gets home. 'What are these numbers in your phone?' she asks. And that's my fault; since I don't have a phone, I ask him to save customers' numbers in his. Then, when she checks his phone, she imagines the worst and loses it. Hey," he called out to Alberto. "Come here and show us that video of your son."

Alberto left the books on the table and walked over to us. He pulled out his phone, slid one finger up the screen, then two, and opened a video of a one-year-old wearing shorts and a T-shirt, dancing—though he could barely stand—and wiggling his hips, some trees in a park in the background. A voice off camera—likely his mother's—was saying, "Rey, *un pasito, un pasito pa' cá, un pasito pa' llá*. Shake your little hips, Rey."

"You've got to see this," Eliezer said.

And the video continued of the little boy who had clearly just learned to stand on two feet rather than crawl on all fours.

"Rey," the voice came, now clapping along to the boy's moves. "Let's see, Rey, one, two. Come on, Rey, baby, show your little belly, go on now." And Rey, teetering, lifted up his little T-shirt with one hand as he wiggled his hips, revealing his tummy and belly button. "Pull it higher, pull it higher," the voice said, and Rey kept lifting his shirt until his little nipples were exposed.

"Did you see that?" Eliezer asked, amused. "Cuban mothers teaching their kids to hustle. A one-year-old male stripper."

Alberto seemed more interested in the video than in Eliezer's comments, his proud-papa eyes never leaving the phone.

"Do you see just how far hustling goes in this country? From the time they can walk, they've got them out flashing in parks."

A customer arrived and put an end to the show. Eliezer went off to greet him, plunging into the mounds of books in the living room.

"So how did you come to Havana?" I asked Alberto.

"That," he replied, turning back to his work tidying up the table, "is a very long story, one I'll save for another day."

Seeing him so focused, organizing books into a grid, Antón said: "Young man, tell me: do you like to read?"

"No," Alberto said. "I don't have time. There's always so much to do here: put everything out front away before we close, pack it in boxes, and put it all back out the next day when the store opens. Then, during the day I need to help Eliezer pick up books and deliver orders."

"Why don't you try poetry? It only takes a minute to read a poem, and you can do that whenever you take a break," I proposed.

"Especially if it's a poem like *The Iliad* or *The Odyssey*," Antón said.

Alberto looked at me, intrigued, as if I were speaking of a far-off land.

"Look," I said, walking over to one of the shelves near the entrance, glancing at titles until I came across Dulce María Loynaz's *Obra poética*. I picked it up and opened it to a page at random.

"Here's a poem by Dulce María Loynaz," I said. "See how short it is? We could read it right now, while waiting for Eliezer to come back. This one's called 'Si me quieres, quiéreme entera.' It's a love poem."

Alberto looked at the page with interest.

"That's not a love poem: it's a horror story, especially here, in the midst of all these dogs," Antón said.

I stood shoulder to shoulder with Alberto and began to read aloud:

"'If you love me, love all of me / not only the parts in light or shadow . . . / If you love me, love me black / and white. And gray, and green, and fair, / and dark—'"

"Gray and green?" Antón interrupted. "What was Loynaz thinking? Have you ever seen a gray and green woman walking down the street?"

"'Love me day, love me night . . . / And early morning in the open window! / If you love me, don't fragment me: / Love all of me . . . Or don't love me at all!'"

"God, she's demanding. You can't love that woman in bits and pieces," Antón said.

Alberto took the book in his hands and reread the poem, silently, absorbed, his lips moving, forming the syllables and words in every verse, without speaking. As I watched him, I remembered that passage in which Saint Augustine describes Ambrose, the bishop of Milan, reading in silence, and it seemed so strange to him to see this gentleman bent over a book, engrossed in reading, not speaking or making any noise, because at the time everyone read aloud. "His eyes ran over the page and his heart perceived the sense, but his voice and tongue were silent," wrote Augustine. That's what Alberto was like, as still and as mute as Ambrose: he looked like a child learning to read, stumbling, forming syllables, words, clipped phrases that

seemed to be made more of sound than meaning, until, all of a
sudden, out of the gibberish came a recognizable phrase, which
he would repeat clearly and fluently. We stood like that for some
time, watching Alberto as he sounded out the syllables in si-
lence: if . . . you . . . love . . . me.

"There are many more poems in that book. You can start by
reading one a day, then two, and so on," I said.

"*Chico,* at that rate he'll never finish," Antón said.

Alberto went back to reading, leaning over the book, nod-
ding his head. He looked like a rabbi over a Torah: rocking back
and forth, back and forth.

"*Pinga!*" Eliezer swore, suddenly coming out from between
the mounds of books. "Nachi peed on the cookie catalog. Al-
berto: bring something to clean it up. Shit!" he said to Alberto.

"Is that another poem by Dulce María Loynaz?" Antón
asked.

The following day, I went back to the bookstore and found Al-
berto at the door, up on a ladder, his head shoved into a corner
of the roof.

"I'm repairing a leak," he said. "If not, it'll get bigger and this
roof will come down, too. It's not hard: I just patch it with a bit
of cement and that's that. But you have to know what to do. Un-
fortunately, Eliezer doesn't know a thing about construction," he
added, waving his trowel for emphasis.

"See that?" Eliezer said, coming out from inside. "Leonardo
DiCaprio turned mason."

Next to the door, a dog was nursing her pups.

"Lucy had her babies," Eliezer said. "We need to buy more
food."

"That's where all the money goes," Alberto said as he climbed down off the ladder, trowel still in hand. "A third to feed the dogs, a third to buy books, and the rest to help the hustlers."

"And Reinier?" I asked.

"Muchacho!" Alberto exclaimed.

"The policeman's in jail. They've had him locked up for three days now," Eliezer said.

"What did he do?" I asked.

"It was stupid," Eliezer said. "He went to the soccer game on Sunday and got into a fight with some guys who beat him up. Reinier broke a bottle and went after them, and everybody got cut up."

"His arm is scratched here," Alberto said, pointing to his shoulder.

"So the police came and took him down to the station. Can you imagine? The police took a policeman."

Eliezer pulled a wad of bills out of his pocket and handed a thousand pesos to Alberto.

"Reina María Rodríguez is launching her book at the Pabellón Cuba today. Go quick and buy ten or fifteen copies. But make sure they're from this collection," he said, pointing to a book on a shelf. "Make sure they're exactly like this one: black cover and gold seal."

"Okay. Be right back," Alberto said.

"I'll go with you," I said.

We left the bookstore, walked up L Street, turned onto Twenty-First Street, and as we walked I said: "Now you can tell me the story of how you came to Havana."

"Muchacho!" he said.

He said he had lived in Bayamo until the age of eighteen, then came to Havana for his military service. He left his girl-friend behind in Oriente Province and went to live in a military barrack near La Víbora. One day, as he was getting a haircut, the barber introduced him to a middle-aged Puerto Rican, who invited him out. They spent a few days together, and this guy fell for Alberto. Once he finished his service and went home, the Puerto Rican kept calling and sending money. He even bought him a motorcycle and a house in Bayamo, and would go visit him every couple of months.

"He fell in love with me," Alberto said.

"And what about the barber?" I asked.

"I never saw him again. This guy I know told me they put him in jail."

Alberto continued his story: his thing with the Puerto Rican lasted a few years, but then the guy started calling all the time, checking up on him, until one day Alberto grew so fed up that he broke up with him over the phone.

"I'll take my freedom over money," he said. "I don't care about money. What I want is to live a quiet life, not have some guy checking up on me all the time. He showed up in Bayamo one day, without warning, and I lost it. I don't like to be spied on."

Alberto met another girl in Bayamo, and the two of them had just moved to Havana a few months earlier. Then he met Eliezer.

"And how did you meet?" I asked.

"At the trial for the murdered Spaniard. I went with my brother; he knew the killer, so the police had brought him in as a witness. And they called on Eliezer because the Spaniard used to go to his bookstore. That's where we met, in court. There we both were, sitting, listening to the trial, when Eliezer pulled out a book by Pedro de Jesús and began taking notes on the blank pages at the back. I was watching him, couldn't believe someone could write that fast. He asked me what I was doing in Havana. I told him I was a carpenter, had just arrived and was looking for work. 'You're a carpenter and I need someone to build book-shelves for my store,' he said, so I went back to the house with him. When I walked in, I said, '*Compadre,* you don't need a car-penter, you need a whole army to straighten things up in here.' But we kept talking, and he told me he paid twenty dollars a day, so that's how I started to work for him. He's a good guy and I want to help him out. With what he pays me, I'm able to support Daykelín and my son, and save a little so that one day I can buy wood to build those shelves for him. Eliezer doesn't have any-one. Well, he's got me and Daykelín. She likes him, too; that's why she cooks for him almost every day. After we close the store, he comes home with me and we all eat together, and Daykelín laughs at his stories. And yeah, he's got the policeman, too; Rei-nier's his boyfriend but he doesn't want anyone to know that, and well, he doesn't have him now that they've put him in jail."

By the time we got to the Pabellón Cuba, it was closing.

"Come back tomorrow at ten," a guard told us.

"Let's go have a drink, and you can keep telling me your story," I said to Alberto.

"Where?" he asked, suspicious.

"Just over here, on La Rampa."

"Okay, but not too far. I've got to get back to the bookstore."

We walked down the stairs and along La Rampa toward the Malecón.

Alberto told me that he was with a Spaniard now, a man who comes every six months and sends money, and things have got-ten complicated because he spends his days at the bookstore and his nights with the Spaniard, and he gets home to his girlfriend at dawn. Daykelín went through his phone recently and lost it when she found messages from the Spaniard.

"What did they say?" I asked.

"I don't know, stupid stuff. He called me *papi,* said a few things. She went crazy, started crying, said I was going to fall in love with him. I said, you're nuts, *chica*. How can you think I'd fall in love with a man? No, that's impossible."

Alberto stayed quiet for a moment, then said: "It's so shameful to have to tell your woman that you're with a man so you can get money!"

"It would be if you were stealing or killing, but it's not shameful to be with another person, man or woman. It sounds to me like you like him."

"I like them both. The Spaniard because I've known him for a long time and he helps me out. And Daykelín because she's the mother of my child."

"Have the two of them met?" I asked.

"No! And they never can."

"But now they both know."

"Yes, but they've never seen one another, and I don't want them to. Is it much farther?"

"No, look. We can sit here, on this patio, and chat a while longer, then I'll walk you back to the bookstore."

We sat outside at the coffee shop on Twenty-Third and O Streets, at a table by the sidewalk. Alberto ordered a beer, and I ordered a mojito.

"Sure, sweetie, right away," said the *mulata* waitress in the typical government uniform: white shirt and black vest.

"One day the Spaniard went to the bookstore with me, but Eliezer doesn't like him. Says he looks ridiculous, all fat and old with dyed-blond hair because he's a hairdresser. But he likes Eliezer, says he's handsome, and he knows how much Eliezer has helped me."

"Enjoy," the *mulata* said, setting our drinks on the table.

The daily spectacle of late afternoons on La Rampa played

out before us: students, hustlers, transvestites, government em-
ployees, tourists, taxi drivers, pioneers. Everyone was heading up
and down the street, a few inches away from our table.

"I like chatting with you," I said to Alberto.

"Take my number," he said.

"I'd like to see you before I go."

"Tomorrow I work at the bookstore. Saturday I'm going to
the beach with the Spaniard."

"Sunday then. I'll take you out for dinner. We could go to El
Cocinero."

"Your place is better," he said. "You can cook me some spa-
ghetti."

"Why spaghetti?"

"I don't know. I just said that but it could be anything."

We continued to talk for a while, now with musical accom-
paniment: a group of musicians had arrived, and the rhythm of
their bongos and clarinet fused with the reggaeton coming from
the taxis along La Rampa. We walked back to the bookstore,
arriving just as Eliezer was closing up.

"Alberto, the radios," he said, pointing to some empty card-
board boxes.

Alberto hurried over to lift them off one of the tables and
began packing them.

"Not like that; like this," Eliezer said, readjusting two radios.
"Unbelievable: you've been closing down every night for a year
now and still don't know how to pack."

I said good-bye and left as they were piling books in empty
beer cases. ("All these boxes here are from either beer or rum
cartons," Eliezer had said to me one day.) I was meeting Wendy
Guerra for dinner at Sia-Kara that night, so I headed back to-
ward the Malecón. As I approached the Habana Libre, my

phone vibrated. A message had come in from Alberto: "u seems like an exelent im glad to met you see you."

"That could be a poem," I thought, remembering Antón.

⸻

The last time I saw Eliezer was a Tuesday afternoon. I was leaving the next day and this time had no plans to return to Havana. I arrived at the bookstore to find him sitting in the doorway, surrounded by his guys: Alberto, Reinier the police officer, an autistic *guajiro*, and two others who had just arrived from the country: their skin leathery from the sun, staring with a mix of curiosity and incomprehension.

"I came to say good-bye," I said to Eliezer. "I head back to New York tomorrow."

"Have I got a gem for you," he said. "You've got to see this. Alberto, bring me the court file."

Alberto went into the house and returned with a big, thick folder full of Xeroxes, which he put in my hands.

"It's the dissidents' court file," Eliezer said. "It's all there: every accusation, the prosecutor's questions, even the brand of cameras and equipment they confiscated. It's the bomb."

"How much?" I asked, flipping through the folder, thinking how this official, bureaucratic language might be useful for my Cuban stories.

"Just imagine. It's priceless. It's the only copy in Cuba," he said, taking the folder out of my hands and setting it on a table.

A puppy—its eyes not yet open—appeared in the doorway, pulling itself along the floor and making strange noises. Reinier picked it up and dropped it back with the others, sleeping on the mother's tummy, in the living room.

"Eliezer told me you'd been in trouble," I said to the policeman.

"Ey," he replied with that smile of his.

"You should have seen the officer who brought him back," Eliezer said. "A *mulato* at least six foot five who could crush your hand when he shook it. Married, two kids, and you know what he said to me? He asked if I could give him a job. Can you imagine? Turns out everyone at the police station wants to work here now."

"They need the money," Reinier said.

"That one wanted to pick up tourists. Can you imagine? Hustling has infiltrated the police force. In this country, there are two kinds of men: on the one hand, there's the Cuban macho, so concerned with protecting his woman's honor that he says, 'I'll never let you prostitute yourself. I'd rather sacrifice myself and do it.' Then there's the lazy-ass Cuban male who spends all day lying around, scratching his belly, and says to his wife, 'Hey, we need a few dollars. Head on down to the Malecón, will ya?' The only difference being who's the whore, the man or the woman."

Alberto and Reinier were playing with Nachi, who had come out from the living room as Eliezer spoke.

"Hustling is no longer taboo in Cuba. Even the police are involved. There are only three taboos left in Cuba, three things that could get you locked up: one, pedophilia, messing with children; two, counterrevolutionary activities, dissidents; three, drugs. Those are the three deadly sins in Cuba. But hustling? No. Prostitution is an entrepreneurial category. Can you imagine? Self-employed sex worker."

"Nachi peed on the dissident file," Reinier said, holding up the wet folder.

"Put it in the sun," Eliezer said, unfazed. "There's a difficult period coming, a 'special period' here at the bookstore. I've got to get ready for all the people who will come once the documentary is out. We've got a lot of work to do. We've got to build bookshelves and repair the roof and renovate the room at the back, make it into a gallery, because now I'll need to show paintings and photographs and have exhibits and organize screenings, because that's what people expect now. It'll be a whole cultural center. And still a dog rescue, and a male brothel, too, because the word is out, and all the foreigners who come these days aren't looking for books or the culture but for *guajiros,* and I've got to adapt, fix everything up back there, so I've got rooms, and the guys won't have to wander around Havana in search of a room, and it'd be a good time to set up a bar, so the customers have somewhere to sit and chat, with the guys, over a beer, but I need to get a license for that and I don't know if they'll give me one."

It was nearly eight o'clock; I had to get home to pack. I interrupted Eliezer's monologue and gave him a hug.

"I'm not sure when I'll be back to Havana," I said.

"Remember," he said. "You stay out of the dark spots. Best to stay in the light."

CONTRIBUTORS

CARLOS MANUEL ÁLVAREZ (born Cuba, 1989) is a writer and journalist. In 2013, he was awarded the Calendario Prize for the manuscript of his short story collection *La tarde de los sucesos definitivos* (2014) and in 2015 he received the Ibero-American journalism prize Nuevas Plumas from the University of Guadalajara in Mexico. In 2016, he cofounded the Cuban online magazine *El Estornudo*. He regularly contributes to the *New York Times*, Al Jazeera, *Internationale*, BBC World News, *El Malpensante*, and *Gatopardo*. In December 2016, he was selected as one of the twenty best Latin American writers of the 1980s by the Guadalajara Book Fair in Mexico. His first collection of journalistic pieces, *La tribu*, was published in 2017 by Sexto Piso.

JON LEE ANDERSON (born United States, 1957) is an American biographer, author, investigative reporter, war correspondent, and staff writer for *The New Yorker* who has reported from war zones in Afghanistan, Iraq, Uganda, Israel, El Salvador, Ireland, Lebanon, Iran, and throughout the Middle East. Anderson has also written for the *New York Times*, *Harper's*, *Life*, and *The Nation*. Anderson has profiled political leaders such as

Hugo Chávez, Fidel Castro, and Augusto Pinochet. He began working as a reporter in 1979 for the *Lima Times* in Peru, and during the 1980s he covered Central America, first for the syndicated columnist Jack Anderson and later for *Time*. He has published the following books: *Inside the League: The Shocking Exposé of How Terrorists, Nazis, and Latin American Death Squads Have Infiltrated the World Anti-Communist League* (1986, Dodd, Mead, coauthored with his brother Scott Anderson); *War Zones* (1988, Dodd, Mead, coauthored with Scott Anderson); *Guerrillas: Journeys in the Insurgent World* (1992, Times Books); *The Lion's Grave: Dispatches from Afghanistan* (2002, Grove Press); and *The Fall of Baghdad* (2004, Penguin Press). He is also the author of the biography *Che Guevara: A Revolutionary Life* (1997, Grove Press). While conducting research for the Guevara book in Bolivia, he discovered the hidden location of Guevara's burial, from which his skeletal remains were exhumed in 1997 and returned to Cuba. He is currently working on a biography of Fidel Castro.

VLADIMIR CRUZ (born Cuba, 1965) is an actor who has appeared in a number of feature films, television series, plays, and shorts. He has also directed films and plays. Cruz studied acting at Havana's Instituto Superior de Arte, graduating in 1988. He is best known for his role in the Oscar-nominated 1993 movie *Strawberry and Chocolate*. He won several awards for his portrayal of the young David, among them the ACE Award (Association of Latin Entertainment Critics of New York). Since 2005 he has also been involved in screenwriting and the production of audiovisual projects, and since 2010 he has run his own theater company. The last play he directed was *Miguel Will*, in 2016, about the lives of Cervantes and Shakespeare. He splits his time between Havana and Madrid.

IVÁN DE LA NUEZ (born Cuba, 1964) is an essayist, art critic, and curator. He was the first director of La Virreina Centre de la Imatge de Barcelona, in charge of defining the project. He was also director of cultural activities at Centre de Cultura Contemporània de Barcelona (CCCB). In 1995, he received the Rockefeller Fellowship for Humanities. He has been awarded the Ciutat de Barcelona Prize for his book *Fantasía roja* (Red fantasy) and the Espais d'Art Prize for the best art review published in Spain in 2006. Among his books are *La balsa perpetua* (1998), *Paisajes después del Muro* (1999), *El mapa de sal* (2001), *Fantasía roja* (2006), *Crítica del futuro* (2006), *Inundaciones* (2010), and *El comunista manifiesto* (2013). Some of them have been translated into German and Italian. His curatorial work includes the exhibitions *La isla posible* (1995), *Inundaciones* (1999), *Parque humano* (2002), *Banquete* (2003), *Postcapital* (2006), *De Facto: Retrospectiva de Joan Fontcuberta* (2008), *Dentro y fuera de nosotros: Retrospectiva de Javier Codesal* (2009), *La crisis es crítica* (2009), *Atopía: El arte y la ciudad en el siglo XXI* (2010), and *Iconocracia* (2015). He has written essays for the retrospective exhibitions of Stan Douglas, Los Carpinteros, Manuel Álvarez Bravo, Vik Muniz, Joan Fontcuberta, Carlos Garaicoa, and Javier Codesal.

PATRICIA ENGEL (born United States, 1977) is the author of three books. Her most recent novel, *The Veins of the Ocean*, was named a *New York Times* Editors' Choice as well as a Best Book of the Year by the *San Francisco Chronicle*, which called Engel "a unique and necessary voice for the Americas." She is also the author of *Vida*, a *New York Times* Notable Book of the Year, winner of the Premio Biblioteca de Narrativa Colombiana, and a finalist for the PEN/Hemingway Fiction Award and Young Lions Fiction Award, and the novel *It's Not Love, It's Just Paris*, winner of the International Latino Book Award. Patricia's books have been translated into several languages and her short fiction has been widely anthologized, appearing in *The Best American Short Stories* and *The Best American Mystery Stories*, among others, and in publications including *The Atlantic*, *A Public Space*, *Boston Review*, *Harvard Review*, *ZYZZYVA*, and *Chicago Quarterly Review*. She has received awards such as the *Boston Review* Fiction Prize; fellowships and residencies from the Bread Loaf Writers' Conference, Key West Literary Seminar, Hedgebrook, Ucross, and the Florida Division of Cultural Affairs; and a 2014 Fellowship in Literature from the National Endowment for the Arts. Born to Colombian parents and raised in New Jersey, Patricia currently lives in Miami and is the literary editor of *The Miami Rail*.

PATRICIO FERNÁNDEZ (born Chile, 1969) studied literature and philosophy in Chile and the history of Renaissance art in the Università degli Studi di Firenze, Italy. In 1998, he founded *The Clinic*, the celebrated satirical magazine dedicated to politics and culture, born on the occasion of the arrest of Pinochet in London, which has become the most read weekly magazine in Chile. He has published the novels *Ferrantes* (2001) and *Los nenes* (2008); *Escritos plebeyos* (2003), a book that collects the best of his editorial columns as director of *The Clinic;* and the collection of feature reports *La calle me distrajo* (Random House, 2012). Fernández currently edits *The Clinic* and theclinic.com; works in radio; and writes about literature, arts, and current affairs in diverse media. Since December 17, 2014, when Obama and Raúl Castro announced the normalization of diplomatic relations, he has traveled often to Cuba in order to report on the changes that started that day.

RUBÉN GALLO (born Mexico, 1969) is the Walter S. Carpenter, Jr., Professor in Language, Literature, and Civilization of

Spain at Princeton University. He is the author, most recently, of *Proust's Latin Americans* (2014), about Proust's Latin American circle of friends in turn-of-the-century Paris. Gallo's other books include *Freud's Mexico: Into the Wilds of Psychoanalysis* (2010), a cultural history of psychoanalysis and its reception in Mexico; *Mexican Modernity: The Avant-Garde and the Technological Revolution* (2005), about the Mexican avant-garde's fascination with machines; and two books about Mexico City's visual culture: *New Tendencies in Mexican Art* (2004) and *The Mexico City Reader* (2004). He is the recipient of the Gradiva award for the best book on a psychoanalytic theme and of the Modern Language Association's Katherine Singer Kovacs Prize for the best book on a Latin American subject.

FRANCISCO GOLDMAN (born United States, 1954) has published four novels and two books of nonfiction. His most recent novel is *Say Her Name,* which won the 2011 Prix Femina Étranger. *The Long Night of White Chickens* (1992) was awarded the American Academy's Sue Kaufman Prize for First Fiction. His novels have been finalists for several prizes, including the PEN/Faulkner Award and the Los Angeles Times Book Prize. *The Ordinary Seaman* (1997) was a finalist for the International IMPAC Dublin Literary Award. *The Divine Husband* (2004) was a finalist for the Believer Book Award. *The Art of Political Murder* (2008) won the Index on Censorship T. R. Fyvel Book Award and the WOLA/Duke Human Rights Book Award. His books have been translated into at least fourteen languages. His most recent book, published in 2014, is *The Interior Circuit: A Mexico City Chronicle.* Goldman has been a Guggenheim Fellow, a Cullman Center Fellow at the New York Public Library, and a Berlin Fellow at the American Academy. He has written for *The New Yorker, The New York Times Magazine, Harper's, The Believer,* and many other publications. He directs the Aura Estrada Prize. Every year Goldman teaches one semester at Trinity College in Connecticut, and then hightails it back to Mexico City.

WENDY GUERRA (born Cuba, 1970) is a Cuban poet and novelist. Guerra has contributed to many magazines and newspapers, including the Spanish daily *El Mundo* (where she wrote the blog *Habaname* for five years), *El País,* and the *Miami Herald,* where she currently writes about arts and literature. Guerra's first collection, *Platea a oscuras,* won her a prize from the University of Havana when she was only seventeen years old. She has a degree in filmmaking from Havana's Instituto Superior de Arte, where Gabriel García Márquez was her teacher in a screenwriting workshop. Guerra's first novel, *Todos se van* (2006), was largely based on her own diaries and followed the young protagonist's childhood and adolescence in Cuba. The novel was adapted into a film by the Colombian director Sergio Cabrera in 2014. In 2006, upon her return to Cuba from Spain, where she had gone to receive the Bruguera Prize, Guerra was asked to step down from hosting her own television show, and although her novels have been translated into several languages, they have never been published in Cuba. Guerra has been a guest lecturer at Princeton University and Dartmouth College. In 2010, she was proclaimed Chevalier de l'Ordre des Arts et des Lettres in France, and in 2016, she was promoted to the grade of Officier. She has always lived in Havana.

LEILA GUERRIERO (born Argentina, 1967) began her journalistic career in 1991, with the magazine *Página/30.* Since then her work has appeared in Argentina's *La Nación* and *Rolling Stone;* in Spain's *El País* and *Vanity Fair;* in Colombia's *El*

Malpensante and *SoHo;* in Mexico's *Gatopardo* and *El Universal;* in Peru's *Etiqueta Negra;* in Chile's *Paula* and *El Mercurio;* in the United Kingdom's *Granta;* in Germany and Romania's *Lettre Internationale;* and in Italy's *L'Internazionale,* among many others. She is the Argentina, Chile, and Uruguay editor for the Mexican magazine *Gatopardo.* In 2005, she published the book *Los suicidas del fin del mundo,* which has been translated into Portuguese and Italian. In 2009, she published a collection of articles called *Strange Fruit.* In 2010, her text "The Signs in Our Bones," published in *El País Semanal* and in *Gatopardo,* received the CEMEX-FNPI Prize. Her book *Una historia seneilla* (2011) was translated into Italian, French, and Portuguese and published in English by Pushkin Press in the United Kingdom and New Directions in the United States. In 2013, she published *Plano americano,* a collection of twenty-one profiles of Spanish and Latin American artists and intellectuals, and in 2015, a collection of her articles was collected in the book *Zona de obras.* She is also editor of a number of journalism anthologies, including *Los malditos* and *Los malos,* published by UDP in Chile.

ABRAHAM JIMÉNEZ ENOA (born Cuba, 1988) is a journalist. He has a degree in journalism from the University of Havana. In 2016, he cofounded the first Cuban online magazine for narrative journalism, *El Estornudo,* which he currently directs. He has collaborated with BBC World News, Al Jazeera, Courrier International, and Univision.

LEONARDO PADURA (born Cuba, 1955) is a Cuban novelist and journalist. He is one of Cuba's best-known writers. He has written movie scripts, two books of short stories, and a series of detective novels that have been translated into more than ten languages. In 2012, Padura was awarded the National Prize for Literature, Cuba's national literary award and the most important award of its kind. In 2015, he was awarded Spain's Premio Princesa de Asturias de las Letras, the most important literary prize in the Spanish-speaking world, usually referred to as the Ibero-American Nobel Prize. Padura has a degree in Latin American literature from the University of Havana. He first came to prominence in 1980 as an investigative reporter for the literary magazine *Caimán Barbudo*. Padura is best known in the English-speaking world for *The Four Seasons*, a detective series featuring lieutenant Mario Conde, a cop who would rather be a writer, and admits to feelings of "solidarity with writers, crazy people, and drunkards." The novels in the series are *Havana Red* (2005), *Havana Black* (2006), *Havana Blue* (2007), and *Havana Gold* (2008). *Havana Black* won the the Hammett Prize from the International Association of Crime Writers. His latest novel, *The Man Who Loved Dogs* (Farrar, Straus and Giroux, 2013), deals with the murder of Leon Trotsky and the man who assassinated him, Ramón Mercader, and is the result of more than five years of meticulous historical research. He lives in Havana.

MAURICIO VICENT (born Spain, 1963) has a degree in psychology and has studied law. From 1991 to 2011 he was the Cuba correspondent for *El País* in Spain. He has also been the Cuba correspondent for *SER* and has contributed to Radio France International as well as other European media outlets. In 1998, he won the International Press Club of Spain's award for the best work of journalism. He was a finalist for the Cirilio Rodríguez Journalism Prize in 1999. He is the author of a book of interviews titled *Los compañeros del Che*, with photography by Francis Giacobetti. He wrote the screenplay for the documentary *Música para vivir,* filmed in 2009 by Manuel Gutiérrez Aragón. In 2011, he directed *Baracoa 500 años después* and in 2014, he published, along with Norman Foster, the book *Havana: Autos and Architecture* (Ivorypress).